Eric Ward's
ST IVES

FROM HIS STUDIO AND BEYOND

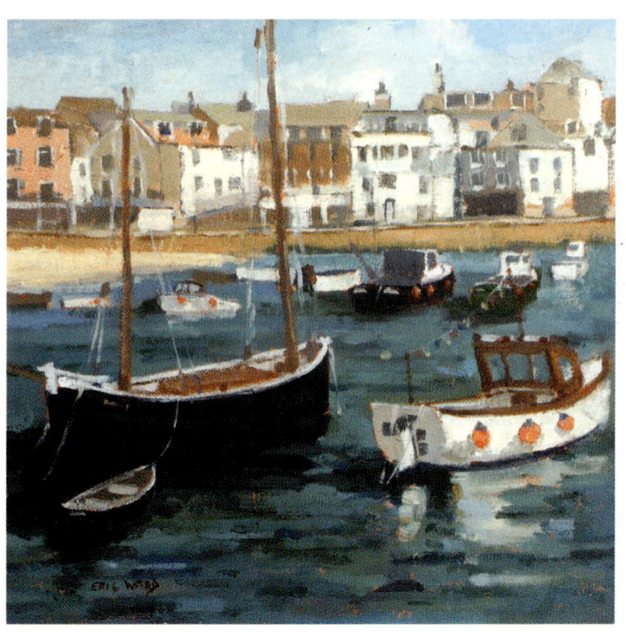

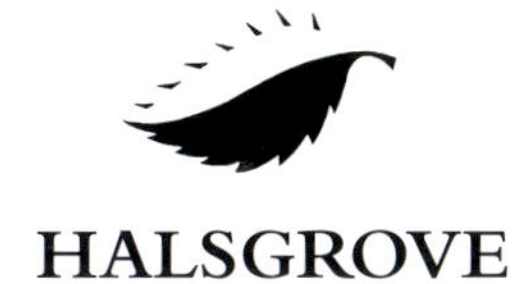

HALSGROVE

First published in Great Britain in 2003

Painting on title page: *Harbour, St Ives,* Oil on panel, 27 x 27cm
P.4: *Pink Geranium,* Oil on panel, 20.3 x 20.3cm
P.7: *Spooky Blues,* Oil on panel, 21 x 18cm
P.8: *Blues at the Western Hotel, St Ives (2),* Oil on panel, 39.5 x 30.5cm
P.21: *Morning Tide, St Ives Harbour,* Oil on panel, 50.8 x 60.8cm
P.59: *Jazz at St Ives,* Oil on panel, 20.3 x 20.3cm
P.83: *St Ives School of Painting,* Acrylic on panel, 39.5 x 30.5cm
P.113: *Looking across Rosevale to Godrevy,* Oil on panel, 25.4 x 25.4cm

Published on the occasion of an exhibition of selected works at the
Belgrave Gallery, St Ives, April 2003

British Library Cataloguing-in-Publication Data
A CIP record for this title is available from the British Library

ISBN 1 84114 262 X

HALSGROVE
Halsgrove House
Lower Moor Way
Tiverton, Devon EX16 6SS
Tel: 01884 243242
Fax: 01884 243325
email: sales@halsgrove.com
website: www.halsgrove.com

Printed and bound by
D'Auria Industrie Grafiche Spa, Italy

CONTENTS

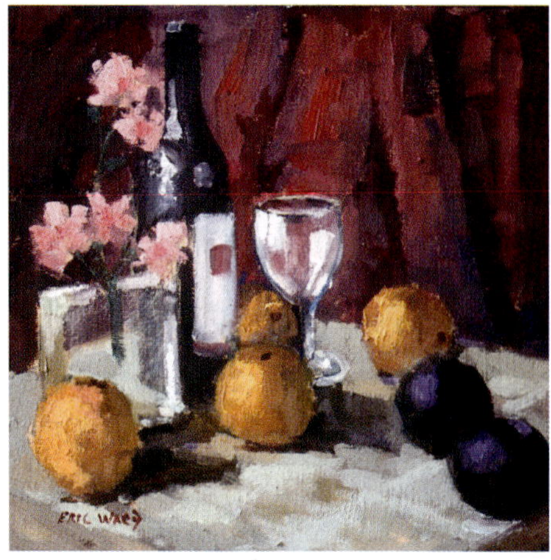

FOREWORD

I first met Eric Ward in 1988 shortly after the opening of our new St Ives Gallery in Lifeboat Hill in December of that year. At that point, Eric, whom I knew as the harbourmaster and coxswain of the St Ives lifeboat, entered not only my gallery but also my life.

At the time we were only exhibiting and selling paintings and watercolours of the early Newlyn and St Ives artists. These were traditional social-realist paintings of the early Newlyn group and early impressionist paintings of the St Ives School, both very different in their outlook towards art. However, one very good institution remained in St Ives that Newlyn did not have, the St Ives School of Painting. It was here, in the mid-1980s, that Eric installed himself to learn life drawing and painting of the nude figure. Under the tutelage of Roy Ray, the principal of the school, Eric was a very fast learner. Despite the lack of earlier formal training, Eric found he had a natural ability for drawing. With the added benefit of a good teacher in Roy he learned not only about drawing but how to construct a good picture. Many can draw but to make the work 'come alive' is another matter.

Eric was very susceptible to the female model. A real ladies' man in the best sense of the word, he loved the female form and very quickly found himself able to portray it in a manner that few far more experienced artists could hope to do. His speedy impressionist sketches in the life school are, I feel, amongst his very best works. Although only studies, taking no more than fifteen minutes each, they totally capture the poise and the life of the model.

Many times I have seen Eric rework and overpaint some of these works, and I feel that they have lost that instant inspiration and magic that was apparent in the original quick sketch. Much better to leave a work a little undone than to come back later and overdo it.

Shortly after our first meeting and general discussion on the merits of a painting and art in general, I asked Eric to bring some of his work for me to see. As a gallery we did not normally handle works by contemporary painters and I seem to recall my remark to Eric which stated that we only sold the work of dead artists. That way, I explained, we had no 'artistic tantrums' which so often happens in galleries showing living artists' work. The dealer and the artist are naturally a million miles apart in their views and quite rightly so. The artist is the creator of a work of art, thereafter the dealer has to do what dealers do best, sell a commodity. Eric, as I soon found out when he brought a selection of his work for me to view, had a different outlook from any other contemporary artist I had met to date. He was a lateral thinker. There was nothing complicated about the man or his work. He simply painted to the best of his ability exactly what he saw and loved: the female figure in all its guises, and still life and many harbour and sea views depicting all manner of boats and weather conditions. I quickly realised that here was an artist who not only painted what he wanted but what other people wanted as well.

I feel confident in saying that Eric has never had to compromise his art to fall in line with what people liked; it was already just what they wanted. He is

4

not an artist trying to break new frontiers in art, he is simply a man who loves to paint all that he sees around him – St Ives. As I have grown to know Eric more and more over the years, I came to understand that where the pavement on the roadside in St Ives ran out was Eric's boundary. To him panic set in at the edge of town. St Ives was to be virtually his sole inspiration for some years to come. Born and bred, schooled and having courted in St Ives, he started life as a fisherman learning about boats, the sea and the weather in all its moods. After fishing he became harbourmaster and his knowledge of the harbour, sea, weather and boats, stood him in good stead. Coxswain of the St Ives lifeboat, decorated on a number of occasions for bravery, who should know more about the town than Eric?

All of this appealed to me when I saw his early work, and it was very easy to see where Eric was coming from. He had a style based firmly on the traditions of Sickert, Dunstan and Ken Howard, who was then based partly in Mousehole on the south coast. Eric learned. All around him was inspiration to draw on. He would look at and appreciate the works of the earlier great artists who had gone before him: J.A. Park, Julius Olsson, Stanhope Forbes and Harold Harvey… and he would learn. He did not copy but developed his own individual style of painting. Even in his very early works, one of which has been hanging in my house since 1989, I could see the beginning of something very exciting: an Eric Ward. In my opinion, this is one of his best early paintings and one which I will never sell. Simple, easy to understand and painted with bold strokes in a slightly low-key palette, it was a nude in a bedroom. This was a subject done many times before but this particular painting was different. It spoke a different language from that of earlier artists. It was quite simply a young girl getting undressed in her bedroom. Years later I discovered the girl was, in fact, Karen, Eric's wife. It was just an ordinary every day occurrence that had been made into an artwork. It is simple, very satisfactory and easy to live with which, for me, is important.

I feel that any work of art should be created for the sole purpose of evoking emotions which enhance and improve one's immediate surroundings and give one that 'feel-good' factor at a glance. Yes, to decorate even. All art has to speak out in some way. Some requires much knowledge and often a lot of self-delusion to understand. Eric's does not. His paintings are simple, direct expressions of things as seen by the artist, hopefully to be of interest to somebody else.

Time passed. The months turned into years and we had been handling Eric's work for some eight years when in 1996 the time came to put on another show for him following successful exhibitions in 1994 and 1995. It is never an easy task, as often work thought to be the best by the artist is not seen as such by the dealer. The creativity of an artist is often years ahead of the thinking of the gallery owner. The 1996 exhibition was to coincide with the BBC programme *Video Diaries, Oil and Oilskin*, the life of Eric Ward, to be screened in October of that year. This was a joint show with another St Ives artist, John Emanuel, and filming started right from the earliest discussions of the show through to the opening evening some ten months and many hundreds of hours of filming later. The result was fantastic. We sold nearly every painting which we had on show and the interest and following for his work increased enormously.

Today, another six years on, Eric's work is selling in galleries all over England. His output is limited only by the amount of hours in a day he can paint. Painting from life, there is no quick and easy solution, just hard work and determination. Eric has this commitment and the base of his subject matter has widened. Commissions, prints, exhibitions and just painting for himself keep him fully occupied.

It is now fourteen years since our first meeting and how he has changed! He is no longer shy of his work. He knows how to give his dealer a bad time and get a fair price for his work. The metamorphosis is now complete. The confidence he has had in his own ability has paid off. The increased size of his studio, with wonderful views overlooking Porthmeor Beach inSt Ives, enables him to paint at his leisure his beautiful still lifes, his nudes, seascapes and portraits. It is certain that he is 'set fair' for the future.

The history of St Ives art colony can be likened to a play of three acts:
Act One – The innovators and the foundling members of the colony: Olsson, Stokes, Grier, Park, Borlase Smart and Fuller, to name but a few. Great painters of their time.
Act Two – The modernists: Nicholson, Hepworth, Heron, Frost, Hilton and Lanyon all breaking new frontiers in British art.
Act Three – Well, this is still being written: there is still a very strong body of good artists in St Ives, and Eric Ward is right amongst them.
From fisherman to harbourmaster, lifeboat coxswain and finally artist. Never has there been a more true 'Son of St Ives'.

Léon Suddaby Somerset 2002

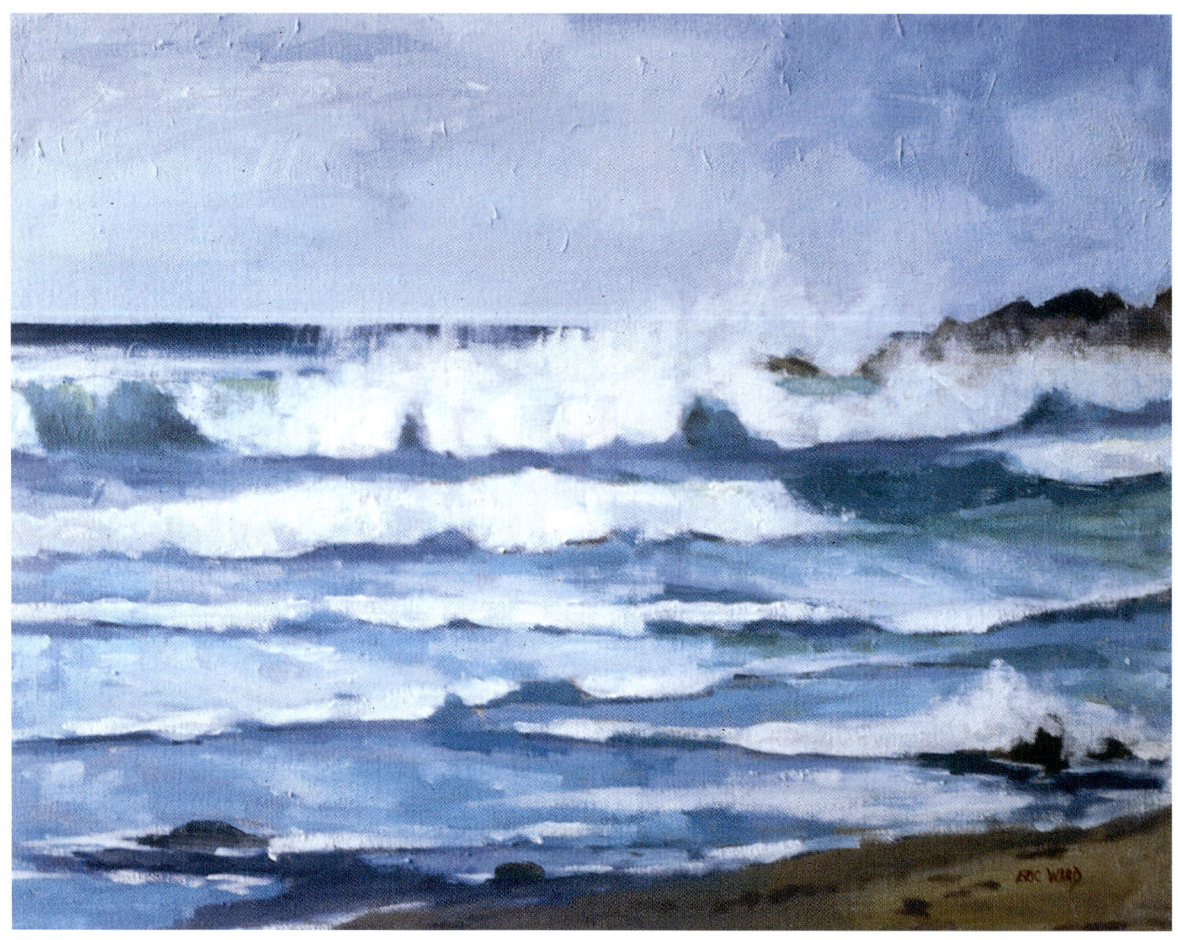

Porthmeor Beach, St Ives
Oil on canvas, 40.6 x 50.8cm

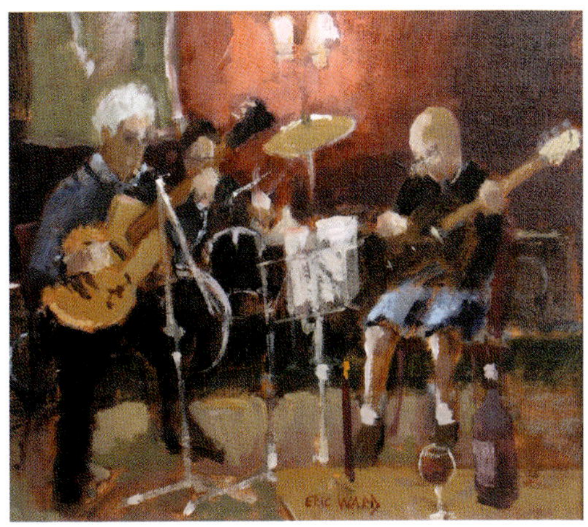

ACKNOWLEDGEMENTS

Firstly I have to thank my wife Karen for everything. My thanks to Léon Suddaby, for helping to make it possible, for writing the foreword and for all the organisation; Roy Ray for all his help and support over the years since I met him in 1985; Chris Install, for introducing Karen and me to the Roseland and Portscatho, and for all his help and friendship; Janet Phillips and Christine Nullmeyers for reading my text and for transforming it into English; Irving Grose and Michael Gaca from the Belgrave Gallery; Nikki Brown and Tony Smith (© Morek Cards) for allowing me to use their photographs. I would also like to thank the many individuals within the artistic community whose help and support over many years has enabled me to make this book a reality. Thank you.

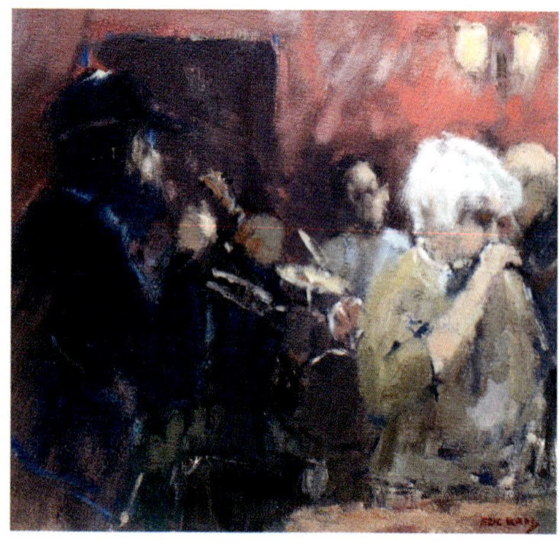

INTRODUCTION

ERIC WARD

I have lived what I would consider to be a charmed life. Without any kind of life plans along the way, things have moved from one thing to another in a generally satisfactory way and I have been happy.

I was born in St Ives on 20 November 1945 at No 3 Dove Street, a small street in the centre of the town behind the Western Hotel, where I would later spend many happy hours listening to jazz and blues. My sister Valerie had been born at Godrevy Terrace some eleven years earlier. Both our parents were amongst the youngest children of large St Ives families, the Wards and the Plummers.

My father was a butcher and slaughterman, and my grandfather a baker. My mother's father was a fisherman, the only grandparent that I remember. By the time I was a small boy he had long been retired and would walk around the harbour, talking to old friends and watching all that was going on. He was always dressed in his brown trilby and an old brown pinstripe suit, with me hanging on to the bottom of the coat so as not to get lost. I suppose I inherited my love of the sea and boats from my mother's family as my father's side was made up of people of the land who were not interested in boats as far as I can remember.

My father's grandparents, Jacob Ward and Susan Agland, originally came from Devon, and settled in Madron in the mid-1800s. Jacob was 6ft 5in tall, the

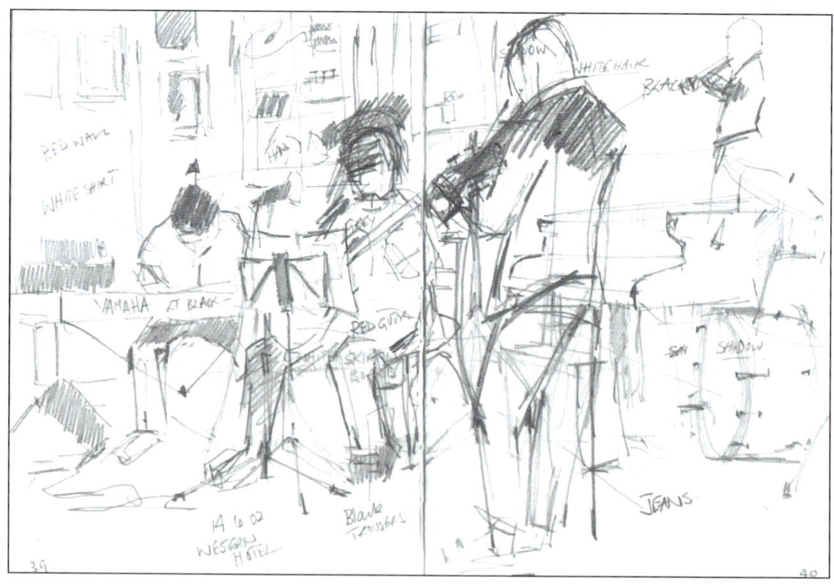

Sketch of musicians at the Western Hotel, St Ives, a favourite haunt for many years.

same height as myself, an incredible height at that time. Rather thankfully, these days young people are getting taller and taller. If nothing else it does make shopping for clothes much easier.

Jacob and Susan had five surviving children, one of whom was my grand-father. Jacob died when Susan was thirty-eight and she later married Alfred Wallis, mariner, scrap dealer and artist. Their coming together is another story but, in 1890, Alfred and Susan moved to St Ives, where the family have lived ever since. Exactly when Alfred Wallis started to paint I have no idea, but his work, with its childlike appearance that later came to be termed 'primitive', was just not considered to be of any value by his family and neighbours at that time. As a result, many were quite casually destroyed, and his surviving works, having been brought to public recognition by the likes of Ben Nicholson and Christopher Wood, are now very expensive.

Sven Berlin, an artist who worked in St Ives at the time of Nicholson and Barbara Hepworth, wrote a book about Alfred Wallis in the early 1990s. During a conversation I had with him it transpired that his wife, who lived with him in the New Forest, had a great-grandmother who was Susan Agland's sister. A very strange coincidence in a very small world. He signed his book for me, 'Almost related'; a treasured possession.

When I was two, my parents decided that life for us all would be much better in America. As with many Cornish families, my mother had a brother and sister living in Michigan. This seemed to be a fairly normal thing, and we set sail for a new life.

Unfortunately for my parents, things did not work out and my mother returned a year later with my sister and me. I never saw my father again and I have no memory of him. Six years later when I was nine, my mother received word that my father had died. The way that my life has turned out, I sometimes wonder what it would have been like had we stayed in America. The thought of being an American citizen seems surreal with my present lifestyle and I am eternally grateful to have missed the Vietnam War. Just a snap decision made by parents when one is a child can and does have an incredible influence on later life.

I attended the local schools and had an idyllic childhood. I consider we were lucky to be the generation to grow through our early years without tele-vision. Children played, and what a playground we had! Sea, sand, boats and, in reminiscences, seemingly endless sunshine. As a small child my mother always took me to Porthgwidden beach as that was her favourite, but as I got older the harbour was our place. It seemed to offer a never-ending supply of things to do. At that time the fishermen dumped their unwanted gear on the Porthmeor side of the Island, just to the far side of where the lifebuoy now stands. Corks, hooks, slates, pot iron and the like amounted to a treasure house for small boys looking to make model boats to sail in the harbour later in the day. Such boats were known as 'Cork-an-barbers' (I have no idea why).

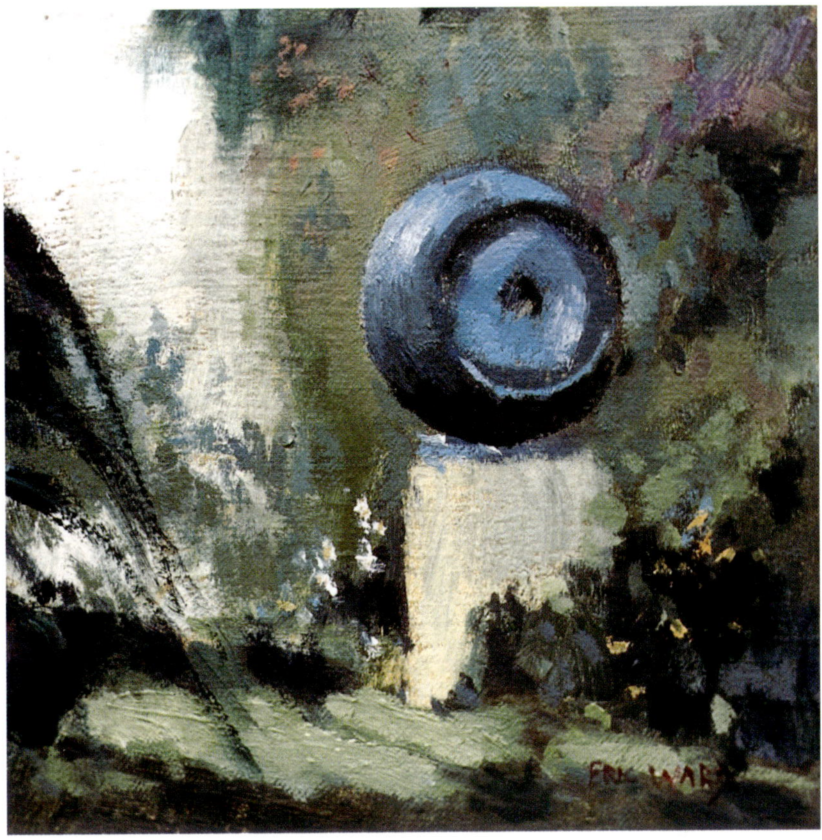

Barbara Hepworth Garden, St Ives
Oil on panel, 17.8 x 17.8cm

Sometimes, for a change or if the tide was out, we would sail them in a pool set amongst the rocks on the south side of Porthgwidden beach, known to us as 'Shark Pool'. When I walk past today it seems very small and unshark-like and, of course, nobody ever seems to play in it.

As we grew older we played cricket and football, and, depending on the season, we climbed cliffs (strictly forbidden), camped and generally had a great time with good friends and family. At school my main interests were art, maths and geography. I have always been puzzled by this because the three do not seem to be connected in any way.

When I was fifteen my mother contracted cancer and died. It was a very traumatic time, made easier by the vital support from my sister Valerie, who by then was married with children, and my father's sister, Aunt Maggie. I owe them both a great debt for my later teens.

Being born at the end of the war into uncertain times, my mother had always wanted me to be a schoolteacher, a job seen as safe and secure. With her death that ambition passed to my guardian, my sister, but it was one that I never really shared. My heart lay with the sea. By this time I had moved from playing to working on the harbour and had become involved with the lifeboat, as a launcher and part of the crew of the new inshore lifeboat.

In my A-levels I managed to fail art, but got an interview at Leicester to train as a PE teacher. The verdict was that my limbs would be too long for gym work and I did not get in. I got another interview, however, at Derby, where, on arrival, I read the legend above the gate of Old College: 'The Diocesan Training College for Women'. We were the third-year of male intake and I had a wonderful three years, at the end of which I returned to St Ives with no focus to my life at all, going from day to day with no thought for tomorrow. I spent an idyllic summer fishing and drinking beer in the local pubs, mostly the Sloop Inn. One evening I was at the bar and had a conversation with a man from South Wales. He was very pleasant and introduced me to his family, including his daughter Karen. The rest, as they say, is history. This year we shall have been married for thirty-five years.

I travelled to Cardiff where Karen was about to begin the last year of a teacher training course, when after only a few weeks, we became engaged. Her mother was none too happy with the arrangement and with hindsight I can see why. Here I was with no job, no prospects and they hardly knew me; my worldly possessions in two suitcases, one for clothes and the other for my books. I shared a room in a lodging house with an ex-Catholic priest and decided it might be time to get my life into some sort of order. I got a job as a police officer after being turned away by the fire brigade, which as I recall was something to do with the difficulties that Harold Wilson, the Prime Minister at the time, was having with balancing his books.

When our twin boys Richard and Zachary were born three years later, Karen and I decided that Cornwall was the best place for them to grow up. I transferred to Penzance and soon realised that the local constabulary was not the place for me. We moved to a farmhouse at Breja, Towednack, just outside St Ives, whilst we waited for a cottage to be renovated at nearby Halsetown. I had a boat built and returned to the sea, and rejoined the lifeboat crew as a signalman, a position now long obsolete. The inshore lifeboat, first established in 1965 and always my favourite, together with the 'big boat', became a large part of my life.

At Breja our only neighbours were a gay couple who ran a business in the town. They were the first gay people we had really got to know as at that time, 1973, it was still unusual for couples to live together. As they had a

telephone and we did not, they became my only contact with the lifeboat, a far cry from today's satellite and pager call-out systems. Many a night Mervyn would be banging on the door to get me up to go to sea, standing there in the cold and dark in his dressing gown. They were wonderful neighbours.

We moved to 73 Halsetown where, thankfully, as least as far as the neighbours were concerned, we did have a telephone and I fished from St Ives, Newlyn and Falmouth, depending on the season.

John Emanuel, the painter, was our next-door neighbour and many happy hours were spent in conversation and playing Scrabble. At this time in the seventies we did not have a television, the only reason being that in Cardiff we rented and when we moved we gave it back. Anyone who has had twins will know what I mean when I say that after the move we never seemed to find the time to get another. We lived at Halsetown for five years, and they were very happy times.

During this time I took part in hundreds of lifeboat services of one kind or another, mostly run-of-the-mill and, in the slow, open boat of the time, usually cold, wet and rather boring for long hours on end. Sometimes excitement did come, and sometimes rather too much, as on the morning of Christmas Eve 1977. We had launched to search for a Danish coaster that reported to be in distress north of St Ives, its exact position unknown. The captain, who had his wife and children onboard, was attempting to make port for Christmas. About 12 miles from St Ives, in darkness and hurricane-force winds, the lifeboat was struck by a high wave. Only the design of the boat

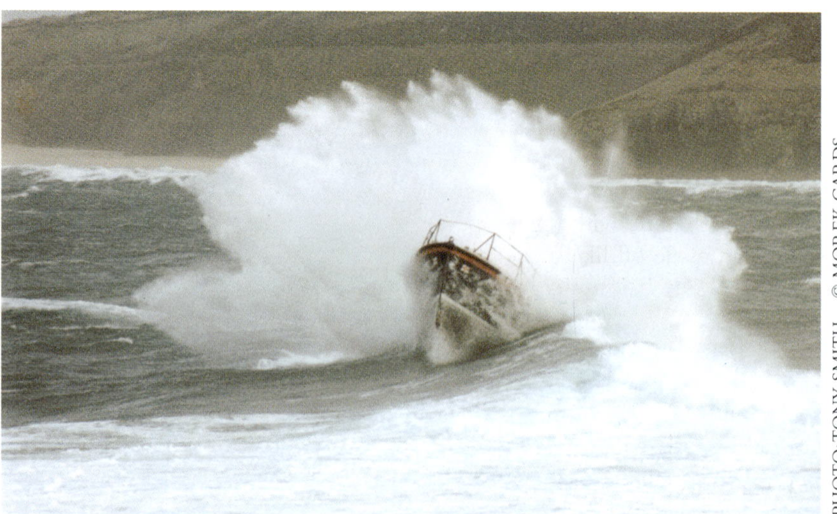

Dramatic conditions – all in a day's work for the lifeboat crew.

prevented a complete capsize. Even so, we were engulfed by water and it was the only time in my life when I thought I might die. Your life does not flash before your eyes, not mine anyway, but I did think about Karen and the children and that Christmas was not the best time of year to drown. Almost as soon as it happened, the boat righted herself; we had a crew count to make sure we were all there and we were OK – wet, cold and frightened, but all right. I have to say that for a few weeks after that I was a little wary about another bad-weather service, but then we went to sea again and things returned to normal. Coxswain Cocking received a silver medal from the RNLI and the crew were awarded valour certificates. On the same night the *Kilmor Quay* lifeboat in Southern Ireland was on service and capsized in horrendous conditions, with one member of crew losing his life. The crew of the coaster we had attempted to rescue, together with the captain's family, were also drowned. It was a very sad Christmas for many people.

There are, of course, many lighter times such as one of our half-yearly exercises with the divisional inspector of lifeboats. His exercise is to make sure that the crew are trained and the equipment works. We had carried out most of the duties without incident and eventually found ourselves beneath the tall cliffs of Hell's Mouth to the east of St Ives. The time had come to exercise the rocket-throwing apparatus which consists of a powerful rocket attached to several hundred feet of thin line. The object is to fire it and gain contact with survivors who cannot be contacted in any other way. It is usual when exercising to aim it over a rock or some other inanimate object, directing the line of fire out to sea away from anything that might be damaged by such a powerful rocket. But the inspector instructed that the line should be fired towards the cliff. Lifeboat inspectors are not to be disobeyed so I dutifully followed instructions, only to watch the rocket soar over the cliff and come to ground in a farmer's field. Thankfully, no pedestrians, motorists or animals were hurt in this exercise. We quickly recovered the line with the spent rocket on the end, no snagging on the way back, and made off like small boys who had committed a misdemeanour and hoped nobody had noticed.

The 1970s were also good times. The children were growing up, Halsetown was a happy house and the fishing was good; plenty of mackerel in the winter and shellfish in the summer. The mainstay of our summer catch was crawfish. They were caught in tangle nets and, as a result, some would be damaged and therefore unsaleable, so the crew would take them home for the table. It seems almost unbelievable now that Karen would cry, 'Oh no, not crawfish again,' as I walked in the door with the creature's orange horns sticking out

of my bag. It's a memory that highlights just how different those days were. By 1979 fishing was less successful and I decided to sell the boat. To pay the bills I worked as a labourer, helping two friends of mine to build a bungalow. That winter I returned to fishing using a small single-handed boat to catch bass from St Ives.

For reasons I will never fully understand I decided to study for what was known as a Second Hand Special, which was in effect a skipper's fishing ticket for certain sizes of boat. This qualification, unbeknown to me at the time, was the beginning of the change in my life. Without it several things would not have been possible and my life would have been different. I did the course at Falmouth and successfully sat the exams in Southampton. I continued to fish on my own and this became important as I was able to do more work for the RNLI without having to consider anybody I was working with.

The year 1982 was a memorable one as I received two bronze medals from the RNLI. The first was for rescuing four young people who were wrecked on the Hayle Bar in a sailing boat in bad weather and heavy surf. The second was for attempting to rescue the sole occupant of the yacht *Ladybird*, wrecked under cliffs three miles to the west of St Ives. Both services were carried out in the inshore lifeboat with me as helmsman, and both crews were awarded valour certificates.

Later Karen and I went to the Festival Hall in London to receive the awards, which were presented, along with other medals, by the Duke of Kent. A good time was had by all. The following year we were invited to attend a royal garden party at Buckingham Palace, which was another memorable occasion, in spite of, or maybe because of, torrential rain.

At this time, the RNLI had a full-time lifeboat crew stationed at Clovelly in North Devon. The boat, known simply as the '70-footer', remained afloat at all times and had two crews. One lived on the boat and one at home, with changeover every two weeks. During the August of 1983 they required a relief crewman for a week and I fitted the bill.

The following November I had a telephone call from the inspector of lifeboats to ask if I would go to Clovelly for the Christmas week, as the

Pictured: Helmsman Eric Ward at the Festival Hall, London, to receive valour awards.

second coxswain had resigned. Being afloat over Christmas is not August. It is one of my favourite times of the year and I like to be at home so I refused. But, discussing the situation with Karen, we had to face the fact that fishing was becoming harder and earning a living in January, February and March is difficult, to say the least. I agreed to do Christmas in return for three months' employment afterwards.

That Christmas week our crew did not stay at Clovelly for long as a poor forecast promising north-westerly gales ensured that we sailed for the shelter of Lundy Island on Christmas Eve. We spent Christmas Day in the lee of the south lighthouse.

During my time there any gales from the west or north-west saw us sheltering behind Lundy, not always alone, sometimes with small cargo ships and Dutch beam trawlers which work those waters at that time of year. As the wind climbed to severe gales and hurricane force we would all huddle behind Lundy for shelter and comfort, as high clouds of foam blew over the island and down into the anchorage. Using our inshore lifeboat launched from the afterdeck we would visit different boats, be invited for dinner and then reciprocate the arrangements. The Dutch were good fishermen and excellent companions. During a brief lull in the weather that spring we ferried about 30 of them ashore and all headed to the Marisco, the only pub on the island. I have never been in a bar before or since and ordered 30-odd pints of lager in one round! On our return they visited the shop attached to the pub and almost bought it out of Puffin teeshirts and souvenirs. I will always

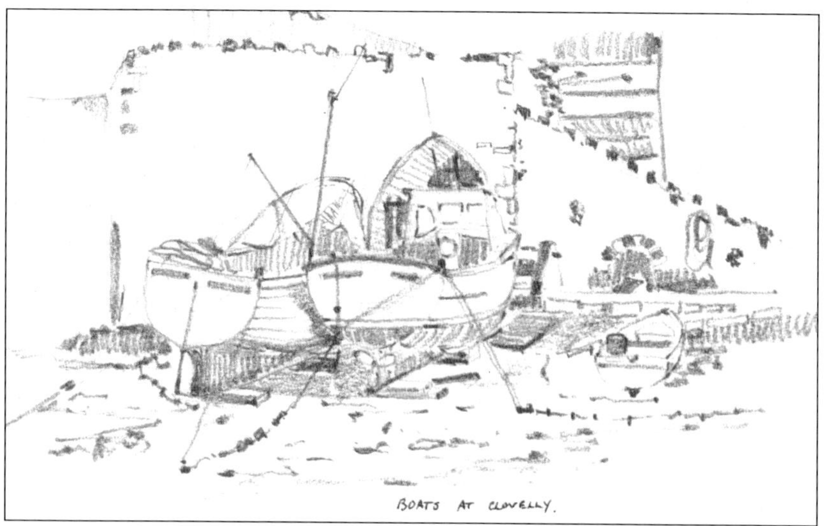

An early 'novice' sketch, executed during lifeboat service at Clovelly, Devon.

remember them walking back to the boats with bunches of daffodils, some with the yellow flowers stuck up under their caps.

The Clovelly position came my way as a result of having the 'skipper's ticket', required by the RNLI because of the size of the boat. It was an episode that proved to be one of the better decisions I have made, in more ways than one. I thoroughly enjoyed my time at Clovelly, the crews were good shipmates and the people of the village were of the friendliest — altogether a good time, with many treasured memories. Having worked on fishing boats, with almost continuous activity, I found the lifeboat a totally different environment, and in order to fill in some of the spare time I bought a sketchbook and some watercolour paints. I sketched and painted Clovelly, the lifeboat, Lundy — anything really. I would sometimes go ashore, at other times paint from the deck of the boat or from inside the wheelhouse, getting in everyone's way, and on fine days travel short distances in the inshore lifeboat. The results were not very good but it was a start. It was the beginning of June before I returned to St Ives and fishing once again.

The following winter, this time after Christmas, thankfully, the second coxswain who had replaced me left for greener pastures and they were short-handed. Without hesitation I returned to the 70-footer to meet old friends, both on the boat and in the village. On a trip to Ilfracombe to pick up supplies I treated myself to a decent box of watercolour paints and a new book. So began another few months of employment interspersed with enjoyable times and painting opportunities.

At the beginning of summer, whilst I was still at Clovelly, the harbourmaster's job in St Ives became vacant. After some hesitation I applied for the position. The hesitation was because I enjoyed life as it was; I was free to do as I pleased, my own boss, the only proviso being that I earned enough to pay the bills and look after the family. Karen suggested I apply, on the basis that I probably would not get the job anyway but I would never be able to look back later in life and wish I had applied for it. I'm sure wives were made to give votes of confidence to their husbands! After the interviews, to my surprise, I was offered the job, which I am sure was down to the fact that I had the qualification of my ticket while the other interviewees did not. It was a huge turning point in my life at the age of thirty-nine and I started work on the harbour on 3 June 1985. I was still a member of the St Ives lifeboat crew and had been the senior helmsman of the inshore lifeboat for some time.

I was determined to carry on with my painting and signed up for an evening class in St Ives. During that winter I was introduced to the St Ives School of Painting, another major milestone that links my work to the present day. I attended my first-ever life class one Wednesday evening despite several moments of being so nervous that I almost never made it at all. I thought everyone would be of a brilliant standard and I did not have a clue what to expect. Of course, I need not have worried as the class was made up of all levels from professionals through to beginners like myself, and had a wonderful atmosphere where everyone was friendly and helpful. If you ever have the chance to attend a life class and are worried about it, be reassured, you will have a great time.

I met Roy Ray who was the principal at that time and we have become life-long friends. Without the School of Painting and the help of many artists in St Ives I would be in a very different position today. Having acquired oil paints, I started out on a journey I have since discovered has no end. I remember wishing I had the ability to paint a picture in a certain way, that being my goal in life. In the beginning improvements came quickly with hard work, but, upon attaining my initial aims, I realised that the goalposts had moved and things were not as simple as I had thought.

My work in the harbour was new and enjoyable. I was, of course, working with the same people as always, but now in a different context. In 1988 the second coxswain at St Ives retired and I took his place. A year later when Thomas Cocking retired, I was appointed coxswain, probably because I was the oldest and the most experienced. So there it was, the lifeboat house on one corner of the harbour, the harbour office on the other and the School of Painting somewhere in the middle. Roy Ray became a driver for both the inshore and 'big boat' tractors as his studio and the school were close to the harbour, and, as he had informed me over a beer one night, he had driven tractors parking Vulcan bombers whilst doing his National Service. This was definitely too good an opportunity to miss!

Being harbourmaster meant I was ashore the whole time, lifeboat duties apart, and I had much more time to paint and enjoy family life. I continued at the School of Painting as often as I could and started to go outside to paint, usually well away from the public. After two or three years I thought my work was perhaps good enough to sell in the local galleries; I tried without success.

One day Léon Suddaby, to whom I had been introduced but did not know, stopped me outside his gallery in Lifeboat Hill and asked me when I was going to bring some work for him to see. I replied that I hadn't intended to as his gallery was rather out of my league. I had never been inside but the

gallery was Bond Street in St Ives, with a £20 000 Stanhope Forbes in the window, and everything else to match. But he liked the work that I took along so up on the wall it went, and started to sell. I had also begun to show work at the New Craftsman, St Ives, and seemed all set.

At this time the lifeboat was requiring more input all round as we had received a new boat. Gone was the old eight-knot 'Oakley', which had served us well and in came the 17-knot 'Mersey', not only twice as fast but offering complete protection for the crew from the weather. Yippee. The boat required more training for all of us, and, being called the *Princess Royal*, necessitated a royal visit for the naming ceremony.

Unusually for such an event, the weather was beautiful and all went without a hitch.

Life, too, was going wonderfully well. I had a job that I enjoyed on the harbour, a new state-of-the-art lifeboat, a great family, and paintings for sale in the local galleries. What more could there possibly be?

AN ARTIST SURFACES

I had retained my single-handed boat when I became harbourmaster but as time went on it was becoming more trouble than it was worth. With maintenance and the general care needed, it was taking up time that I could use for painting, so with reluctance I sold it and decided to put the time to better use. This again was a major decision as I had owned a boat of one sort or another for many years. It was almost like making a break with one lifestyle to give time to move into another, a symbolic gesture. To emphasise the point even more to myself I used the money to purchase a painting by J.A. Park, a particular favourite of mine and a great impressionist painter who lived in St Ives for a long period of his life.

Around the same time I met someone at the School of Painting who was to become a friend and influence the subject matter of my painting; artist and gallery owner Chris Insoll from Portscatho, in the south-west of Cornwall. I knew him from the life room at the School of Painting but got into proper conversation with him one day on St Ives harbour where he was painting. He informed me that he owned a gallery, liked my work and would be pleased to have some to show and, hopefully, sell. Naturally, I was delighted, and Karen and I took work over to him on a Saturday afternoon in July. St Ives was packed to overflowing with visitors of all descriptions so we were surprised and delighted with the relative peace and tranquillity of Portscatho and the Roseland. Since that time we have discovered many jewel-like villages on the south coast and visit regularly. I have painted the area many times, sometimes with Karen reading her book, and at other times with Chris and painters from the area. It is a joy to be able to sit and paint outside without being known to anyone. When you are harbourmaster and lifeboat coxswain it is pretty impossible to sit outside around the harbour and paint. Too many people know you, too many people always seem to want something and to interrupt.

Occasionally I will stay over at Portscatho for a few days, sleeping in Chris's studio and painting all day. Food is usually taken at the local pub along with other necessary refreshment. There is no telephone, no interruptions – absolute heaven. Chris has shown my work regularly since that time and he has been very important in my development as a painter.

Up to this point all my work had been completed using acrylic paint. I had started using oil paint in the life room, but when I started to paint outside, in a far less controlled environment, the results were a terrible mess! I discussed the problem with Roy Ray who asked what ground I was using. I informed him that it was board or canvas primed with acrylic primer, at which he suggested I get some acrylic colours and use them for the initial underpainting and composition, and thus solve one of my problems. The paint would dry almost immediately and when satisfied I could carry on with the oil paint.

I was already tinting my grounds with two acrylic colours, burnt sienna and ultramarine blue, the sienna for landscapes and a combination of the two to make an earthy green for figures. Painting on a white ground has some advantages, and is used by some painters, but I still prefer painting on a tinted ground. Being able to complete a painting is a very complex process, and involves solving a number of problems. One of these is the overall tone of the painting. Generally, the darker the ground the more low-key the work will be, so the ground is invaluable in this respect. It also means that all of the canvas does not need to be covered with paint. The ground acts like the cement in a wall holding the work together. I was lucky enough a few years ago to see a show by the master of low-key painting, Walter Sickert. To be able to see where the paint had not been fully applied was both very interesting and educational.

I had my two acrylic colours and things started to go well, so well in fact that I bought more and more acrylic paint and less and less oil paint. Eventually, over a period of time, I was using acrylic paint exclusively. This was the case for about ten years, with the result looking very much like oil paint. Now I am working with oils, except for the small figure studies done quickly from

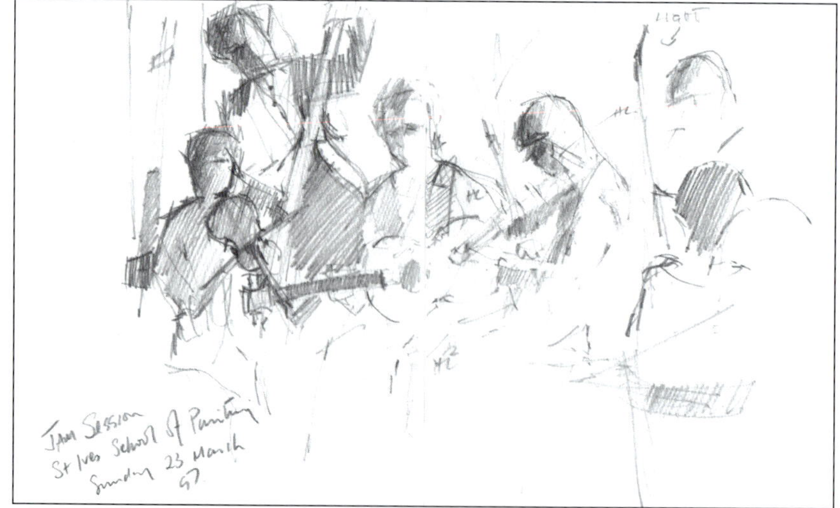

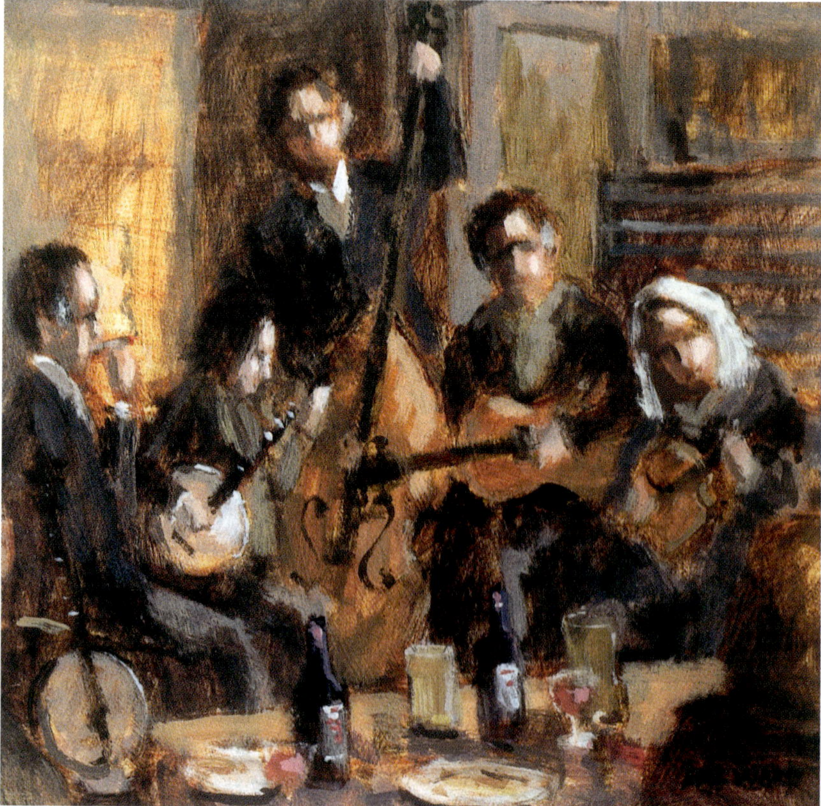

Top: *Preliminary sketch for a favourite subject.* Above: *Jam Session, St Ives School of Painting* Acrylic on panel, 25.4 x 25.4cm

the model. How this transition took place is another story that I come to later. My subject matter became more and more varied. I had added land and seascape painting to my figure work and now expanded even further into areas such as still life, interiors, pubs and musicians. I started to look at everything with a painter's eye. Even if I was walking along in the sunshine certain objects and views would be exciting. Light and how to represent it became all-important.

I started to carry a sketchbook with me when I visited music venues, pubs and the like. I already had completed hundreds of drawings in the life room but these new drawings were to use in the completion of paintings at a later time. It was a very steep learning curve. I was attempting to make finished little drawings in their own right, but when I came to use them as a basis for paintings, they did not contain enough of the information I needed. Over the years, by trial and error, I have learned what is needed in a drawing to be worked into a finished painting. Sometimes it may require a second or third visit and usually takes several drawings, together with notes. I am afraid I never have found a short cut for this; it is just continuous practice.

I also use photographs to help with painting. I know that this is frowned upon in certain quarters but sometimes it is the only way to collect information. One has to be aware of its limitations and resist slavishly copying the image. Of course it is always better to paint and draw directly. That five-minute drawing is five minutes analysing and thinking about the subject, but photos have their place alongside everything else.

Thanks to the various roles in my life I received a certain amount of publicity, which resulted in my first one-man show at the Hallam Gallery in London. This was also the first time Karen and I stayed at the Chelsea Arts Club, a place that has become very important to us and where we have spent many happy times. This first time we were guests of Roy Ray who had travelled to London with us for the show. A couple of years later Roy proposed me as a member and I was accepted. New friends and good times have been the order ever since.

The show at the Hallam went well despite a heatwave, a Tube strike and total gridlock of the London traffic. The three of us walked from the Chelsea Arts Club to Upper Richmond Road as any sort of public transport was unavailable. Thankfully, I had advertised the show with the RNLI and many people who lived in the area turned up. The RNLI has a complex fund-raising organisation with committees everywhere, including London. The Hallam show taught me a lot and was a great deal of fun; I sold work and all was well.

I had a major one-man show in the Sims Gallery, St Ives, in 1994, comprising over 70 paintings. Léon Suddaby, the gallery owner, offered the show because he thought that as a serious painter I should get a large body of work together. I shall always be grateful for that advice as it put me mentally into another gear and moved me on. The exhibition was a great success and Léon wanted me to follow it up with another the following year.

John Emanuel had also had a successful solo show, just before mine, and we decided to have a two-man show. John paints figures in a totally different way from myself so the theme of the show was 'Two views of the human form'. It, too, was a great success and the following year we had another show together.

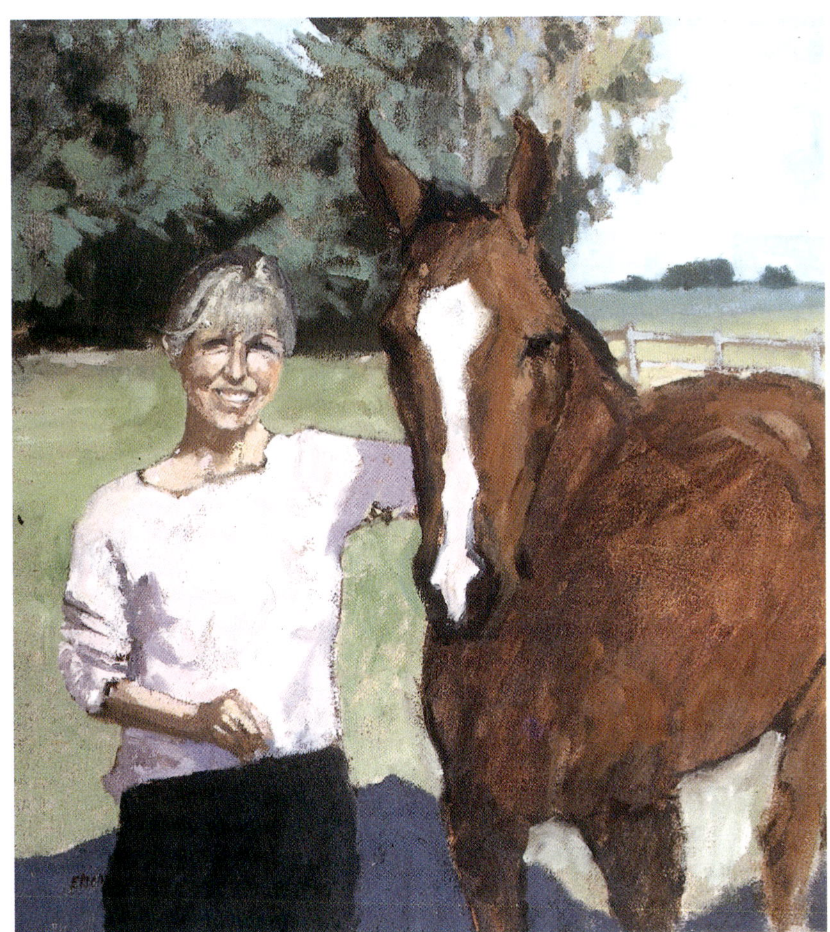

Annie and Mieke
Oil on canvas, 35.5 x 30.5cm

Life is very strange; the thought of exhibiting paintings together when we were neighbours at Halsetown and I was a fisherman would have seemed crazy.

During this period I was contacted by the RNLI who wanted to know if I would be willing to make a video diary for the BBC. The remit from the BBC was to make an hour-long programme on the daily life of a lifeboat coxswain. I discussed it with Karen and decided to give it a go, especially if I could publicise some of the painting in it. The idea of a video diary is that the person making it takes charge of all of the filming, meaning no BBC crews, no cameramen, or other personnel. It was all filmed using Hi 8 equipment, with the lifeboat crew doing much of the work.

After a couple of false starts we settled down to it and the project went well. As with all things to do with lifeboats they never travel to any set plan. Karen always insists that anything to do with boats always takes three times as long as anything else and is always chaos! (She is not a boat person.) Predictably, the presence of cameras and equipment on the lifeboat meant that nothing dramatic happened. We went through what is known as a quiet time.

Incidents would happen at other stations nearby and occasionally make the national news. This would elicit an immediate phone call from my editor Clare, 'Is that you? Is that you?' 'Eerr, no,' would be the inevitable reply. Clare visited St Ives many times and has become a good friend of ours. She was brilliant throughout the making of the diary and without her it probably would not have been made at all.

We did eventually find incidents to fit the bill, as well as domestic life and painting finding their way into the footage. My second show with John took centre stage. The diary was broadcast in 1996 and I was very surprised by the response. It was reviewed well in some of the national newspapers and letters poured in from all over the place. I still have people coming up to me to say how much they enjoyed the programme and how they still watch it before they visit St Ives. I even met a nice lady on Paddington railway station who told me how much she had enjoyed the programme, as a result of which she and her family had moved to Cornwall and how pleased they were at having done so. The power of TV is truly amazing!

There were hours and hours of film that were unused and I still have the tapes in a large box in my studio. It was recorded over a year in St Ives so may be interesting to someone in about fifty years time! The RNLI were pleased with the result and gave me a silver-coloured statuette of a lifeboat man which was presented at the London Boat Show in a little ceremony that Karen and I attended. Clare said it was my very own Oscar, and Oscar he has been called ever since.

There are, inevitably, very sad times with the lifeboat service when lives are lost. These times are made even worse when they involve people that you know and have worked with. All lifeboatmen will have to deal with death and the handling of bodies throughout their careers. I am not sure that you ever get used to it and it is especially poignant when you have had contact with the person the day before.

The other side of the coin brings times of high emotion and elation. Shortly before I retired from the RNLI on August Bank Holiday 2000, Karen and I were at home watching television, because I hate Bank Holiday pubs and restaurants, when just before dark my pager went off. I immediately went to the lifeboat house where I was informed an eleven-year-old boy had been washed down the river at Hayle, an estuary two miles east of St Ives. It was his birthday and the boy had been playing with his brother in a gully at the side of the river. It was ebb tide on a very high spring tide and as it fell, the two boys got nearer and nearer to the river. Eventually the sand gave way and he was in a torrent of water and swept away. A rescue helicopter and the inshore lifeboat were also tasked and made their way to the incident. We launched the lifeboat and made our way towards the mouth of the Hayle river.

Having worked in this area for many years, I am well aware of the tidal streams coming out of Hayle and over the sand bar at its entrance. I stopped the boat and decided to commence my search about a mile from the bar itself as it seemed to be the most likely place to find the boy. We had been searching for about ten to fifteen minutes in the growing darkness when the second coxswain shouted to me from the bow that he could hear something. He pointed in the general direction from which he thought the sound had come and I ran the boat up alongside a small terrified boy in his swimming trunks, about one mile from the shore. The crew pulled him from the water and as they carried him past me into the wheelhouse he was still screaming at the top of his voice. Until you have heard someone who is so utterly terrified scream for their life, you have not heard anyone scream. It was an experience that was very emotional and one I will remember for a very long time. He later wrote to thank us with a lovely letter, in content rather like a thank-you note for a Christmas or birthday present, a typical child's letter. I have the greatest admiration for him for being able to keep it together and stay afloat in an impossible situation whilst being swept out to sea, in the growing darkness, and alone. It is the sort of situation that as a rescue service you only get one chance at and, thankfully, we got it right.

When I became interested in printing and etching I was lucky enough to receive tuition from a very good painter called Roy Walker. He had already helped me with painting and now he taught me the process of etching. Roy was a man who had time for everyone and was an inspiring teacher. Sadly, he became ill in 2001 and died at the end of that year. He is sadly missed by many.

I enjoyed etching very much and set myself up in my studio with all the necessary equipment, including a press, soon afterwards. Etching and printing is a whole new world to explore, and, as with painting, I bought many books on the subject and attempted to learn all I could. Unfortunately, time is at a premium and I cannot give the printing the attention I would like. I had to decide whether to be a painter who printed or a printer who painted. I chose the former. My etchings are primarily in black and white and I found using pure tone in the prints a great help and influence in my painting. I do think the two complement each other and I hope at some stage to be able to give more time and energy to printing.

One of the many great advantages with painting and the art world in general is the friendship and comradeship that develop. Over the years Karen and I have made many new friends and had the opportunity to expand our social life. This was helped along by our children growing up, my change in lifestyle, and our move in 1979 from Halsetown to our present address at Ocean View, St Ives. There were no plans for the move here, in fact, we were supposed to be going to look at a house elsewhere in St Ives. I came in from sea and found a note from Karen directing me to Ocean View instead. Karen saw the house with its wonderful views and I knew we would be moving in! Another important feature was its easy walking distance to everything in St Ives.

Roy Ray, mutual friend Andy Davidson and myself discovered that we had a shared interest in Chinese cooking, which naturally developed into many social gatherings. The largest of these were at the School of Painting where the three of us would cook for up to 16 friends. Small hurricane lamps that I had used in my fishing days to mark dahn buoys were pressed into use to give the wonderful old building an even more atmospheric feel. The fun, laughter and good times always went on well into the small hours.

I painted more and more, surrounded by people who were supportive and encouraging. But even with such people around, painting is a very strange discipline because when you are at work you are essentially alone. The problems are yours to solve and decisions concerning the way the work will go are down to you. It is very easy to become too involved to the point of it being detrimental to the work itself. A great antidote to this is, of course, the harbour and the lifeboat crew. Both these things have a very successful knack of bringing you back to the reality of the world.

More people began to see my work and I had a one-man show each year, as well as showing in different galleries. My work began to be shown

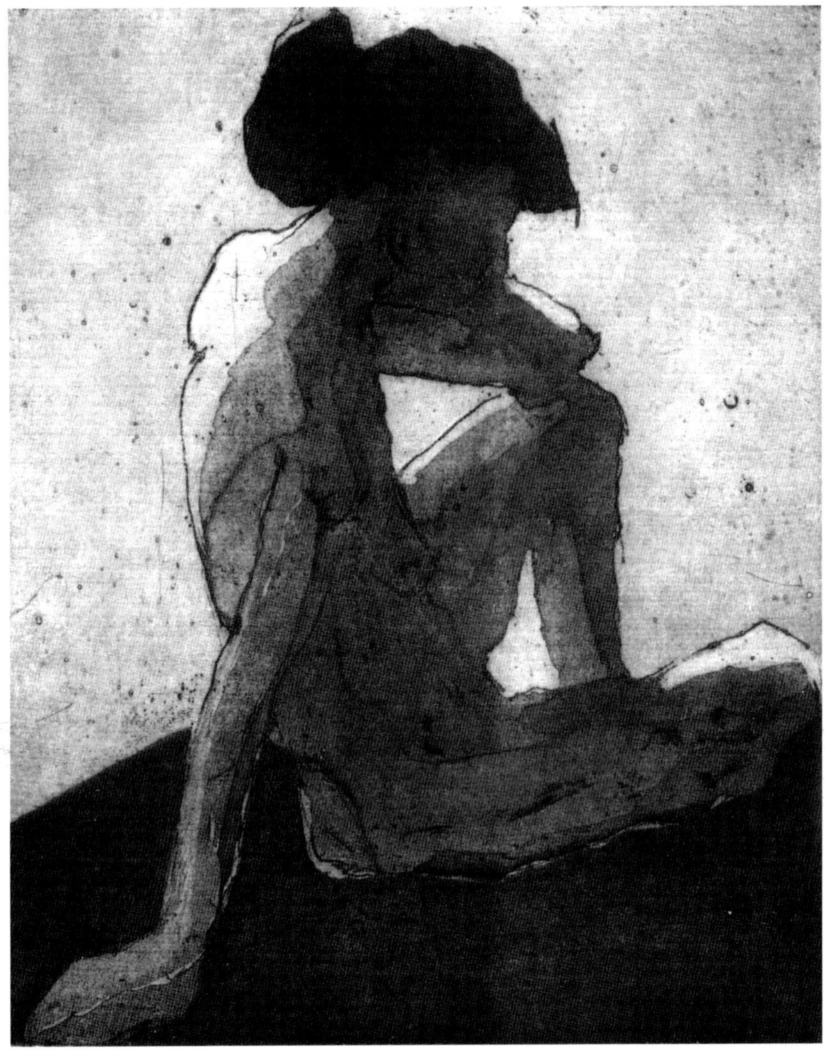

Christine II, etching, steel plate

throughout England and I exhibited in shows in Germany and Holland. During 1998 I had a second London show at The One Below Gallery with Henry Dyson Fine Art. Gradually, I began to get to know people who had collected my work. This process does take quite a while as galleries and dealers guard their customers' identities very jealously. There is one exception known to me and that is the New Craftsman at St Ives. After a while you meet people, names crop up, you see people are at previews and you get to know them. It is something I rather enjoy. I am sure that, even under torture, Léon Suddaby would not give up his client list but he is not without

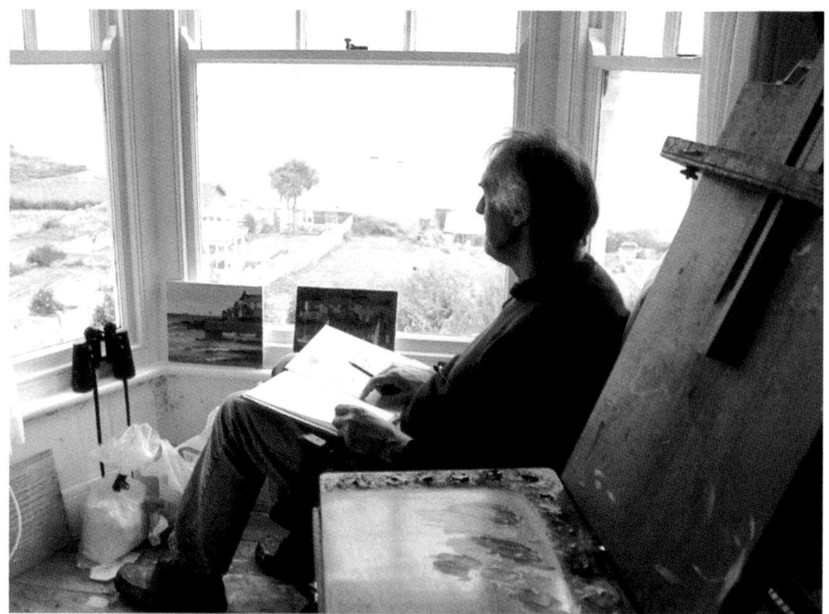

The artist's studio with 'ocean view'.

generosity. Three or four years ago, late on a Saturday afternoon, Léon turned up at my door with a car full of goodies that he was more than happy to share! He had been to Devon and had cleared an artist's studio where he had bought everything. The paintings were for him and all the other stuff was to be mine. There was paper, inks, brushes, a radial easel, which never made it to the studio, and tubes and tubes of perfect but very old oil paint. This was oil paint in tin-like tubes with long-forgotten makers' names – romantic oil paint.

The easel stands more or less where Léon put it down in the sitting room. Karen immediately laid claim to it and it now boasts a painting on display, plants entwining their way around and over it, and one of Karen's favourite hats atop. Its just as well I did not really need it!

When dealers appear unannounced, bearing gifts and with no discussion about money, apprehension spreads throughout the artist's body like a well-administered drug. A small voice at the back of the mind constantly reminds one that perhaps in the long run it is going to be cheaper to buy all the stuff in the King's Road. All these thoughts are then put aside as he surveys the paints. Shortly afterwards I just had to get out my oil palette and use some of these beautiful things. Needless to say, my euphoric mood was soon dashed in despair. Having used acrylic paint, with different techniques, for so many years the results did leave something to be desired. I persevered

and quickly relearned a great deal about oil paint in the following months. A great proportion of my work is now done using oil paint and I continue to learn every day. It is such a challenging material: it makes you want to wake up every morning and paint more and more. There are always new aspects of it to explore and boundaries to push. Wonderful!

In 2000 I reached the retirement age for the lifeboat service. There was a little local publicity in the newspapers and on local television; I had a last launch in the boat and a quite 'illicit' fun trip in the inshore lifeboat. I had officially retired from that in 1995. It is a young man's boat, but still very enjoyable.

This retirement is, of course, giving me more of that most precious commodity, time. When the public see a lifeboat go to sea they quite naturally think that is all there is to it. How far from the reality of it all they are. With new and faster boats the training of crews is obviously more intense, especially so since the wheelhouses are now full of the latest electronic equipment.

I am often asked if I miss the lifeboat service and I can honestly say that I do not. I have an incredibly full life and my retirement came at a time when I was ready for it. Things have worked out very well indeed. As well as not having to shoulder the responsibility, it is the small things that make life a joy now that I am no longer the lifeboat coxswain: going to bed and knowing that, unless the house burns down, you will still be there in the morning; being able to undress at night and put your clothes in the laundry instead of placing them at the foot of the bed ready to climb back into; not being called out in the middle of the night from a deep sleep.

Every time this happens you get up and get dressed, your mind working overtime. What are the weather conditions? What is the state of the tide for launching the lifeboat? What are the sea conditions? Where is the casualty? How difficult will it be to get there? You get yourself to the lifeboat house. Which members of the crew are available? Has the tractor driver arrived? The honorary secretary is bombarding you with information as you pull on your wet-weather gear and lifejacket. The boat is launched, radio contact made with the coastguards, and sometimes with the casualty. More information from the crew manning radio, radar and satellite positioning equipment has to be assimilated. Orders are given, assessments made. Fifteen minutes ago you were fast asleep and now you wish you could clean your teeth.

Throughout the thirty-six years I was with the RNLI, life was made much easier for me by my wife Karen. She accepted it from the beginning as part of my life and never seemed to worry about it. This was a huge godsend as I do not think I would have coped very well with a wife who was perpetually worried about me when I was at sea. Even Karen would agree that there have been rare occasions over the years when I have been called away at inconvenient times, but worrying is something she never did.

Shortly before I retired we went for a meal with one of our sons to a local restaurant in St Ives. It was the end of October, dark, the rain lashing the windows and the wind howling to gale force. We were coming to the end of our meal when my pager went off. Karen looked across the table at me, fork poised, and said quite calmly, 'leave money'. My son, expertly trained by his mother, said, 'It's OK Dad, I have some money.' Later I joked that a 'be careful, dear' might have been nice but that is how it has been and I am very grateful for it.

During the nineties I painted more and more, taking my paints further afield. We stayed at the Chelsea Arts Club on many occasions and if not too loaded with other things I sometimes took my box and kit with me. Painting on site in London was a revelation. I expected to remain totally alone to get on with the job. How wrong I was. Almost the instant I had set up, people came to talk to me. One lady even wanted to know where I had got my paintbox as her husband painted and she wanted to buy him one for Christmas.

Even in an early Sunday morning St James's Park people stopped, sat next to me and engaged me in conversation. So much for reserved Londoners. Whilst in that seemingly empty St James's Park an old lady stopped in front of me on the other side of the path and proceeded to feed the squirrels. It was a charming scene and no problem to me at all. That was until approximately 25 French students appeared and congregated in front of me to watch the old lady feed the squirrels, completely blocking my view. As this went on for some time I had a polite word, they moved further along the path and I continued with my painting. I must say they were all very chirpy and bright so early on a Sunday morning, not at all like students in my day. On another occasion I had plans to paint in Green Park but they were abandoned because unbeknown to me it was the morning of the London Marathon. Generally though, I have had few problems and people are interesting and polite.

The millennium arrived in St Ives with a huge fanfare, as I suppose it did everywhere else. I still cannot quite come to terms with watching it happen in Sydney, Australia, just before I was about to go out to celebrate the same event. St Ives celebrates the New Year in style, with many visitors and fancy dress the order of the day, or maybe I should say night. Rather thankfully the doom-mongers' predictions of financial meltdown, and even worse the end of the world, failed to occur and life carried on much as before.

The year 2000 was the first for many years that I did not have a one-man show. This was not a deliberate decision, just that nobody asked me. I was quite pleased not to have any deadlines to meet and continued to supply work to galleries that were showing my work on a regular basis. I continued to paint outside on the south Cornish coast whenever I could and had painting days out around St Ives with the painter and printer Hilary Gibson.

Hilary and I have been friends since she came to St Ives from Brighton in 1994. She sat for me as a model when I did one of the shows with John Emanuel and during one of our conversations she told me she enjoyed working outside. Since then, weather permitting, we have had painting trips around St Ives. Gurnard's Head became a favourite spot, the cliffs and coves around the area being particularly beautiful, with the sea in sunlight a mixture of the most wonderful colours. Painting on the north coast means the light is usually behind you illuminating the subject matter to the full, a totally different light from working on the south coast. There, looking into the sun, the light leaches the colour from the surface of the sea giving a silvery appear-ance. The deep colours seen on the north coast are sometimes missing and paintings are different. Both can be incredibly beautiful and their variety is endless, making a painter's life very interesting.

Since receiving those unexpected oil paints from Léon I have felt confident enough to take them outside. I am experienced enough now not to get into the terrible mess of years ago, but with painting, other problems occur.

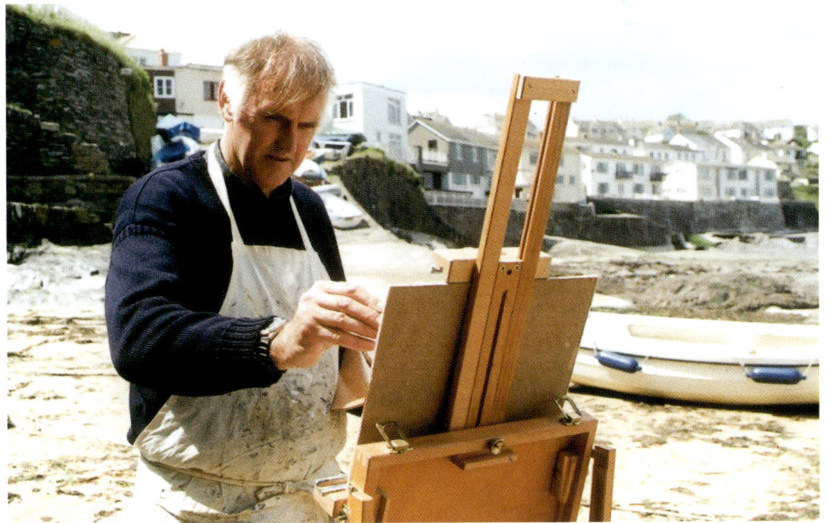

The artist at work.

Nothing is ever simple or easy when you have a paintbrush in your hand. As you solve one set of problems you move into the next.

The new problem was quite simply that finishing an oil painting in one sitting outdoors did not give me the result I required. I had come to enjoy the experience and the end results in the studio of painting oil paint on to dry oil paint. This, of course, is impossible to do in one sitting. You either return several times with the same weather and light, not always possible, or you finish the work in the studio. I am sure this has been done by painters over the years and, after all, the painter is creating a picture not slavishly copying what is in front of him.

As always with painting it is a balancing act. Sometimes things work well and sometimes they don't and get scrapped. Certain materials give you the results you want but are difficult to use, other materials work sometimes but not others. I feel that every time I pick up a paintbrush I have issues to explore. Even when things do not work out I put it down to experience and hope that I have learned something from it.

Even though I did not have a one-man show in 2000 I did take part in two group shows, one at the Glasshouse Gallery, Truro, and the other at the Rainyday Gallery in Penzance. I continued along these lines in the early summer of 2001 with a three-man show at the Maltby Gallery in Winchester. This was special for me because the other two painters were my old friends Roy Ray and John Emanuel.

I am very pleased to report that, during 2001, Peter O'Neil decided to reopen his Out Of The Blue Gallery at Marazion, and offered me a September one-man show. This proved to be a big success and a very happy experience for me, helped in no small way by Peter's very approachable personality and relaxed 'party' attitude to show previews. Not always the most tranquil of occasions for artists.

Once again a south-coast gallery had brought good luck, adding to my success at Portscatho and also Mid Cornwall Galleries at Biscovey near St Austell – one of my first supporters and a very encouraging promoter for many years. It is always very heartening when galleries approach with requests to show your work, and John Golding at the Fowey River Gallery suggested a one-man show for July 2002, a wonderful excuse for many visits to Fowey to 'work'. Salcombe on the South Devon coast was one of the places I had often visited when delivering lifeboats for the RNLI, it being one of their regular stopping-off points. It had become a town I knew quite well, its people too, but, of course, from the sea.

When in October 2001 I received a telephone call from Mandy at the Cove's Quay Gallery, Karen and I decided to hire a car and pay her a visit. Even after dozens of visits in the past, it was, by road, like approaching an unfamiliar place for the first time. This feeling was immediately dispelled as we walked from the car park and I encountered several old friends. Passing a small pleasant hotel called the Old Porch House, I informed Karen that I had stayed there many times. She replied that she had long been under the misapprehension that I had always roughed it whilst away on lifeboat trips. Another cover blown! Salcombe, as always, is a joy and Mandy is arranging for Karen and me to stay there in order to paint in the port and surrounding area. I have to say it is something we both anticipate with pleasure.

Much of my life appears to have been accidental, events happening without much planning behind them and, thankfully, they have mostly turned out OK. I do have an ambition today that was missing in my early life and that is to be a good painter. Those two words seem so simple, yet represent achievement that is complicated and elusive, and the exploration that is full of excitement and enjoyment. When I awake each morning I have that wonderful feeling that in the day ahead I am going to have many more things I want to do than I can possibly have time for. That feeling is one of the things I love about painting.

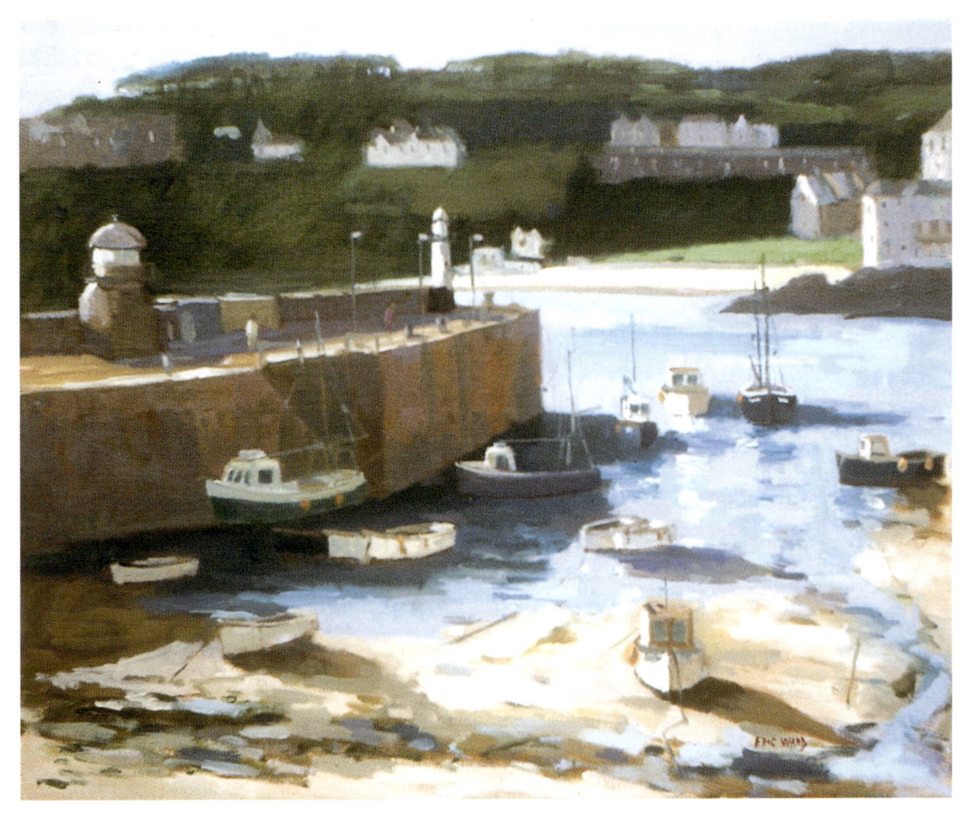

BOATS & HARBOURS

Boats and harbours have always been my world, my playground as a boy in St Ives and workplace as a man. As a fisherman my working life began in St Ives, then later Newlyn, Penzance and Falmouth. Work with the RNLI took me farther afield, to ports and harbours all over Britain. Now, as a painter, I visit old haunts and new, see old friends and meet new – with easel and oils instead of fish and boats. Very different and exciting.

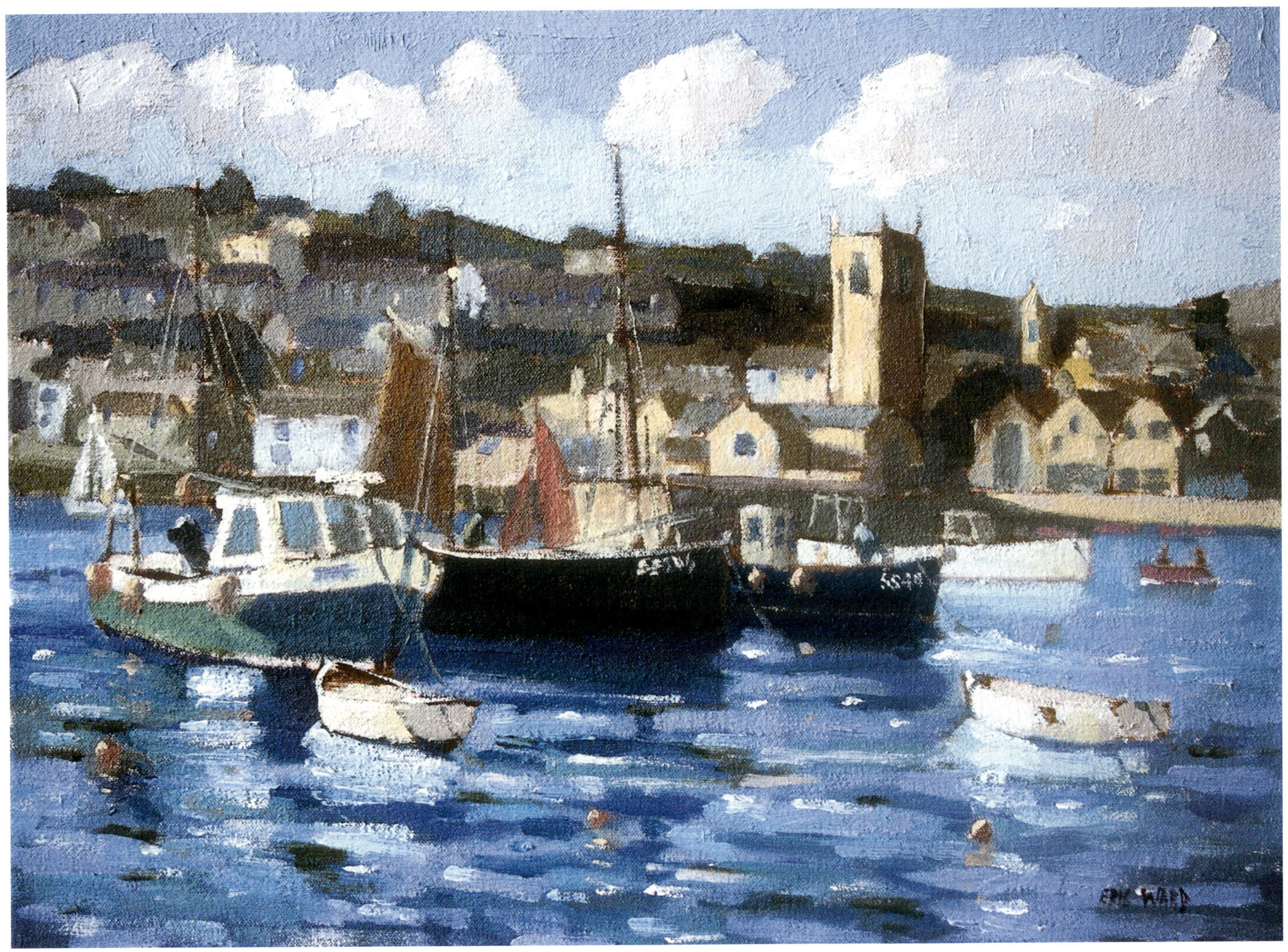

Sunny Day, St Ives Harbour
Oil on canvas, 30.5 x 40.6cm

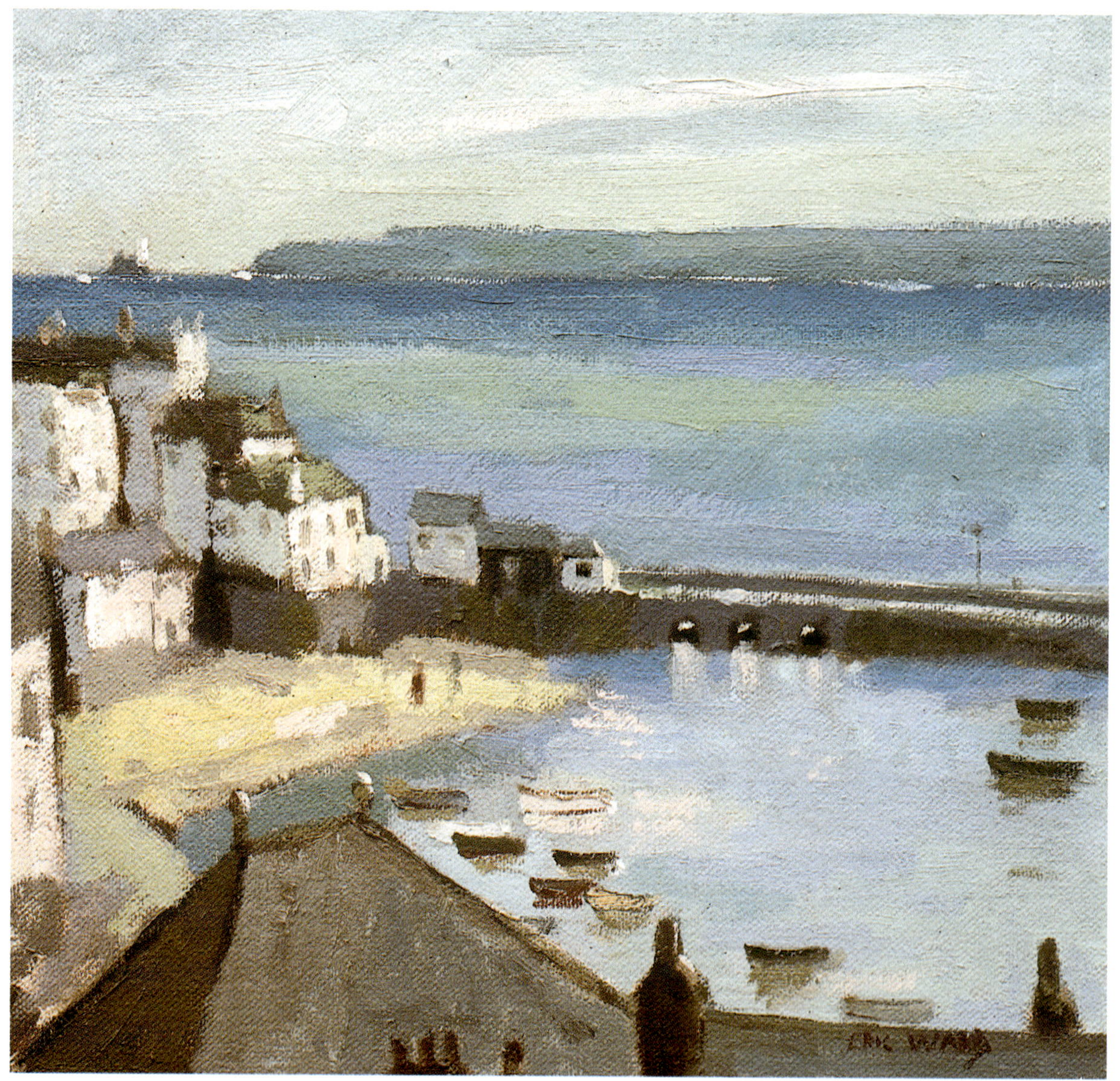

St Ives Harbour
Oil on panel, 25.4 x 25.4cm

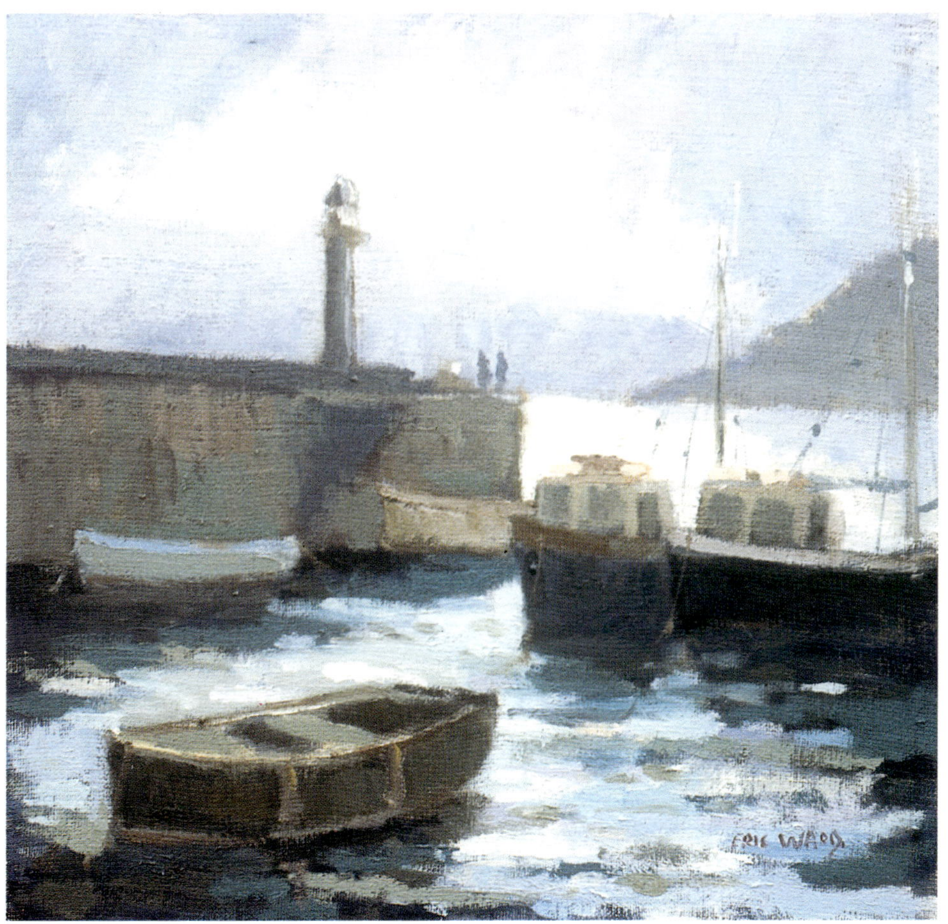

Early Morning, St Ives Harbour
Oil on panel, 25.4 x 25.4cm

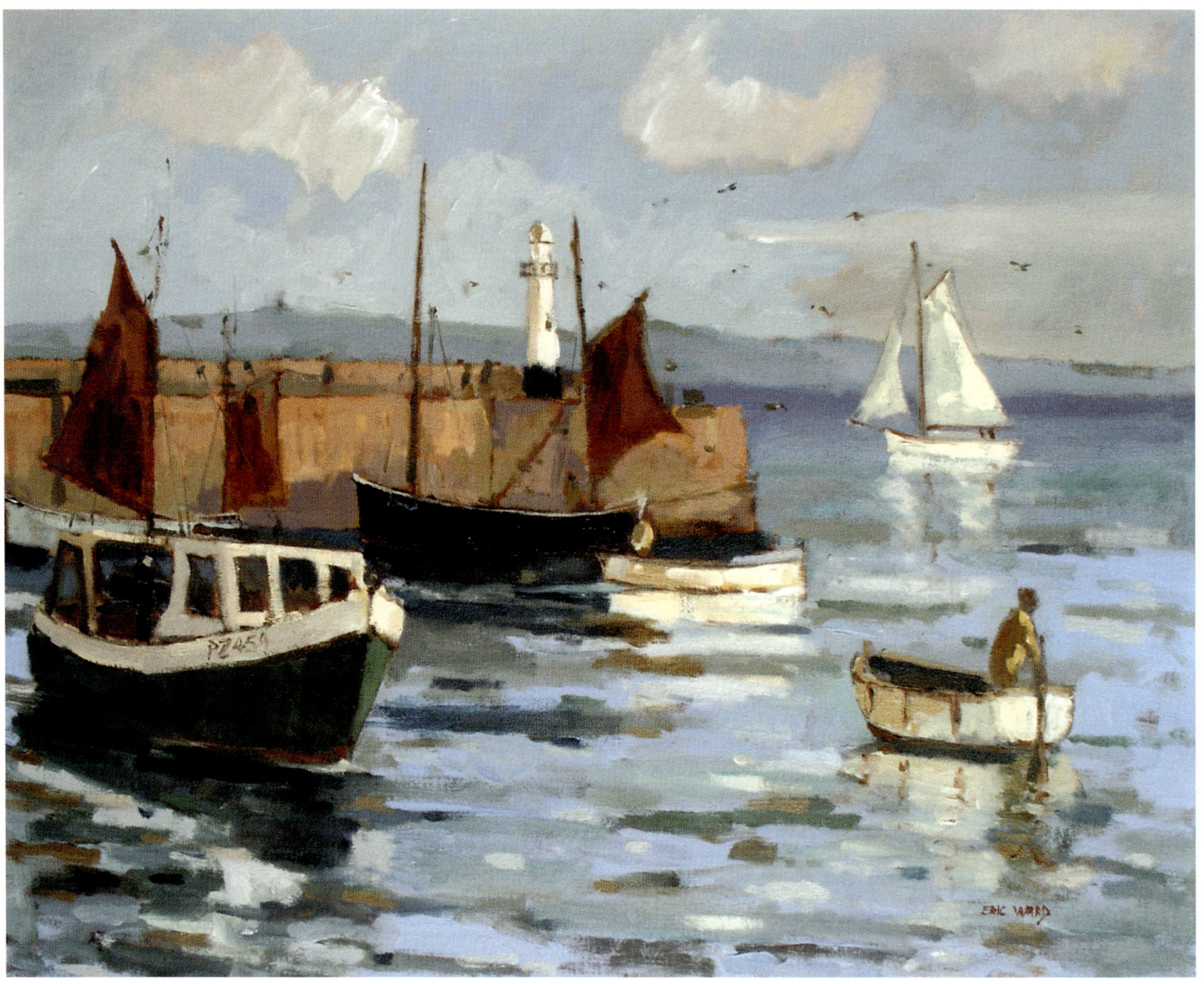

St Ives Harbour, Afternoon Sunshine
Oil on linen, 50.8 x 60.8cm

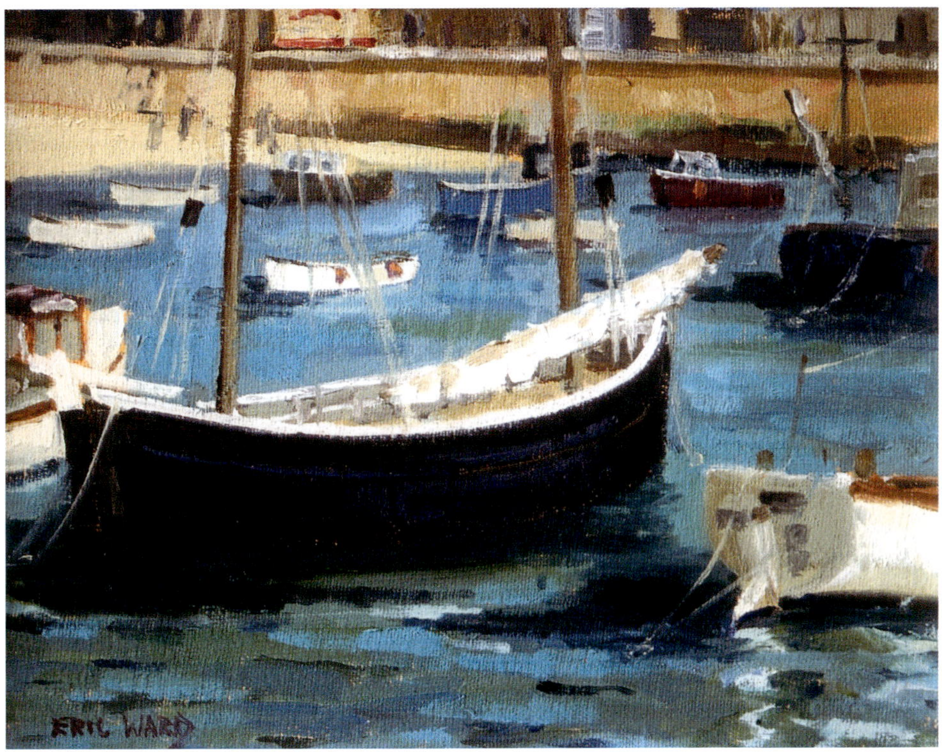

The Dolly Pentreath *at St Ives*
Oil on panel, 20.3 x 25.4cm

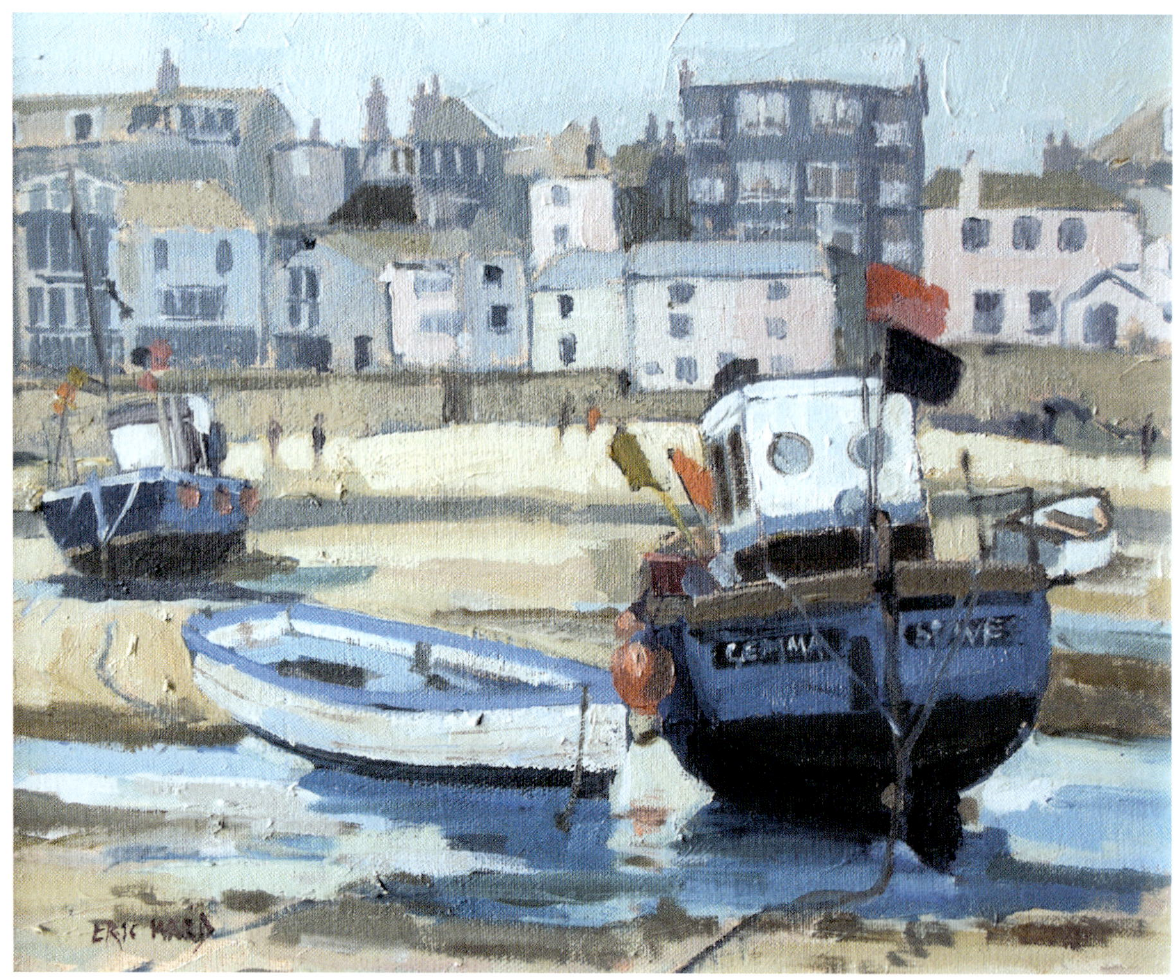

Low Tide at St Ives Harbour
Oil on panel, 25.4 x 30.5cm

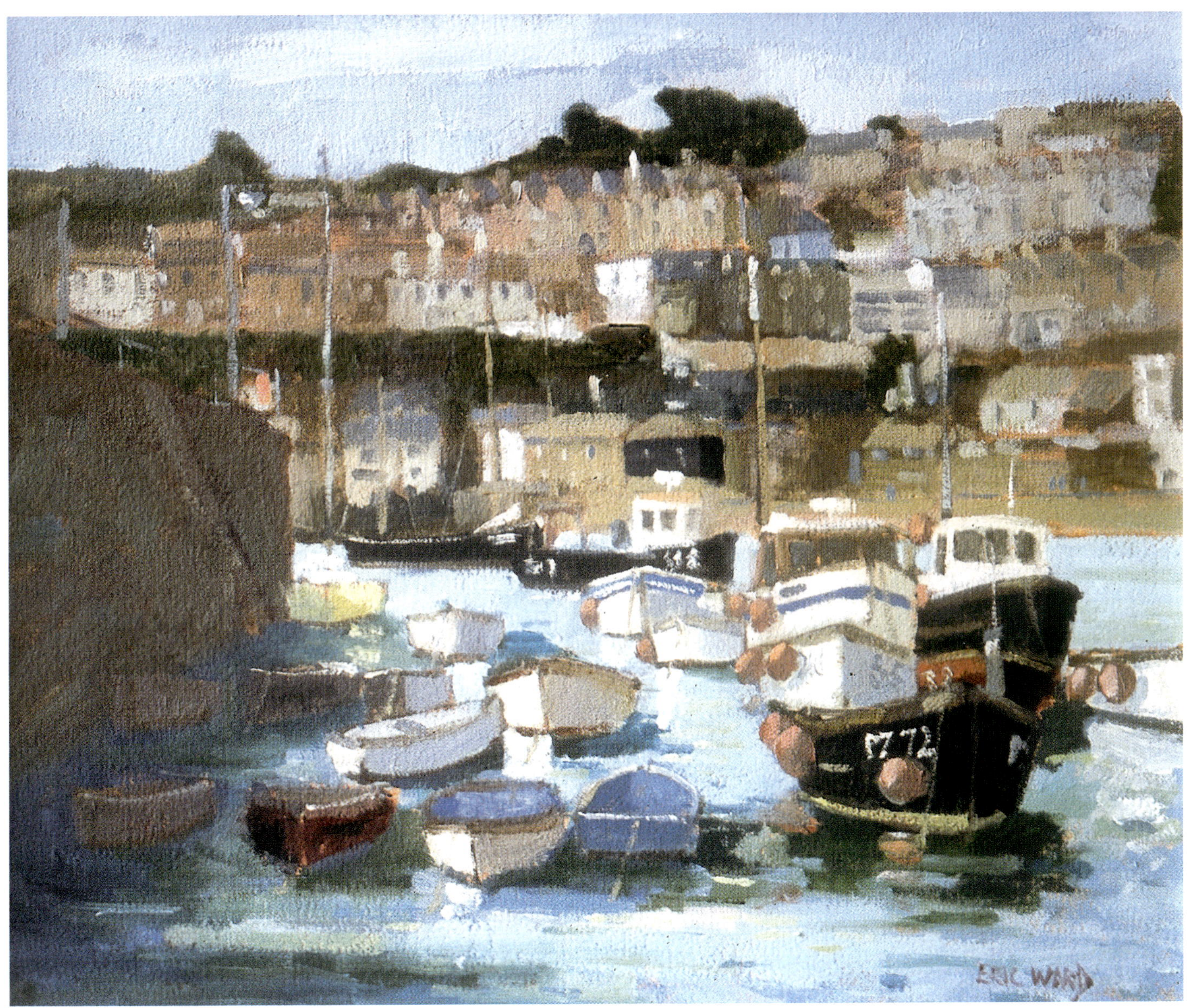

The Yellow Yacht, St Ives Harbour
Acrylic on paper, 30.5 x 35.5cm

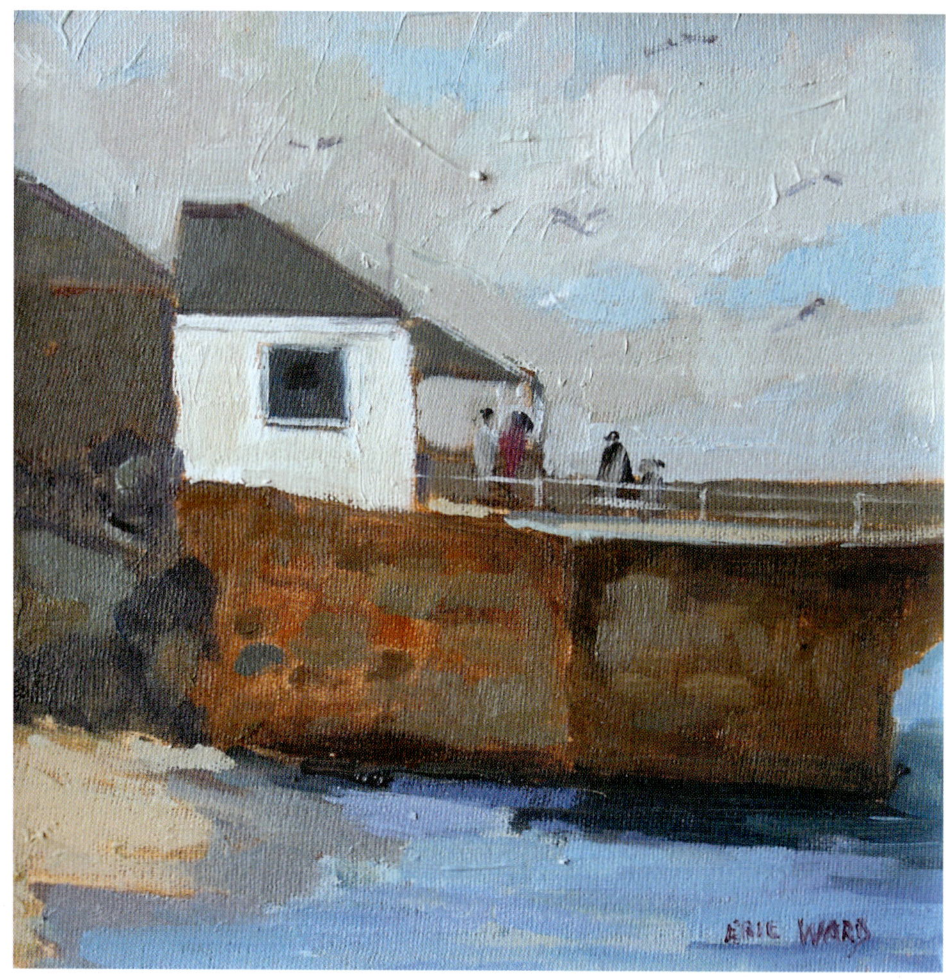

The Harbour Office, St Ives
Oil on panel, 20.3 x 20.3cm

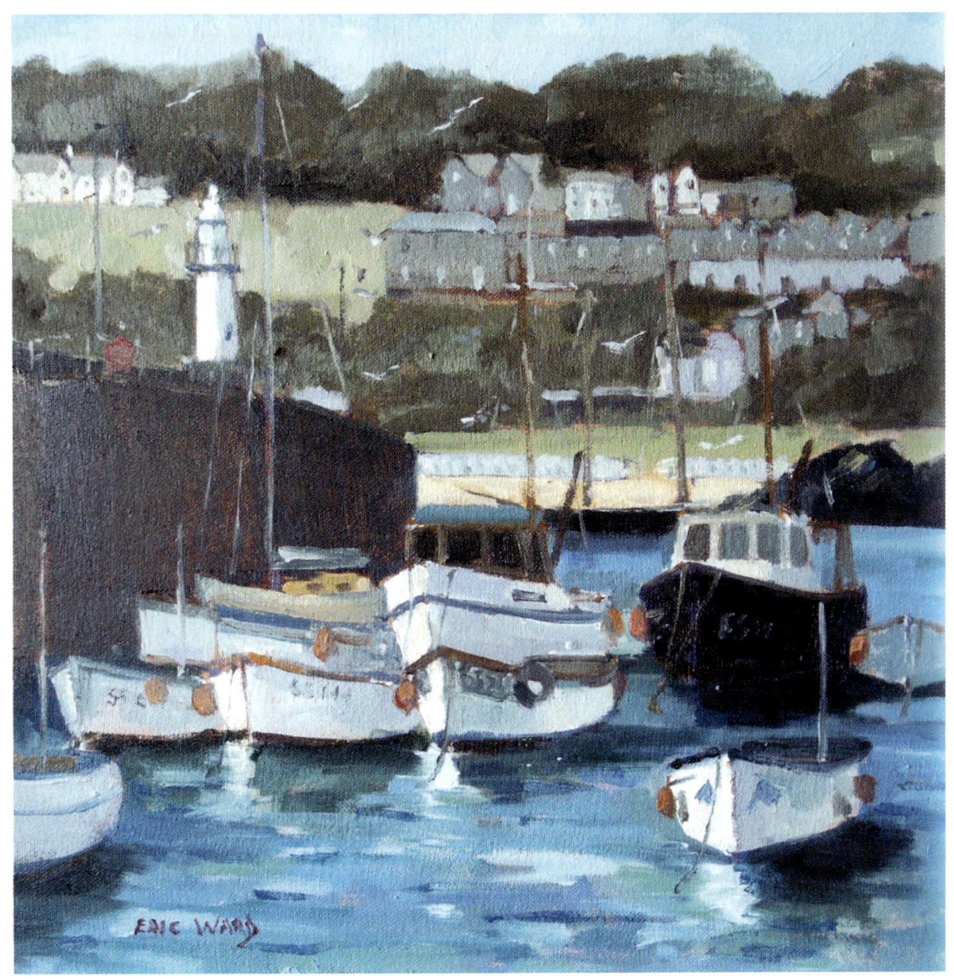

Fishing Boats, St Ives Harbour
Oil on panel, 30.5 x 30.5cm

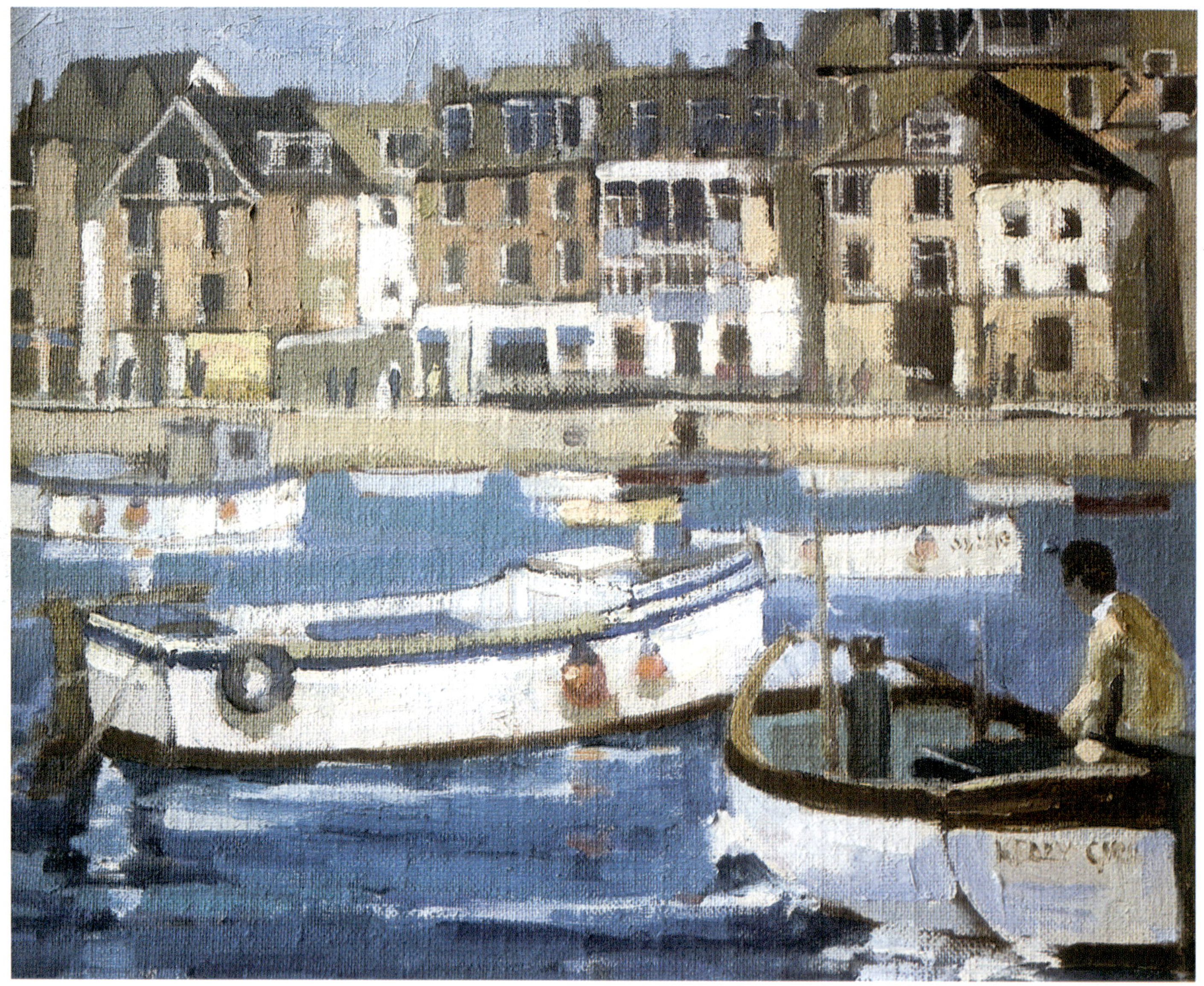

The Wharf, St Ives
Oil on panel, 25.4 x 30.5cm

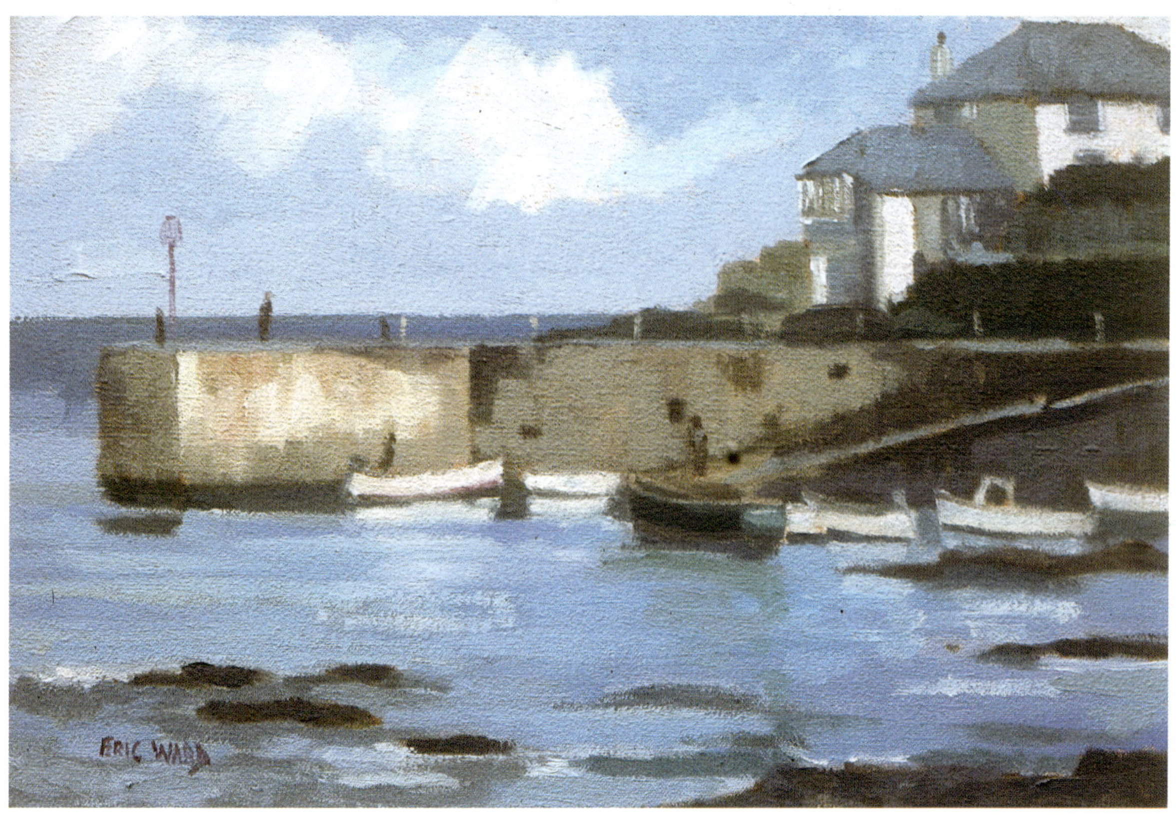

Portscatho Harbour
Oil on panel, 25.4 x 35.5cm

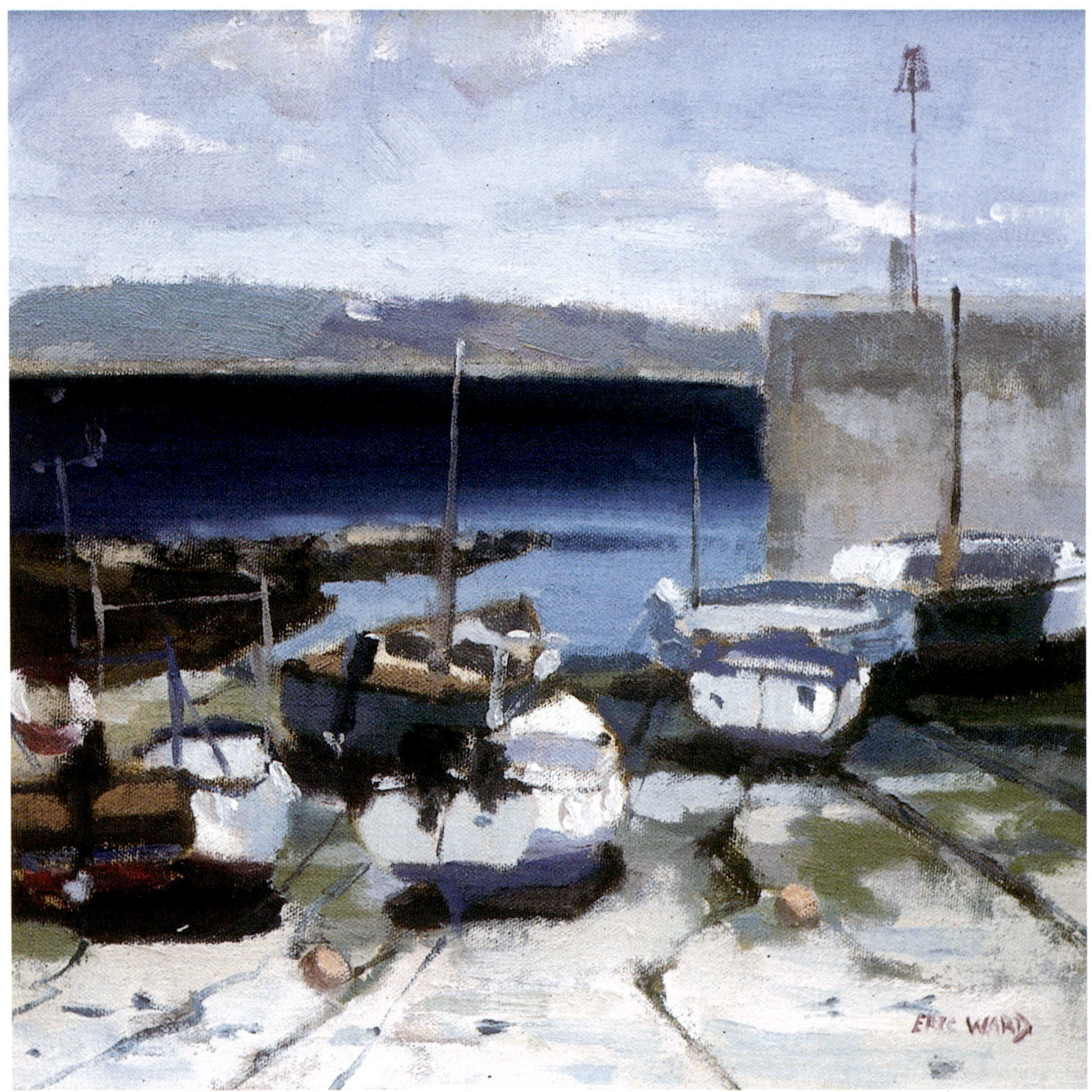

Low Tide, Portscatho
Oil on panel, 27.9 x 27.9cm

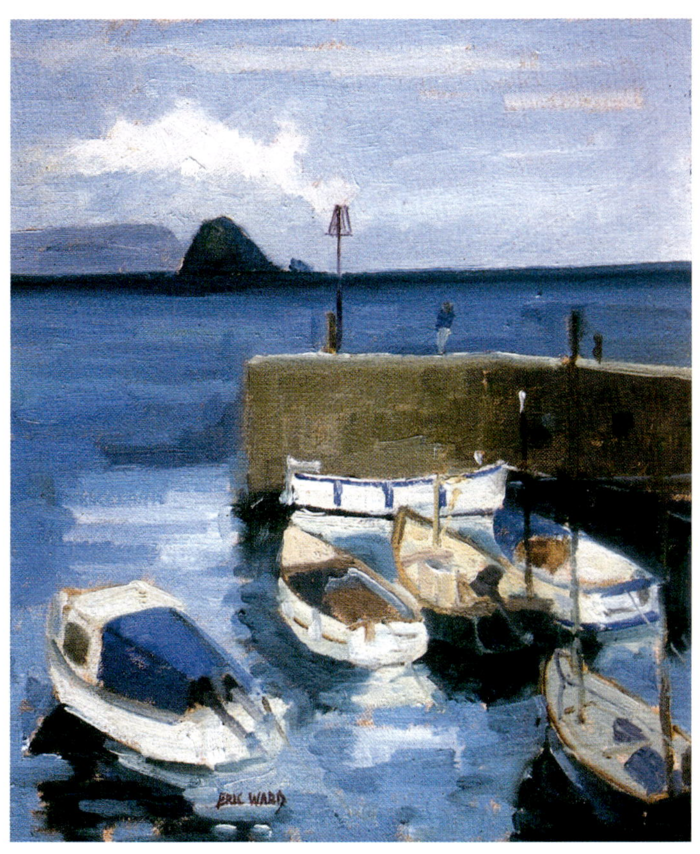

Portscatho Pier
Oil on panel, 30.5 x 25.4cm

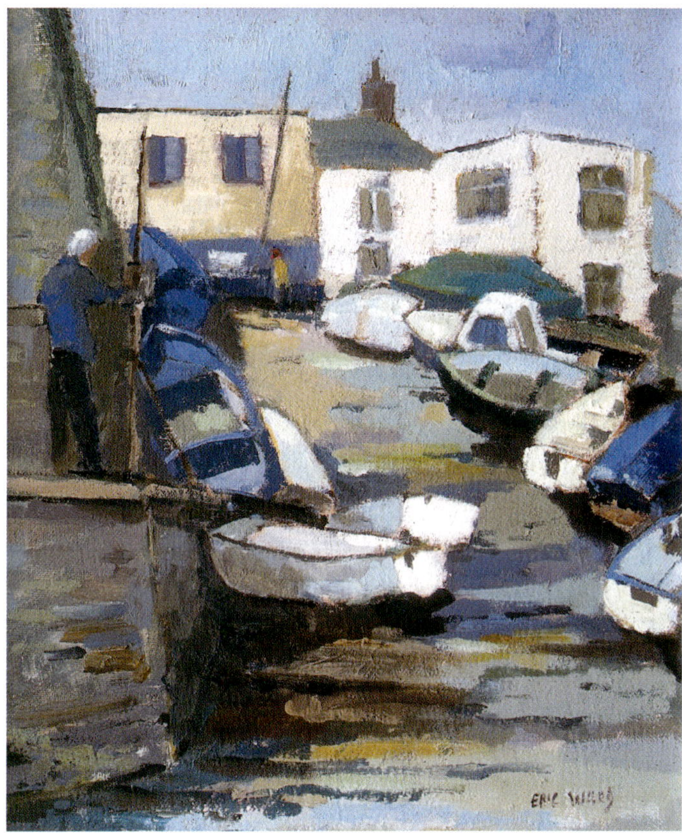

Trevor Felcey at Portscatho
Oil on panel, 30.5 x 25.4cm

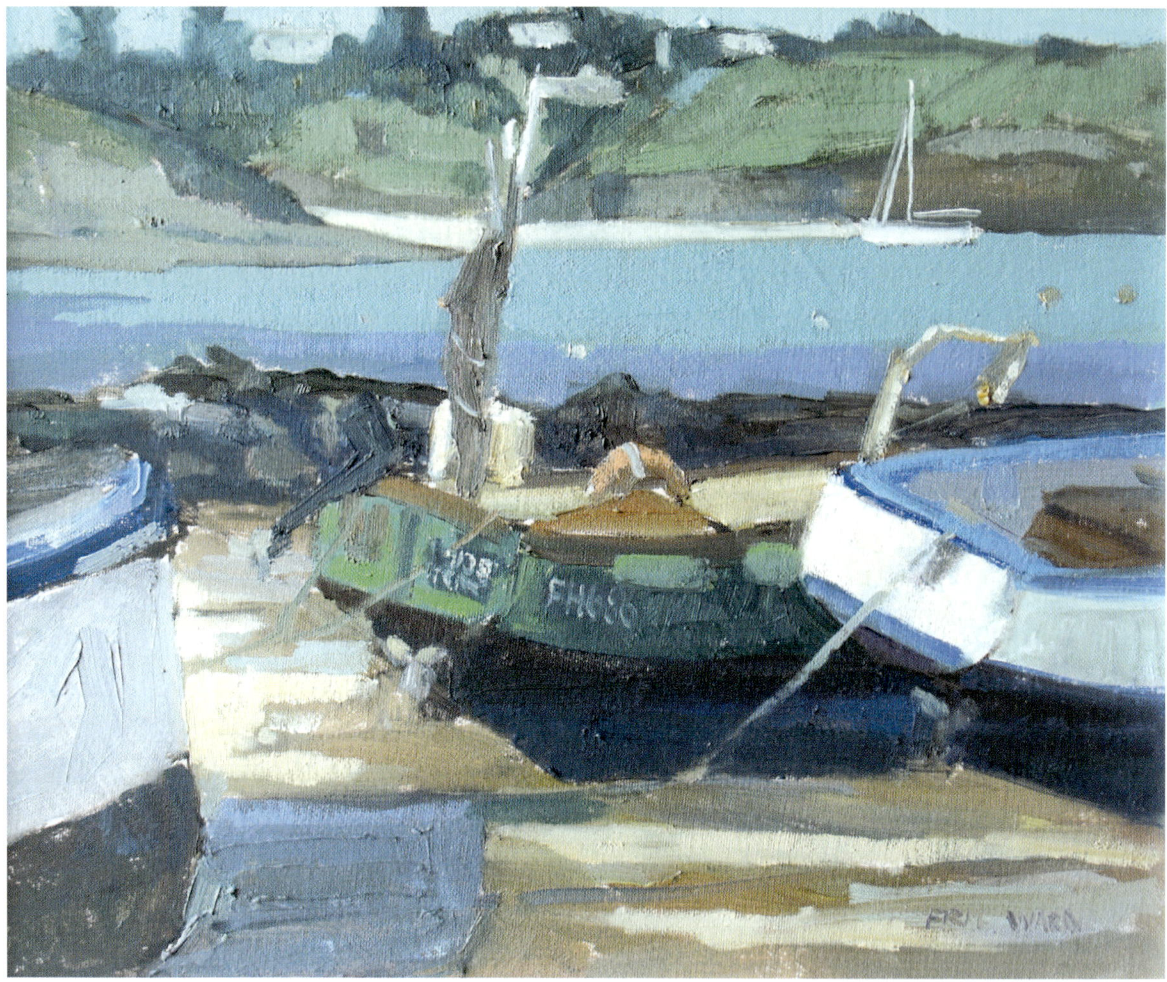

Boats at Portscatho
Oil on panel, 25.4 x 30.5cm

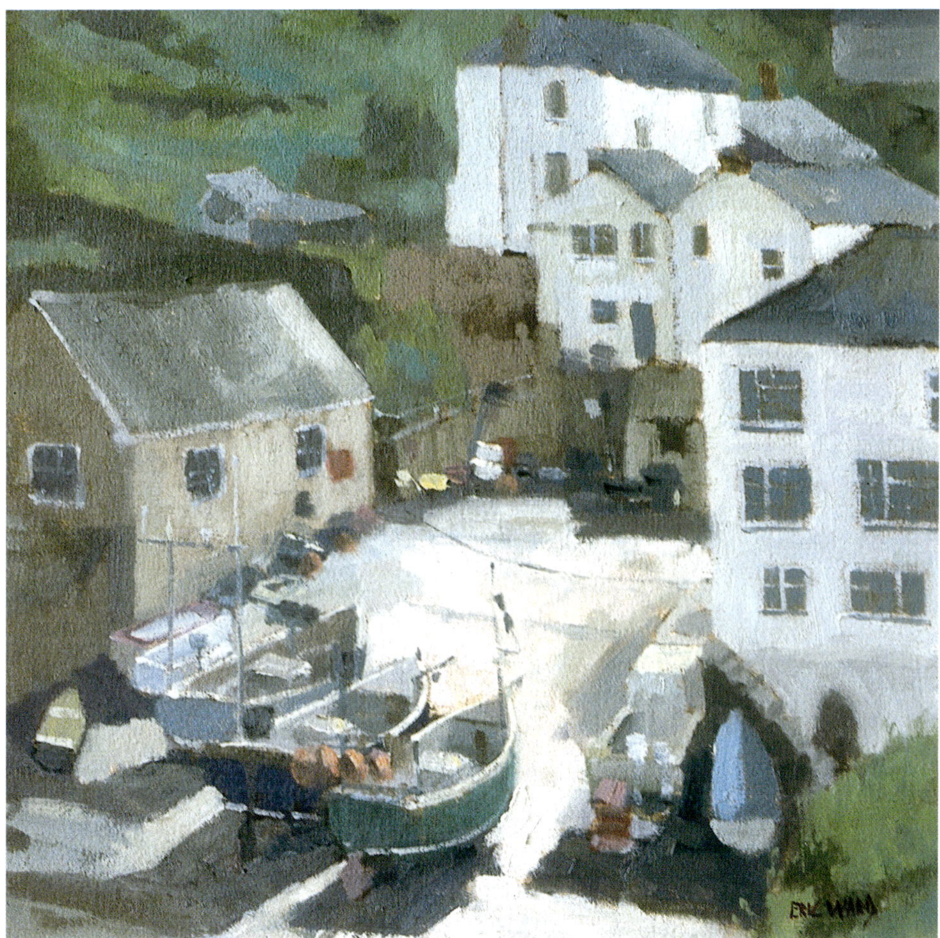

Portloe, Cornwall
Oil on panel, 35.5 x 35.5cm

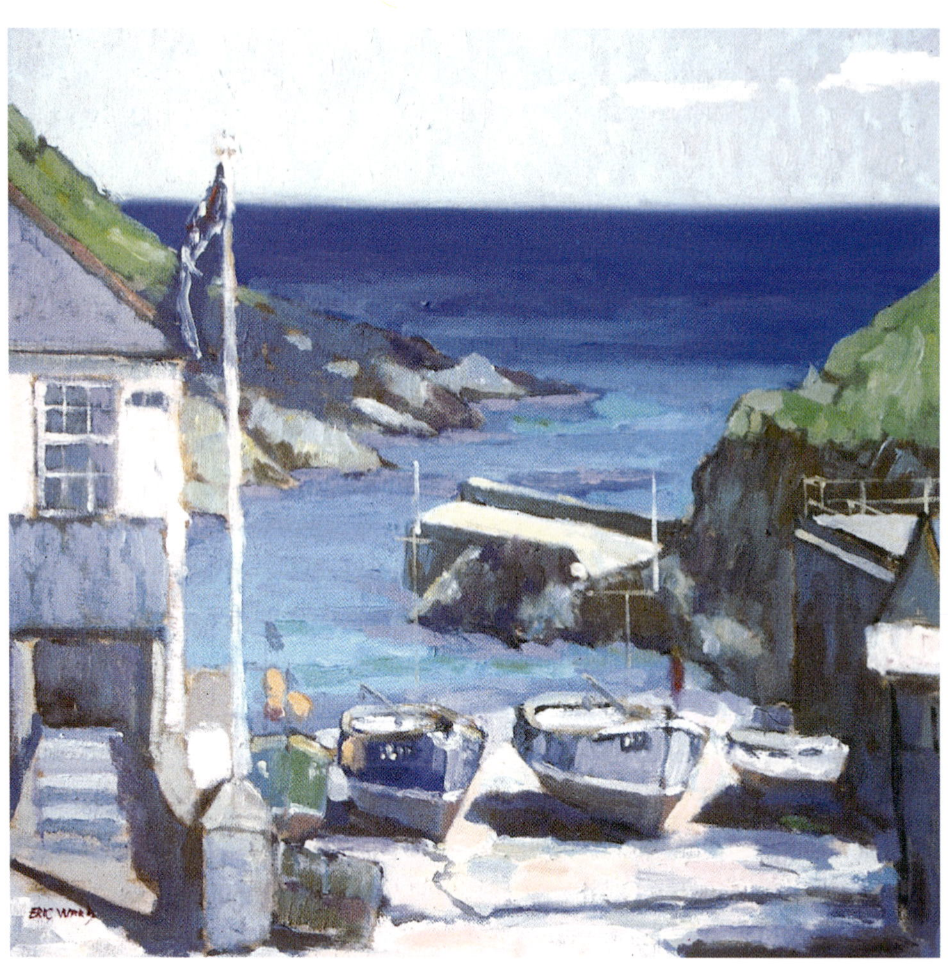

Boats on the Slipway, Portloe, Cornwall
Oil on panel, 40.6 x 40.6cm

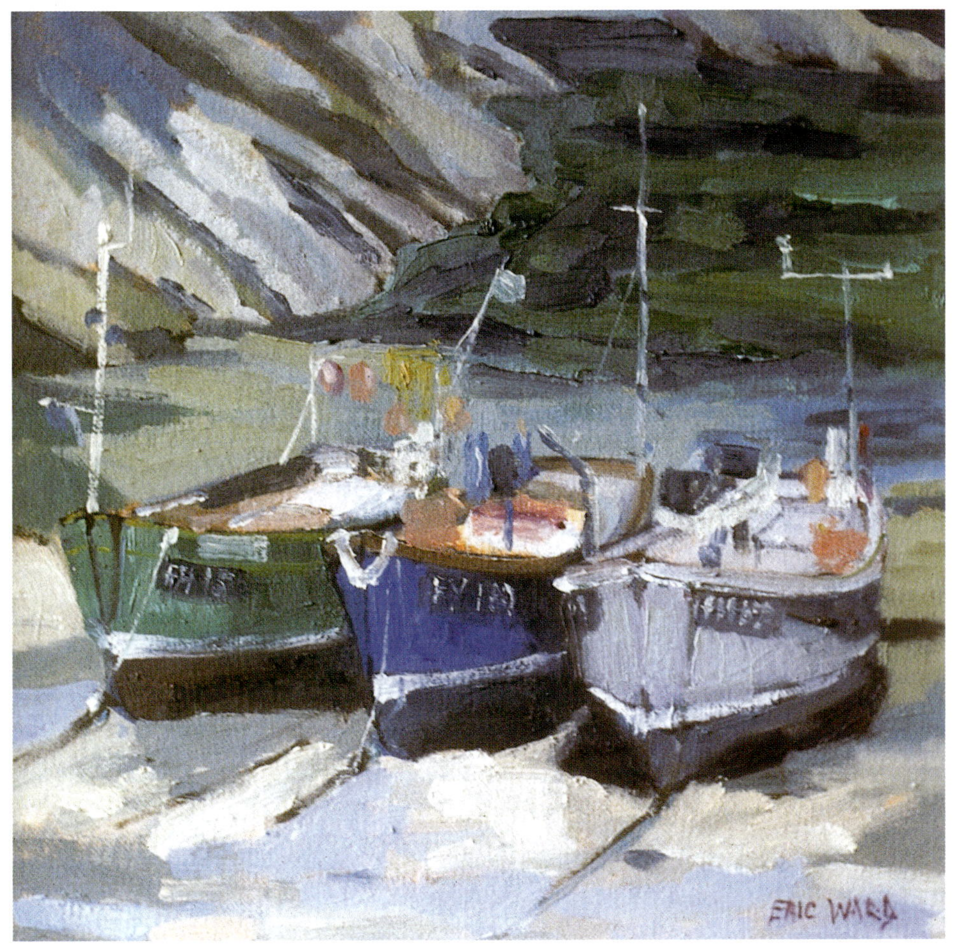

Fishing Boats, Portloe
Oil on panel, 25.4 x 25.4cm

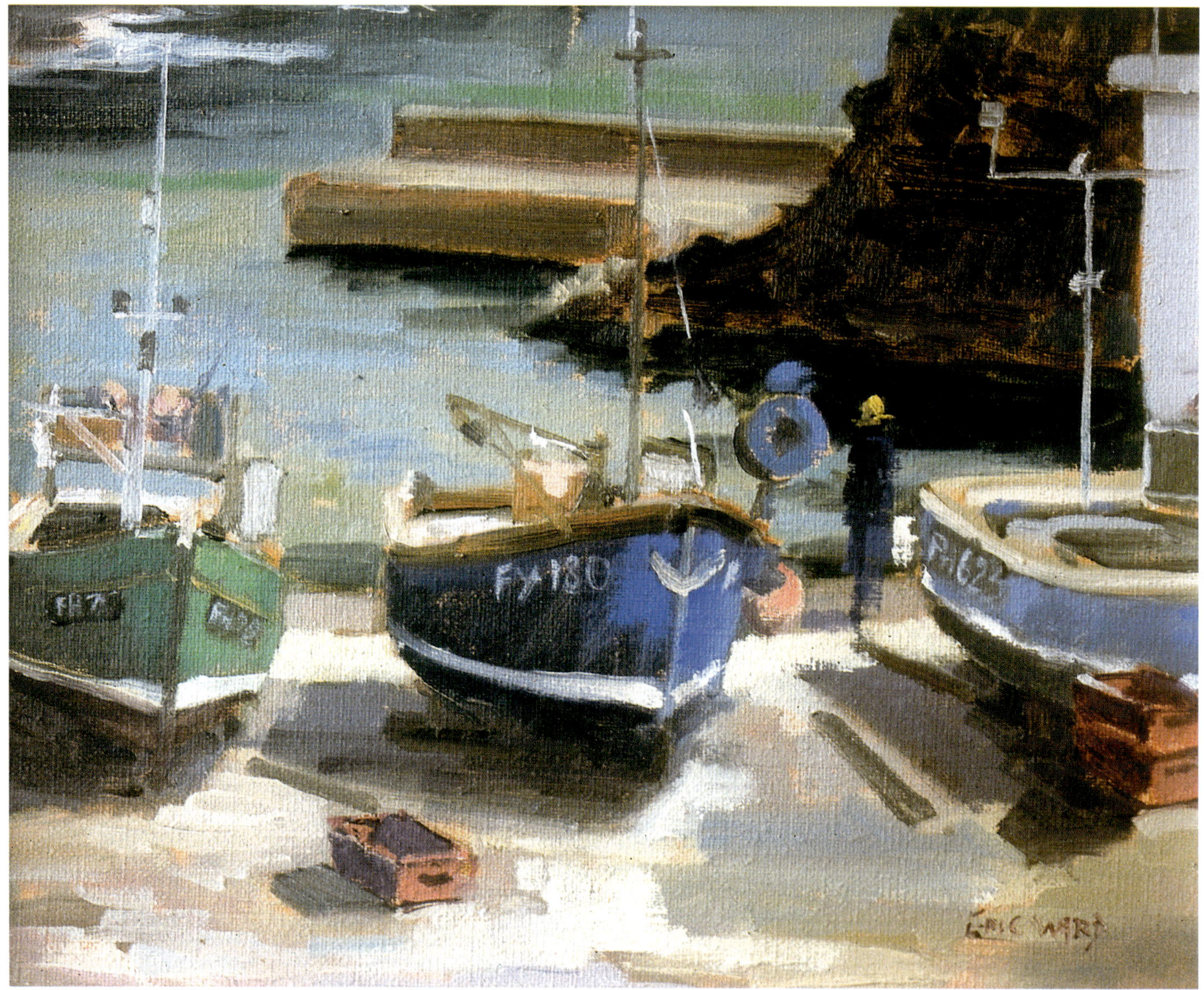

Karen at Portloe
Oil on linen, 25.4 x 30.5cm

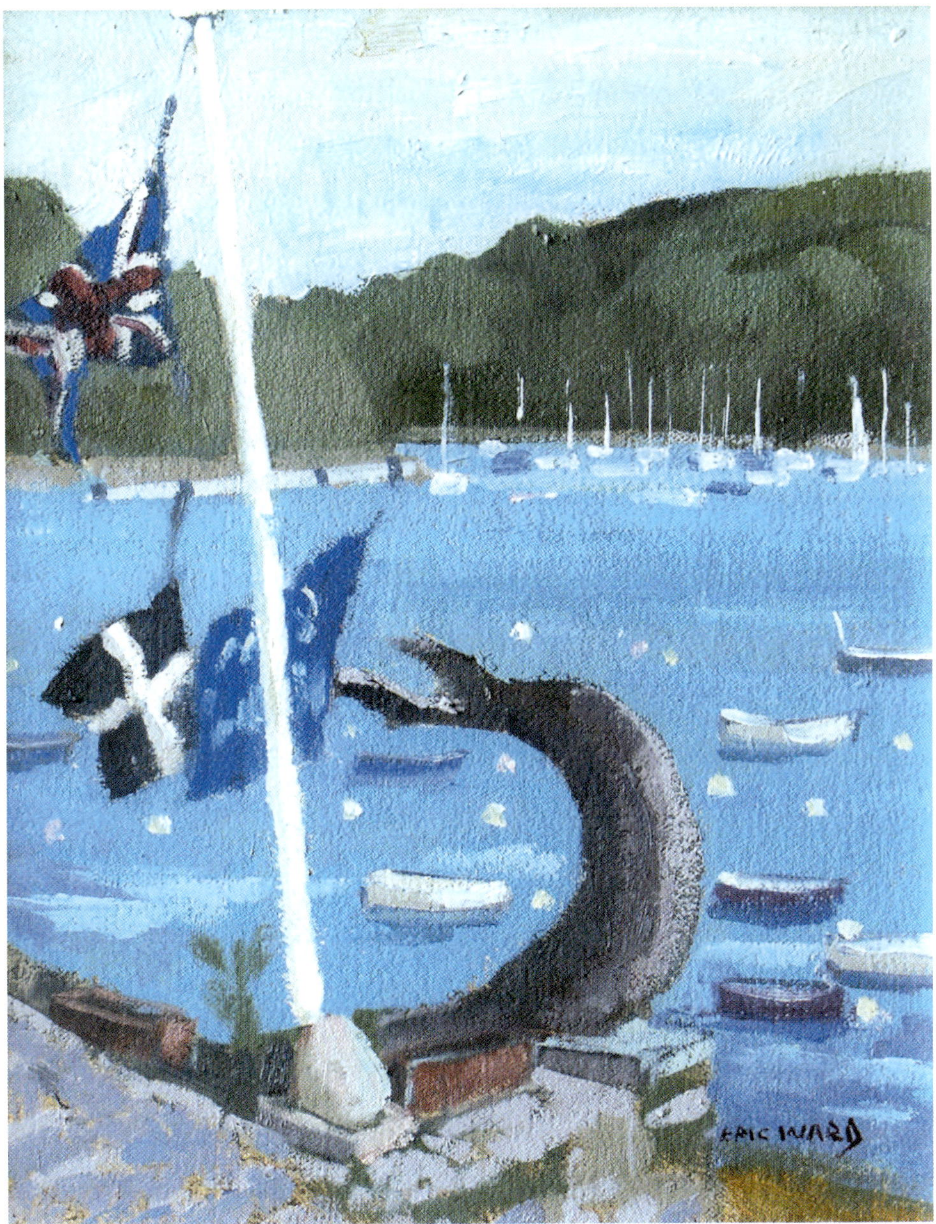

Flags at Fowey
Oil on panel, 25.4 x 20.3cm

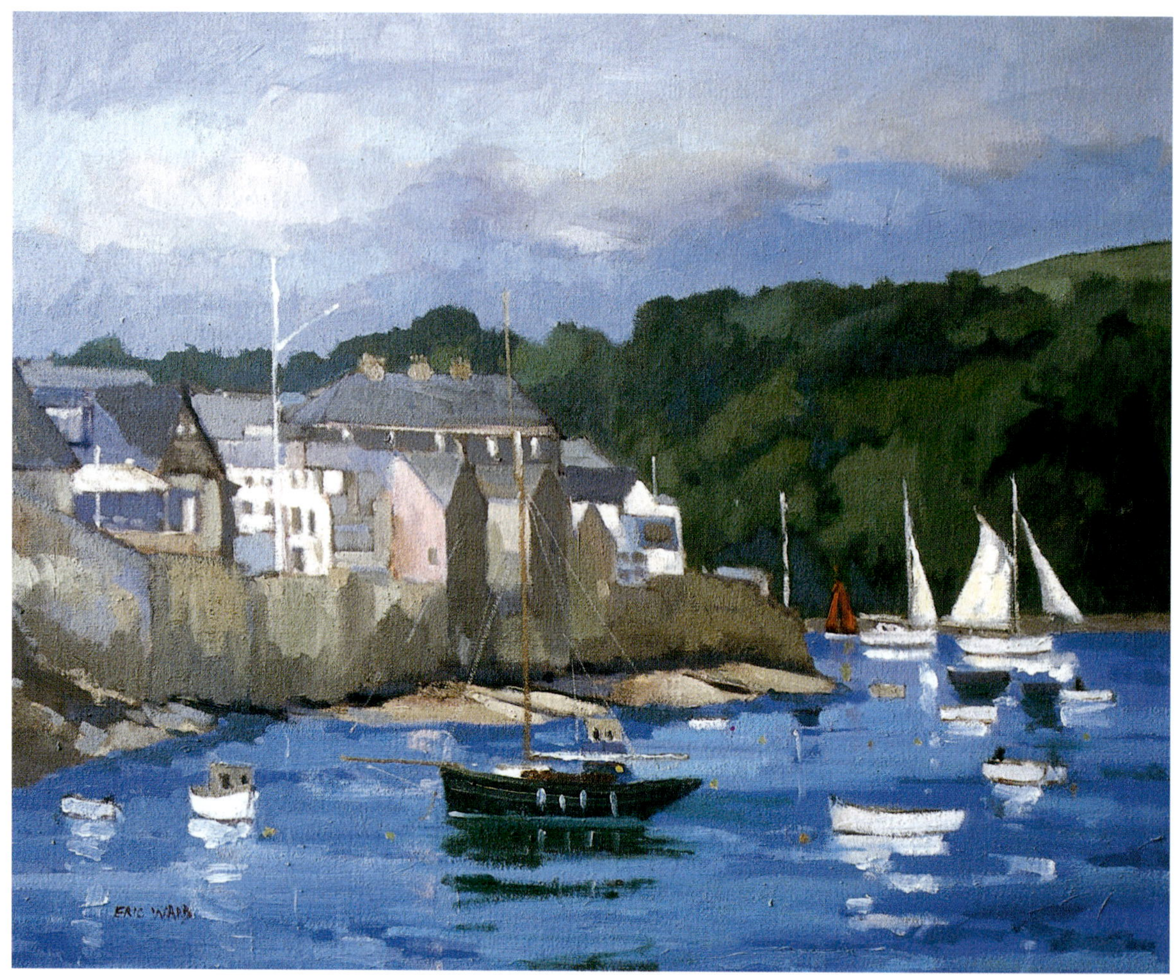

Summertime on the Fowey
Oil on linen, 50.8 x 60.8cm

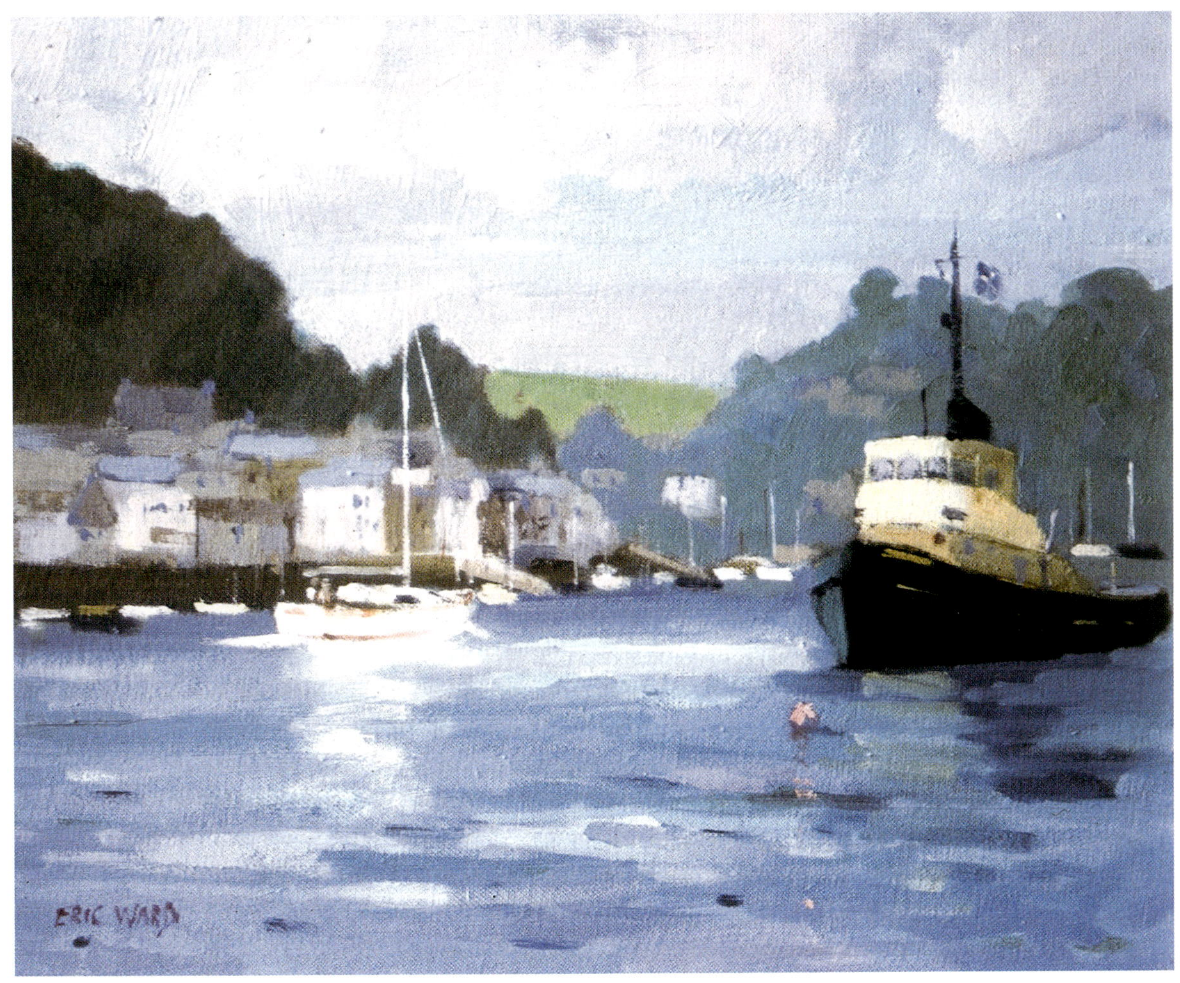

Tugboat and Yachts, River Fowey
Oil on panel, 25.4 x 30.5cm

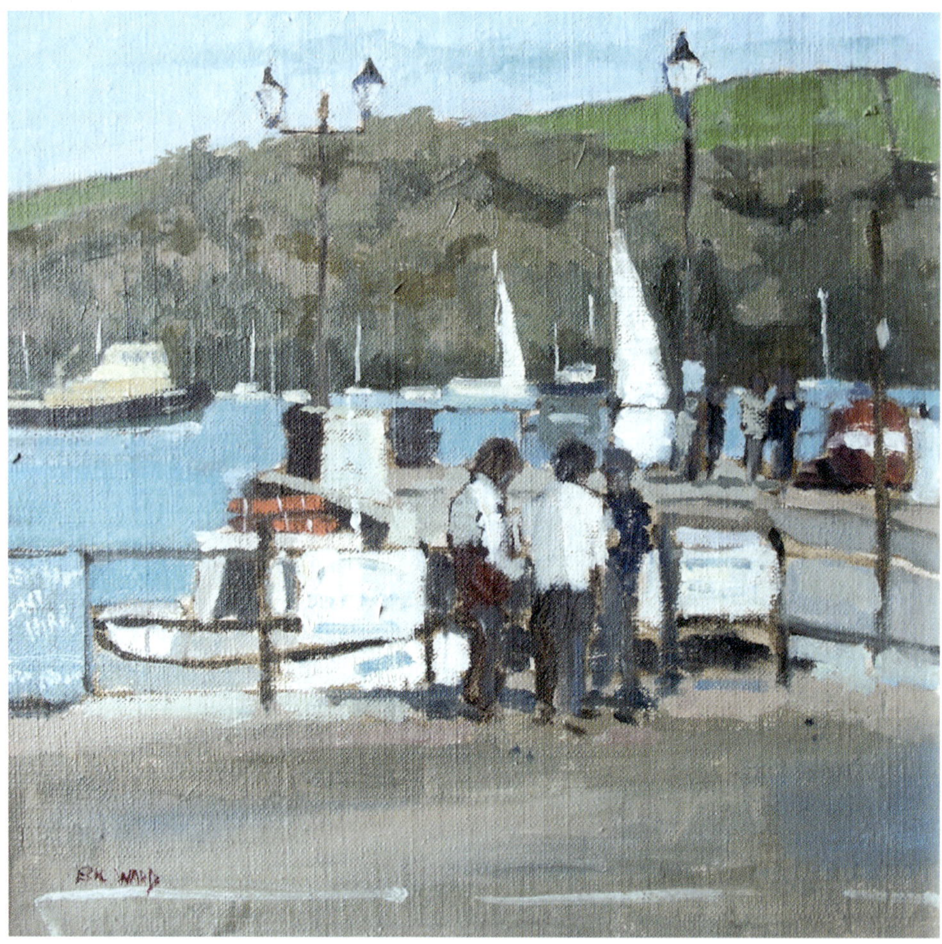

Discussing the Day, Fowey Pier
Oil on panel, 35.5 x 35.5cm

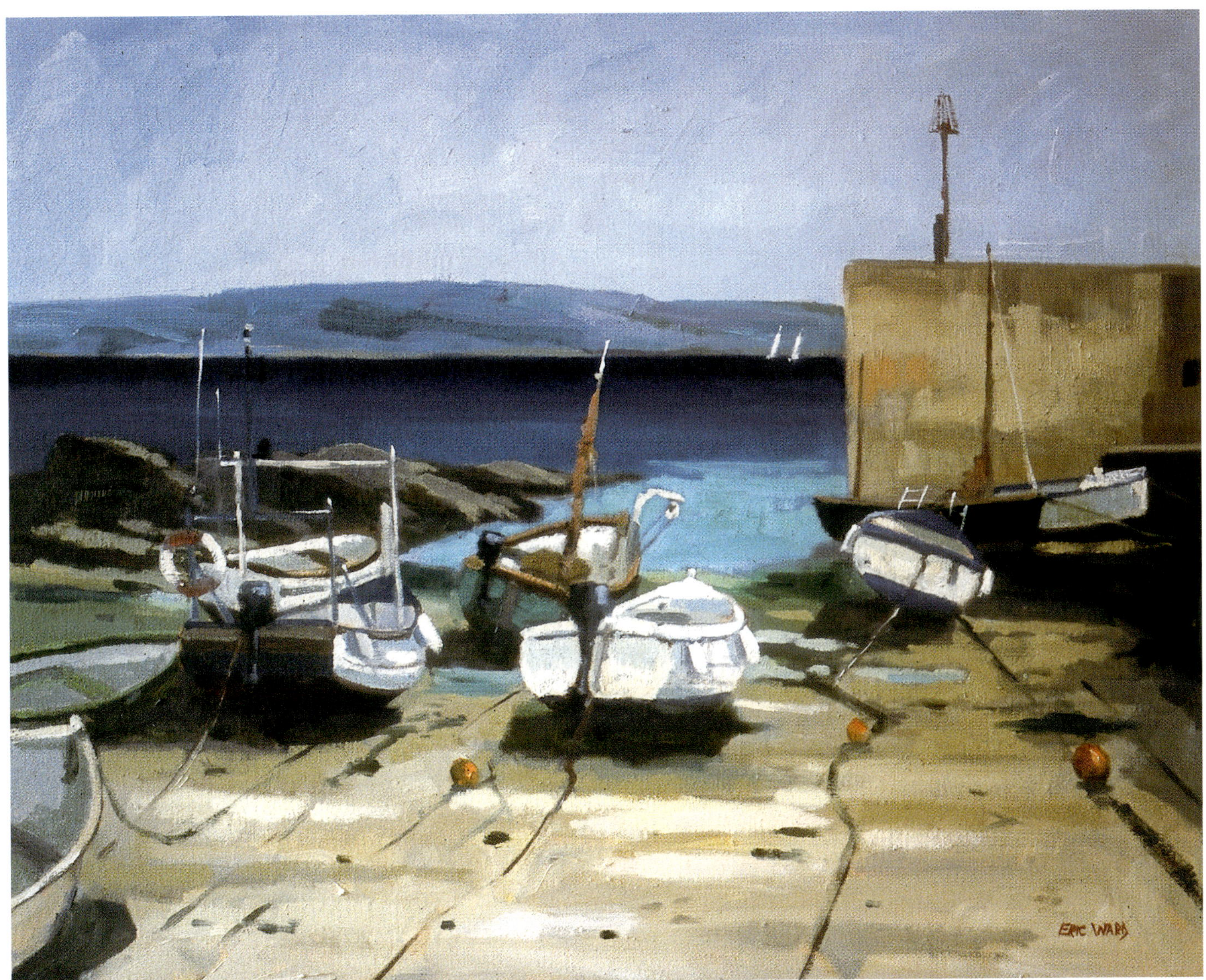

Boats at Portscatho
Oil on linen, 50.8 x 61cm

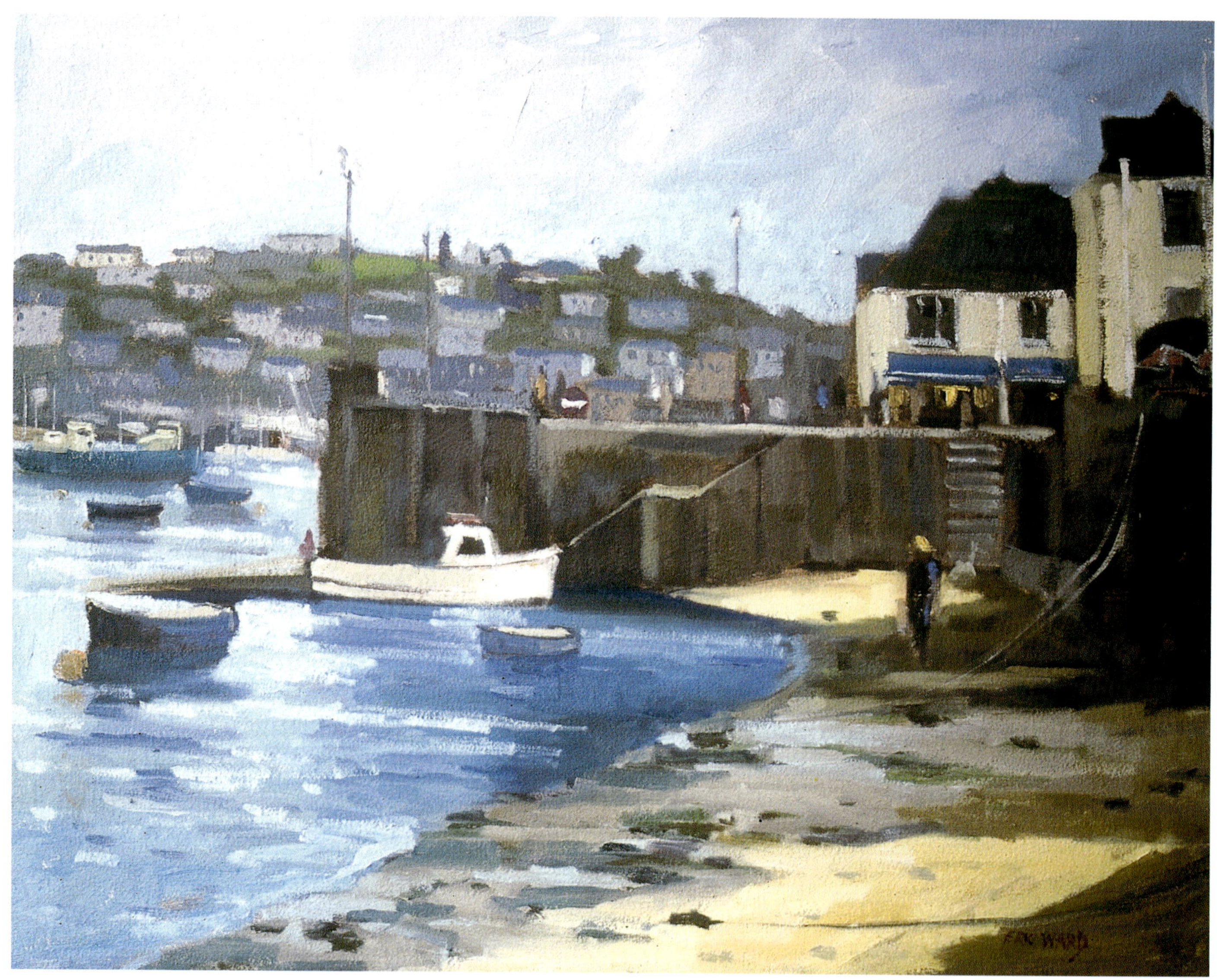

River Edge, Fowey
Oil on canvas, 50.8 x 60.8cm

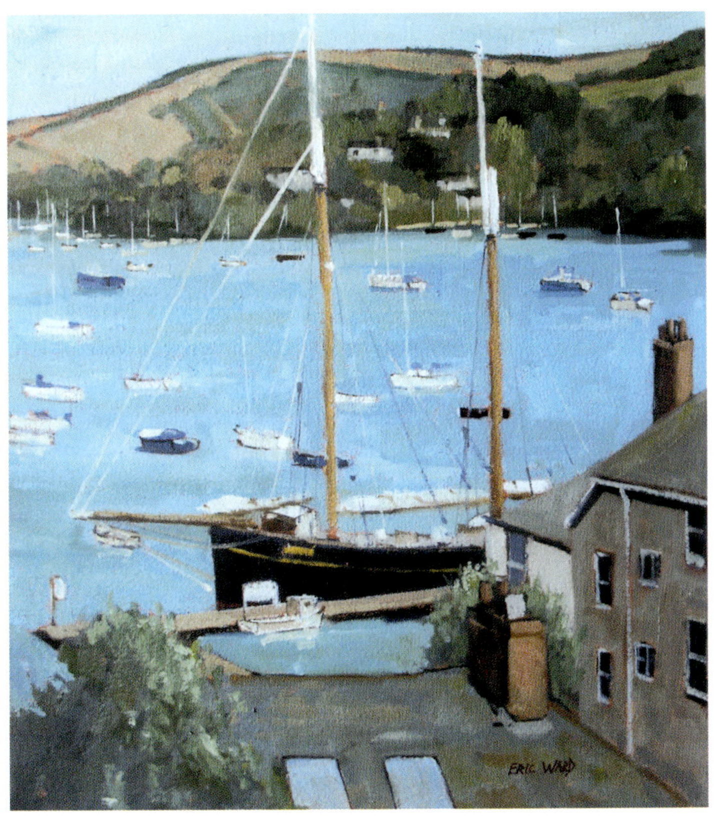

Lotus *at Salcombe*
Oil on canvas, 40.6 x 35.5cm

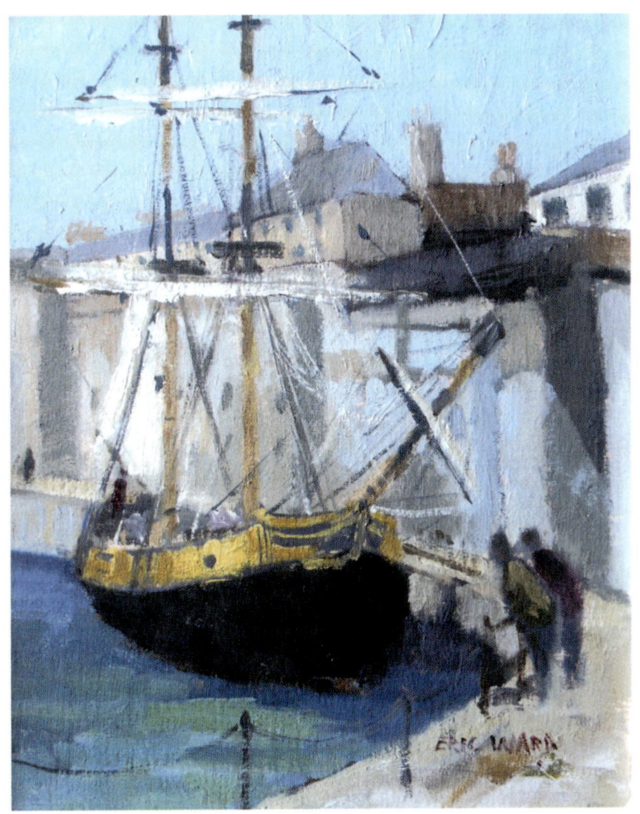

Phoenix *at Charlestown*
Oil on panel, 25.4 x 20.3cm

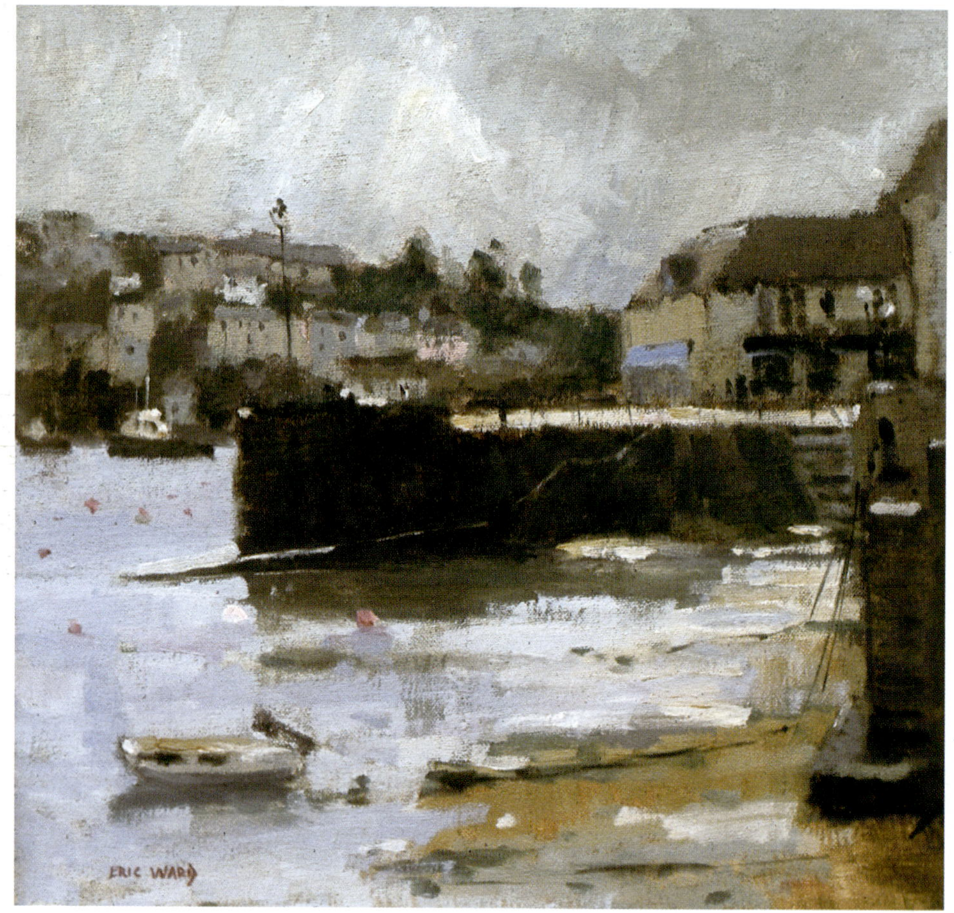

Fowey, Cornwall
Oil on panel, 30.5 x 30.5cm

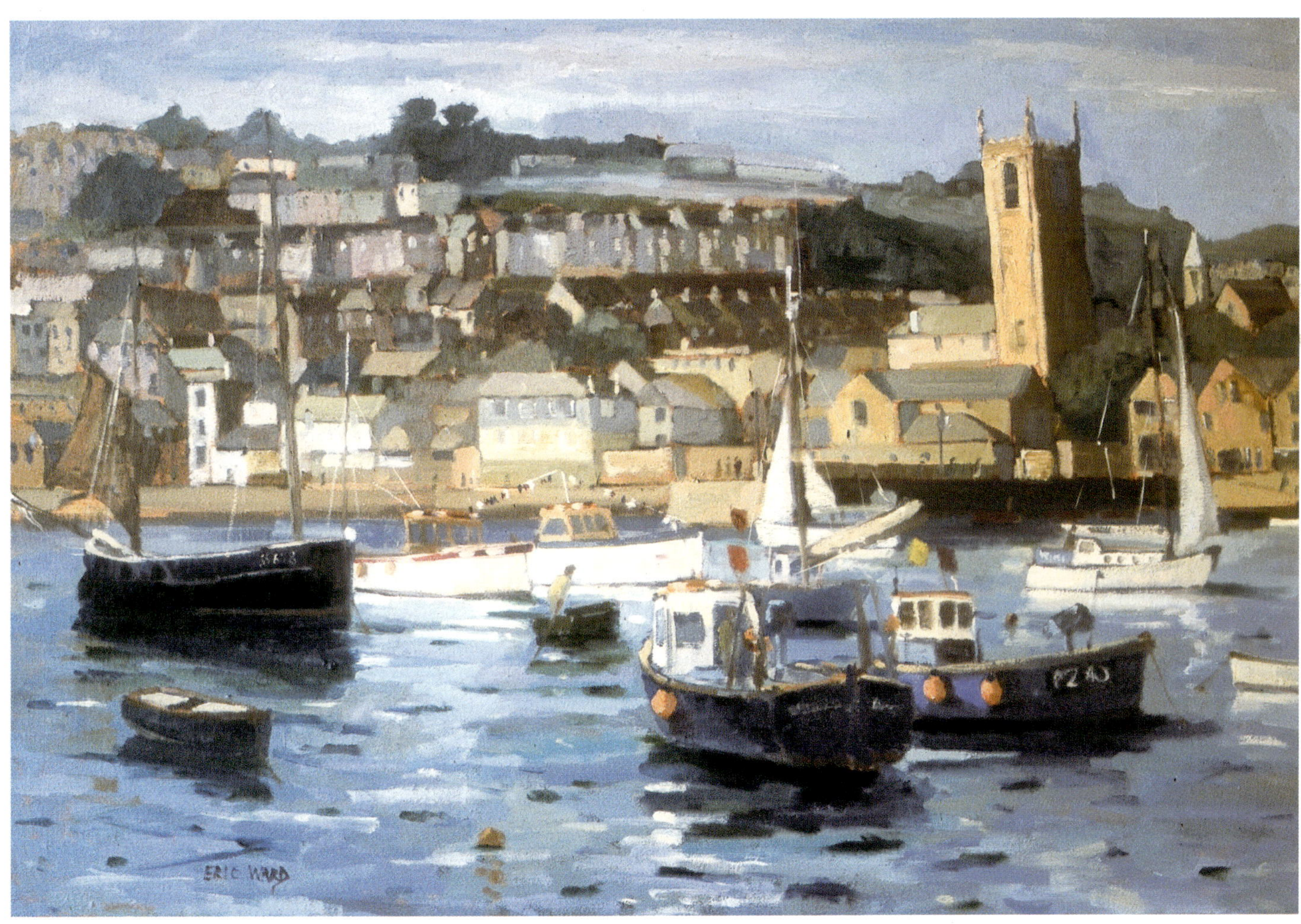

Summer Harbour at St Ives
Oil on canvas, 50.8 x 71cm

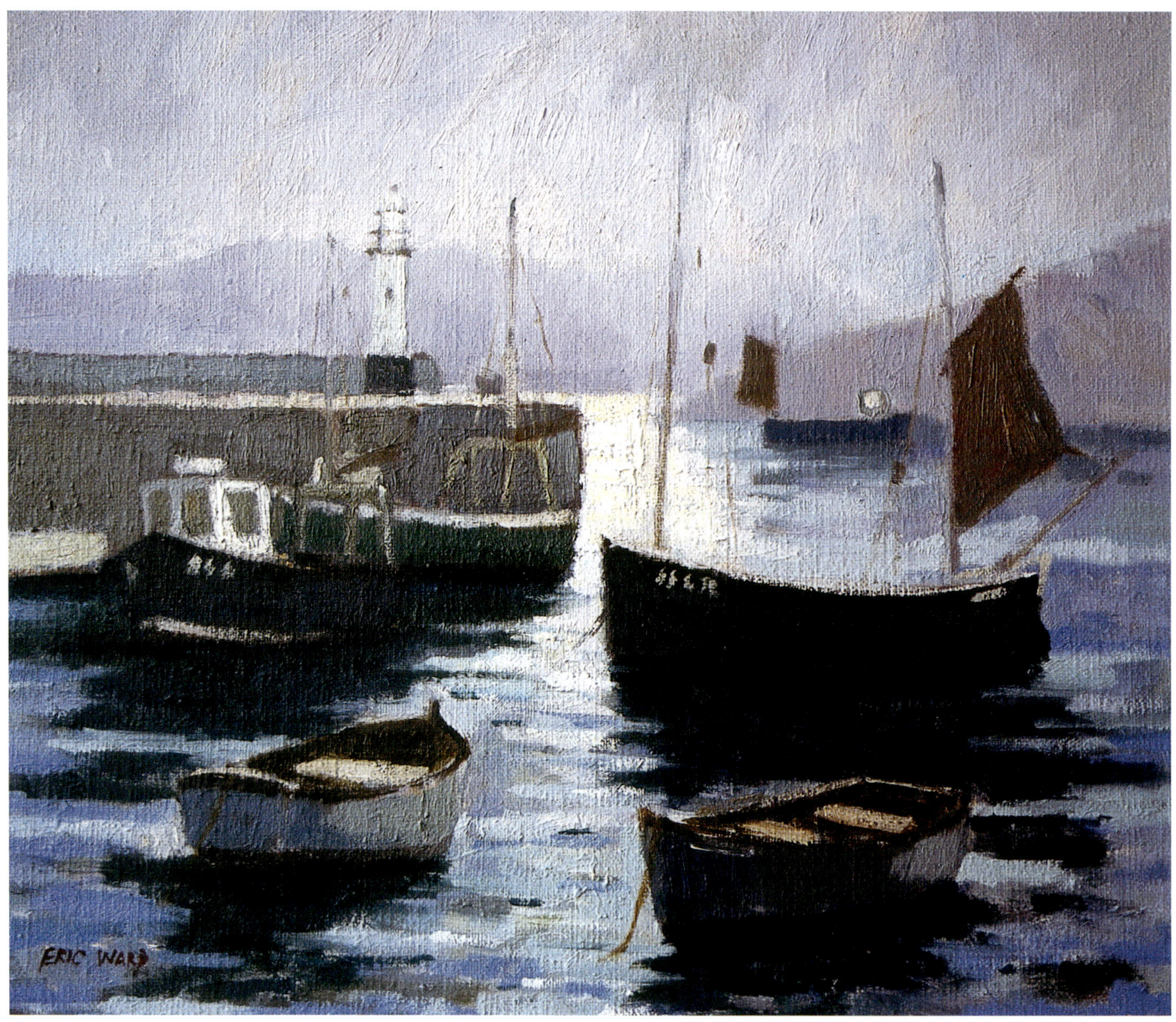

Boats on the Early Morning Tide, St Ives
Oil on linen, 30.5 x 35.5cm

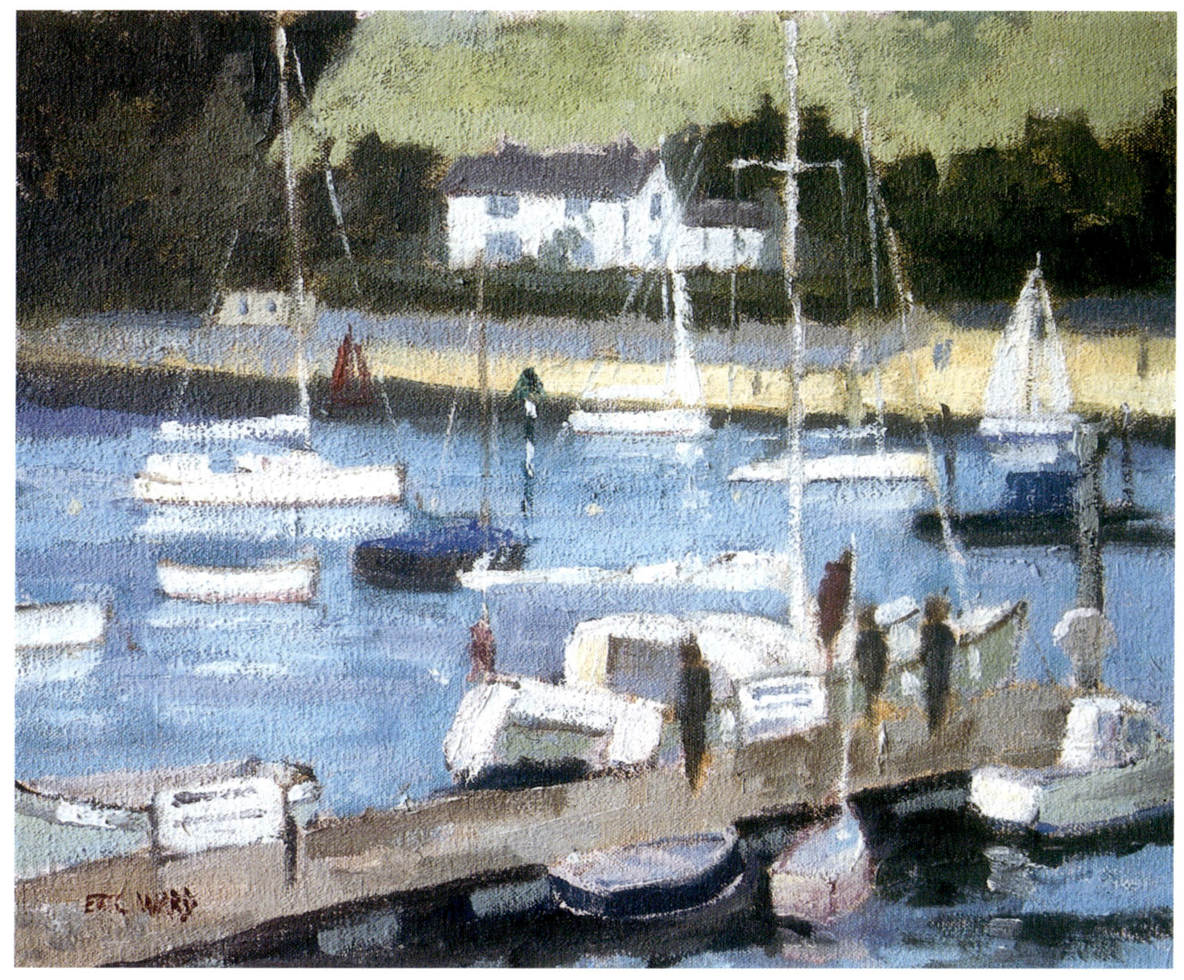

The Pontoon, Salcombe
Oil on canvas, 25.4 x 30.5cm

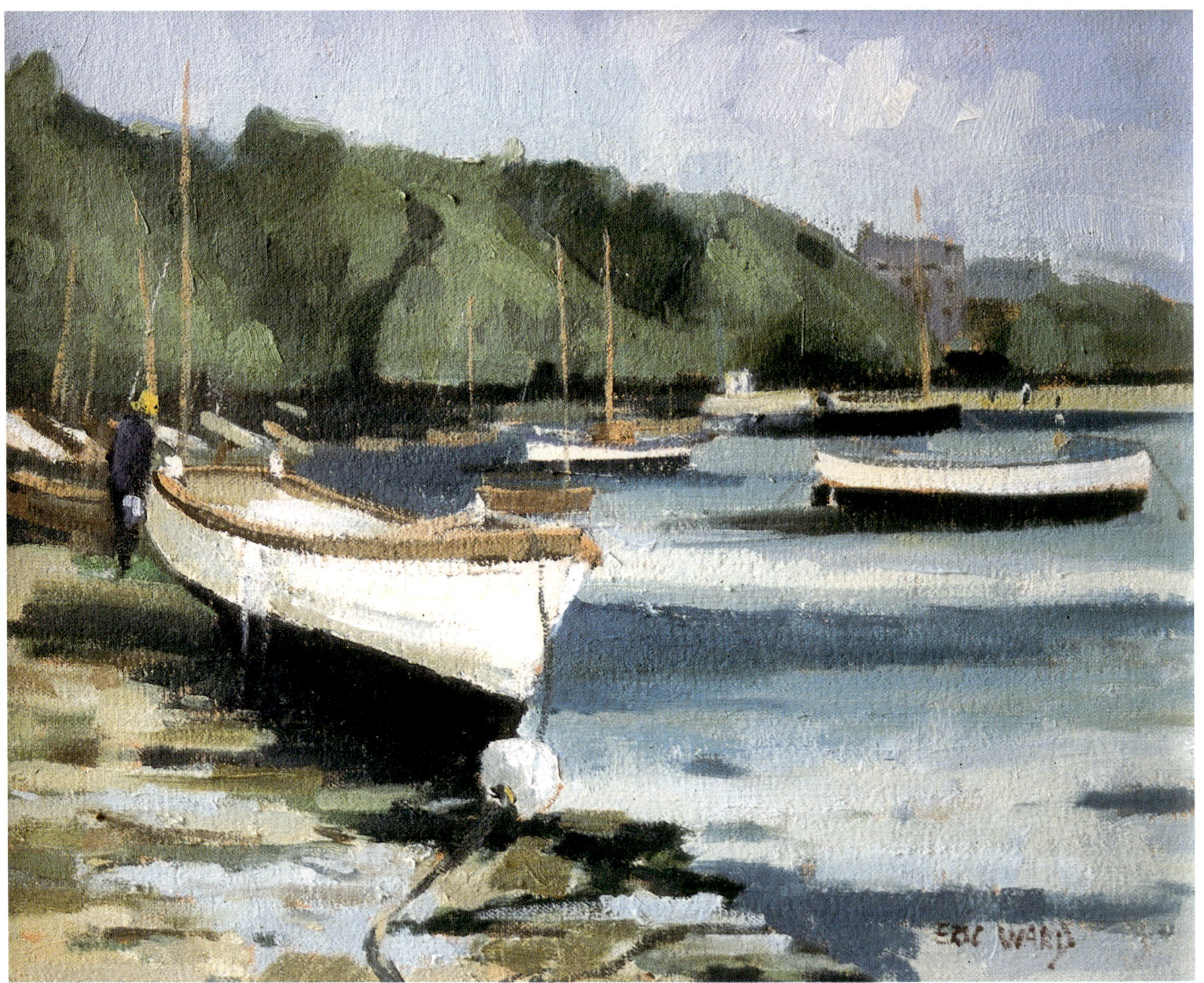

Bantham, Devon
Oil on canvas, 25.4 x 30.5cm

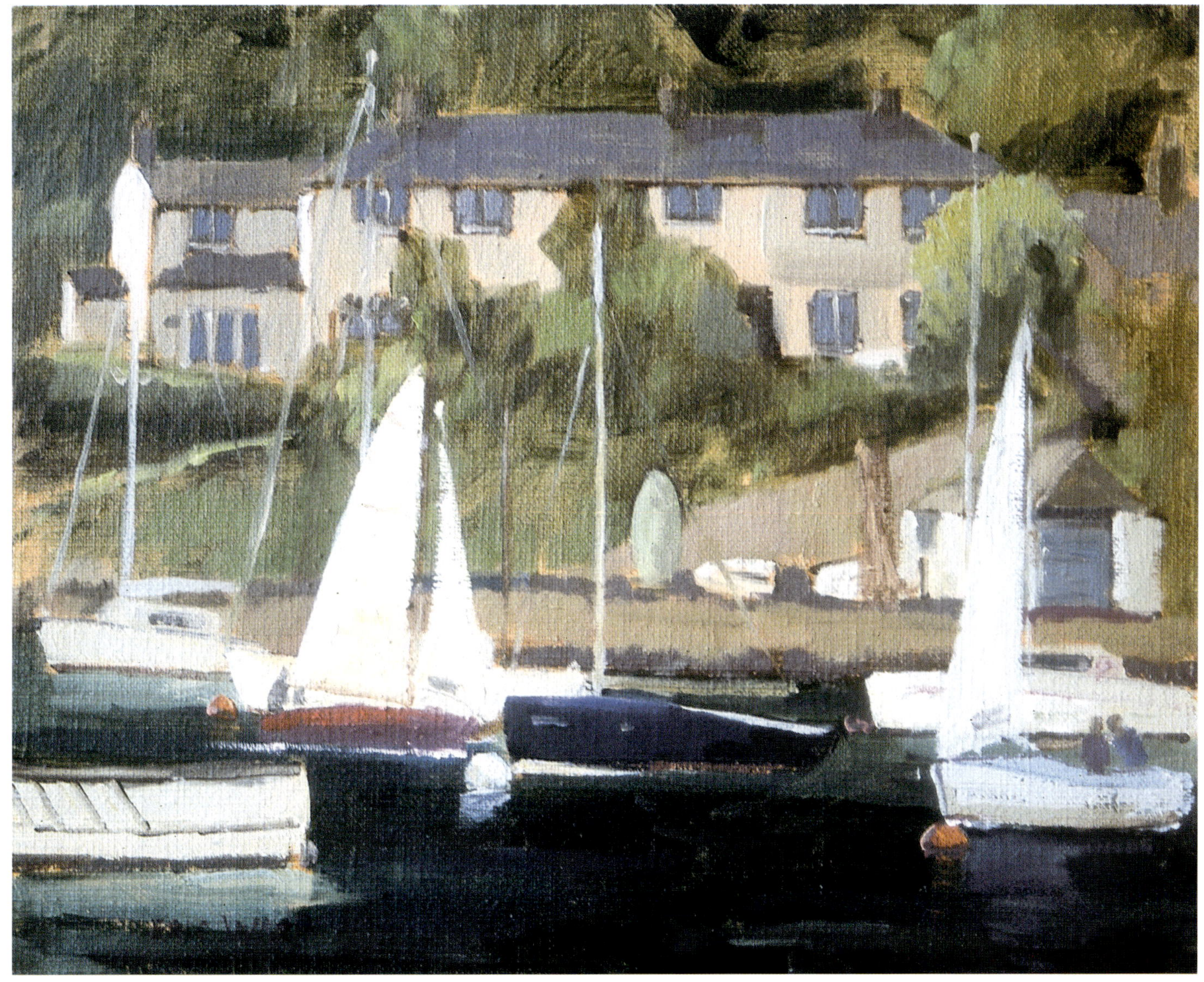

The Harbour, Newton Ferrers, Devon
Oil on panel, 25.4 x 30.5cm

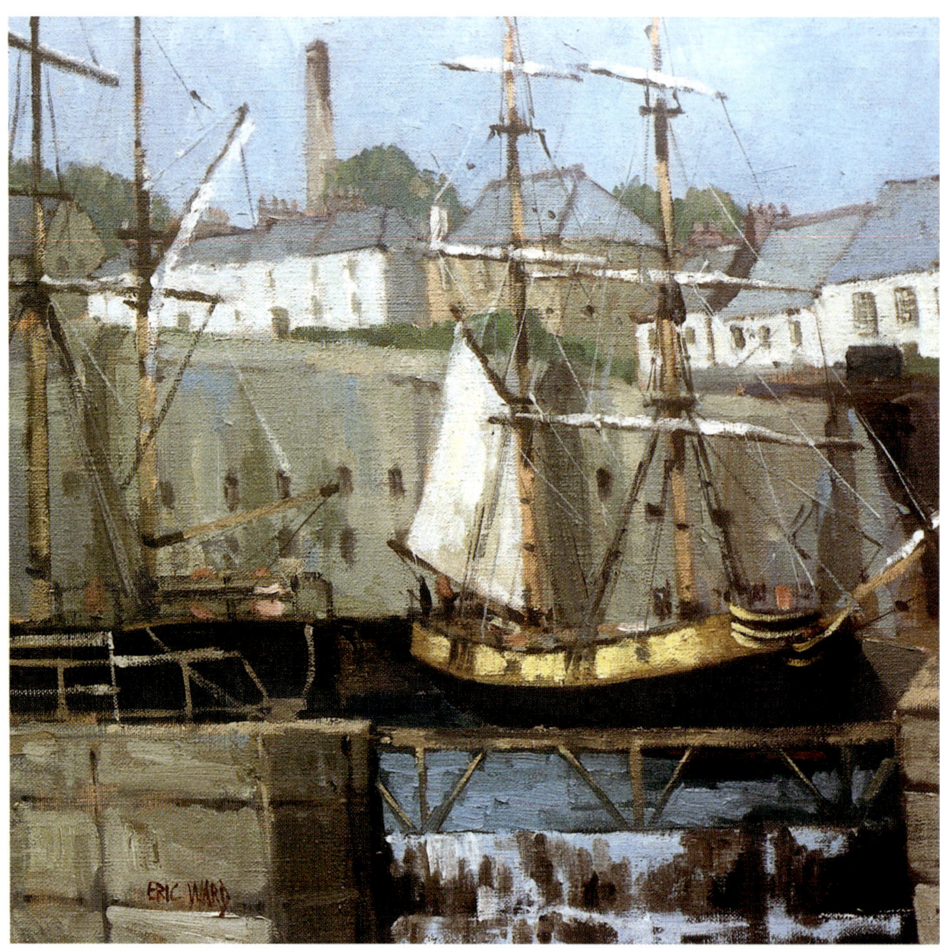

Phoenix, *Charlestown*
Oil on canvas, 40.6 x 40.6cm

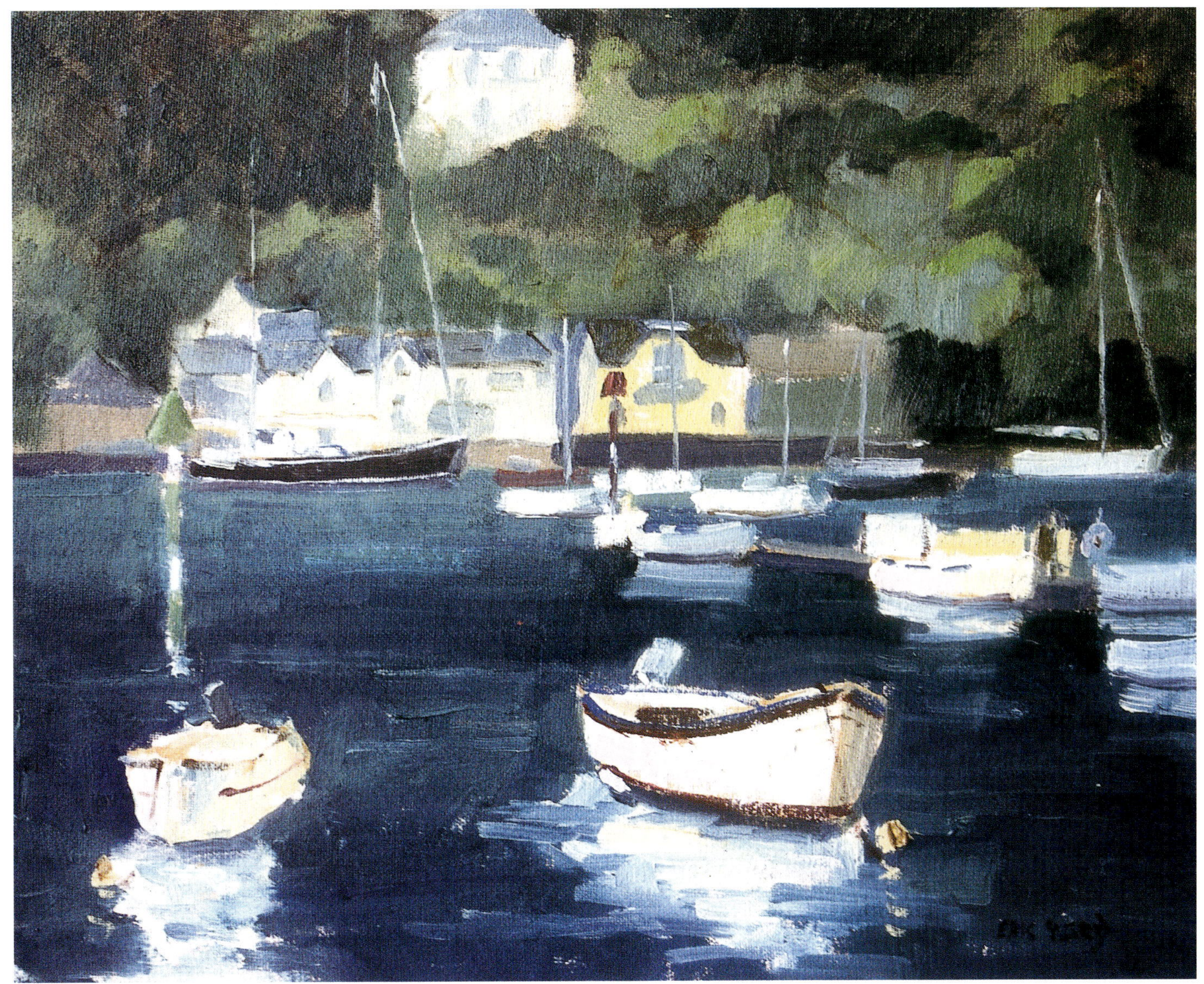

Early Morning at Salcombe
Oil on panel, 25.4 x 30.5cm

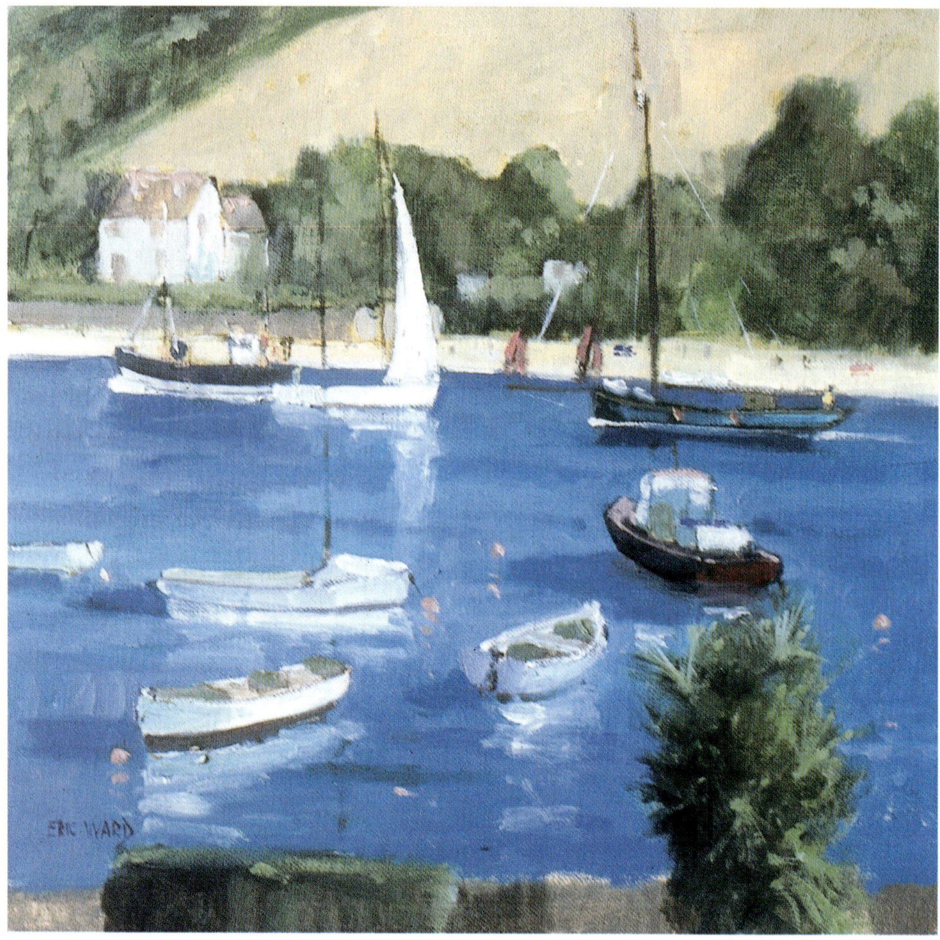

Busy Salcombe
Oil on panel, 27.9 x 27.9cm

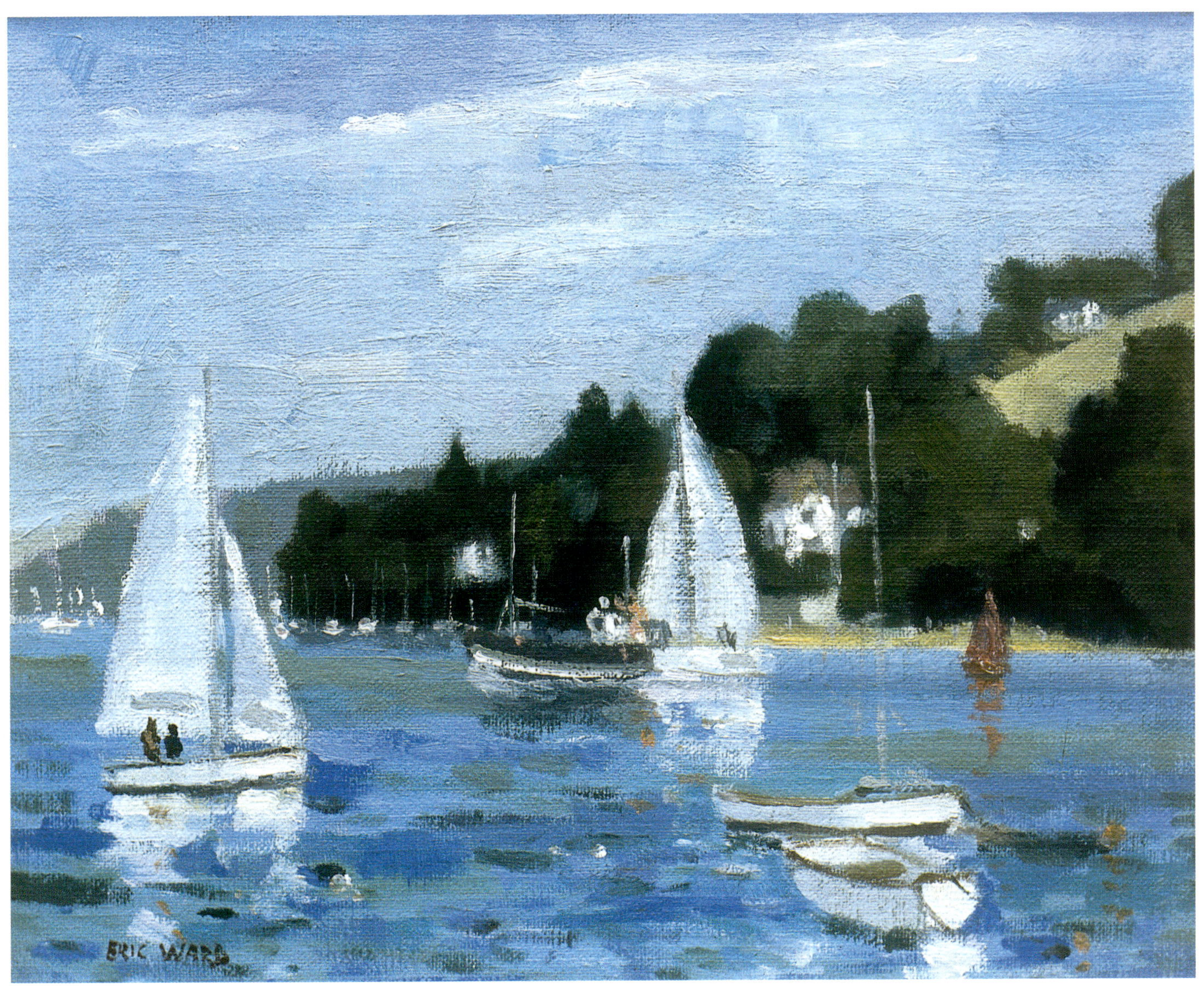

Boats on Salcombe Estuary
Oil on panel, 25.4 x 30.5cm

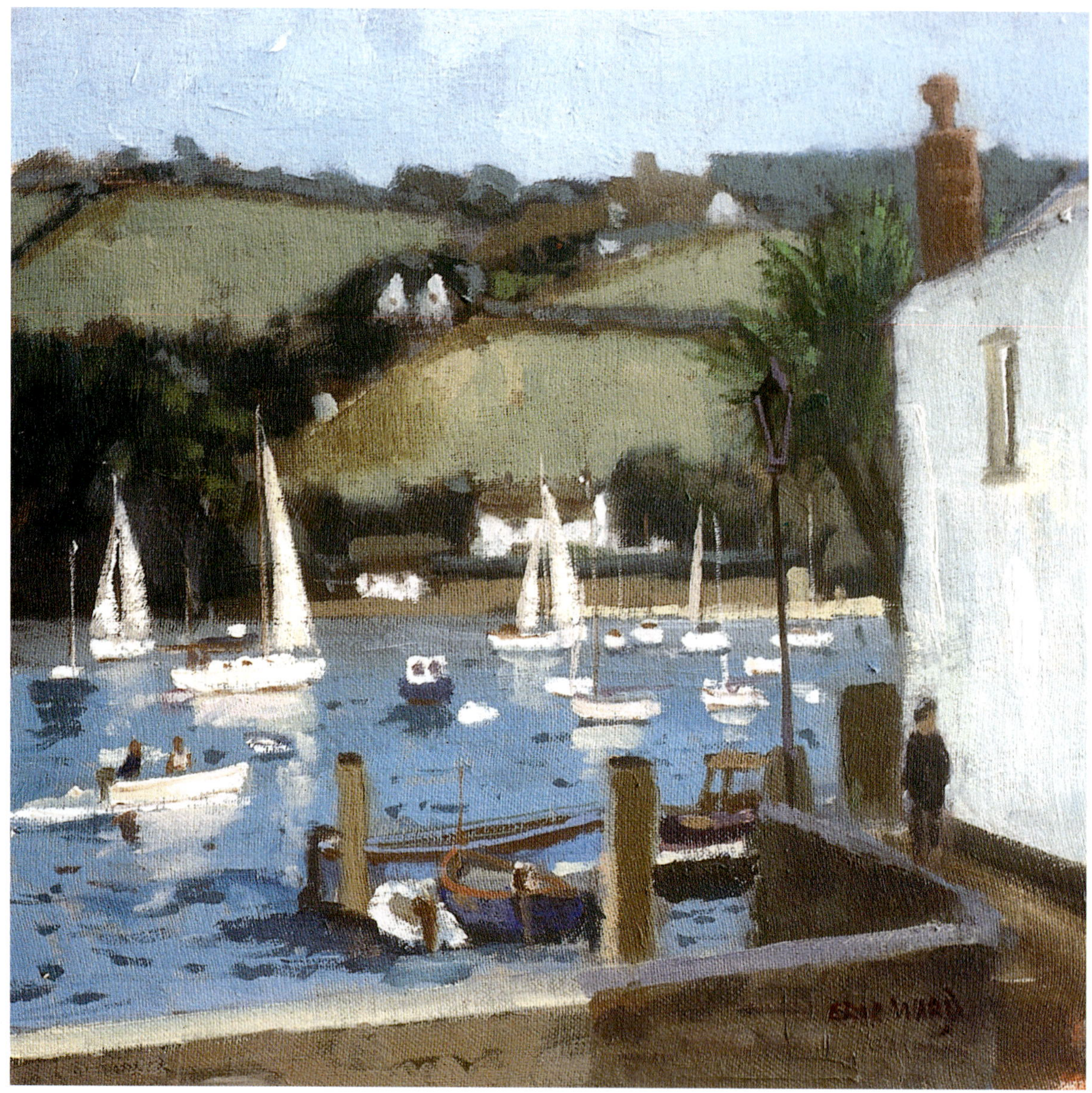

Sailing Boats at Salcombe
Oil on panel, 25.4 x 25.4cm

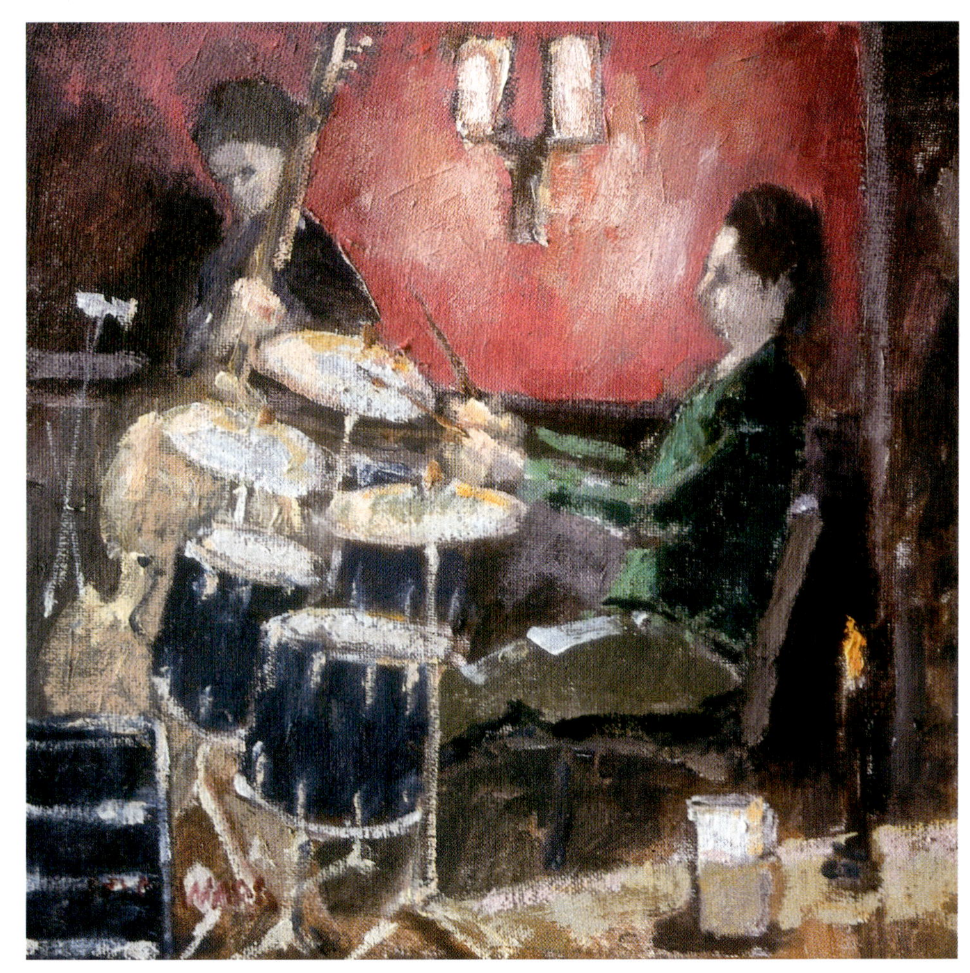

PUBS, CLUBS & MUSIC

Pubs, clubs and music invariably means people; people at leisure having a good time. From an artist's viewpoint, it is fascinating: the different body language, subdued lighting, performers with instruments, miniature still lifes on tables – everything an artist could want. The art of sketching and making notes in such places becomes second nature as ideas for paintings occur from all directions. A great way to spend time.

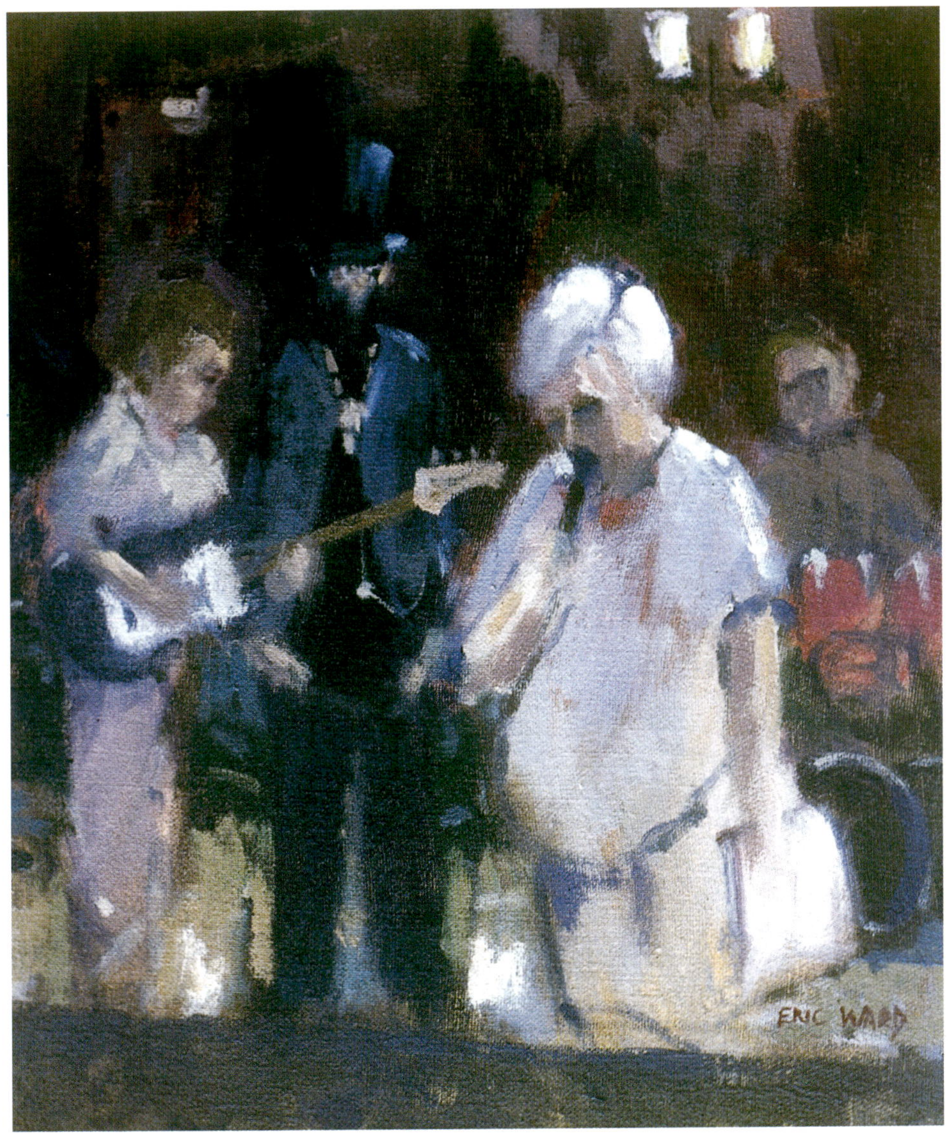

Blues at the Western Hotel, St Ives
Oil on panel, 30.5 x 25.4cm

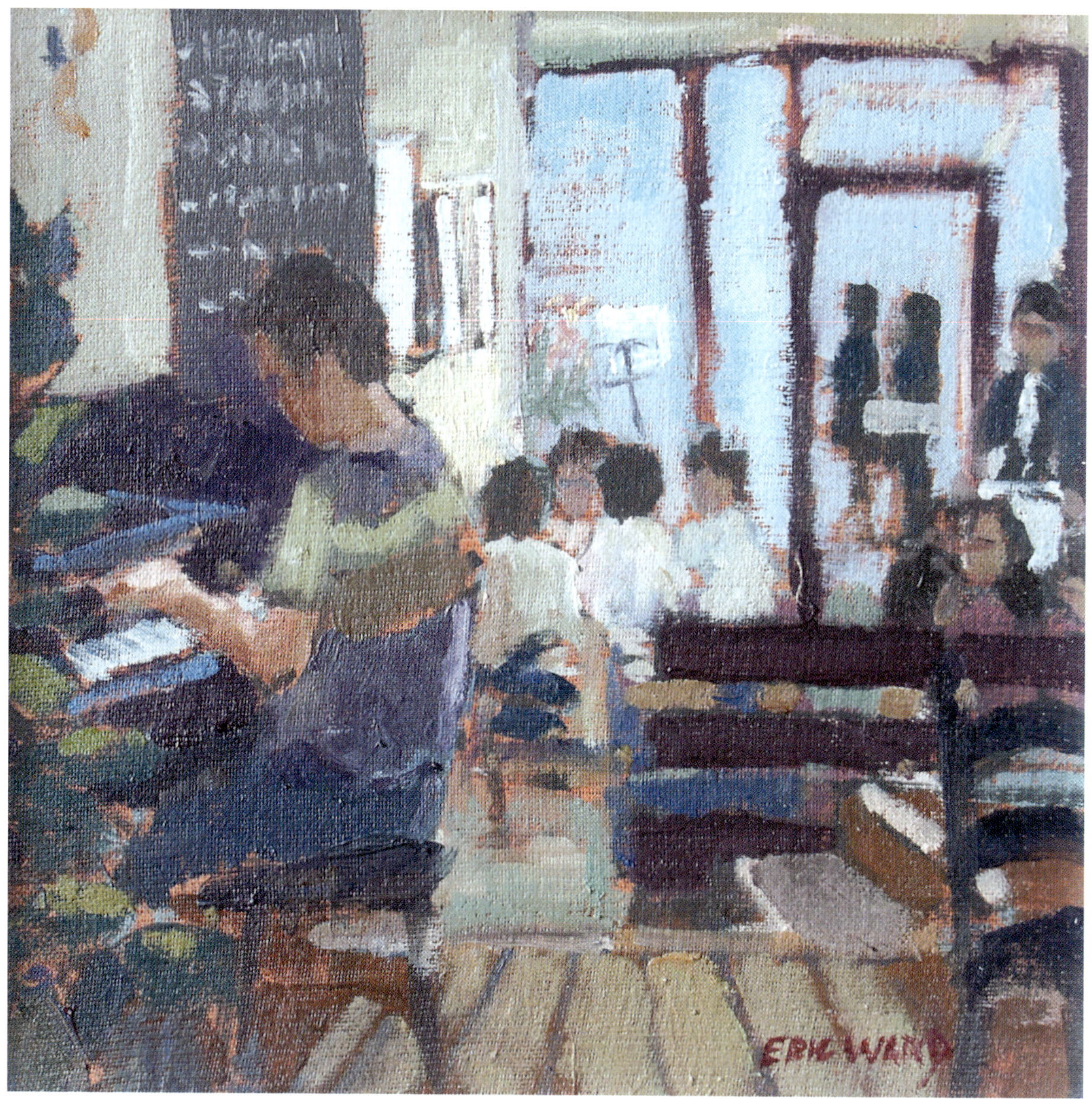

Music at 'Frets' Bar, St Ives
Oil on panel, 20.3 x 20.3cm

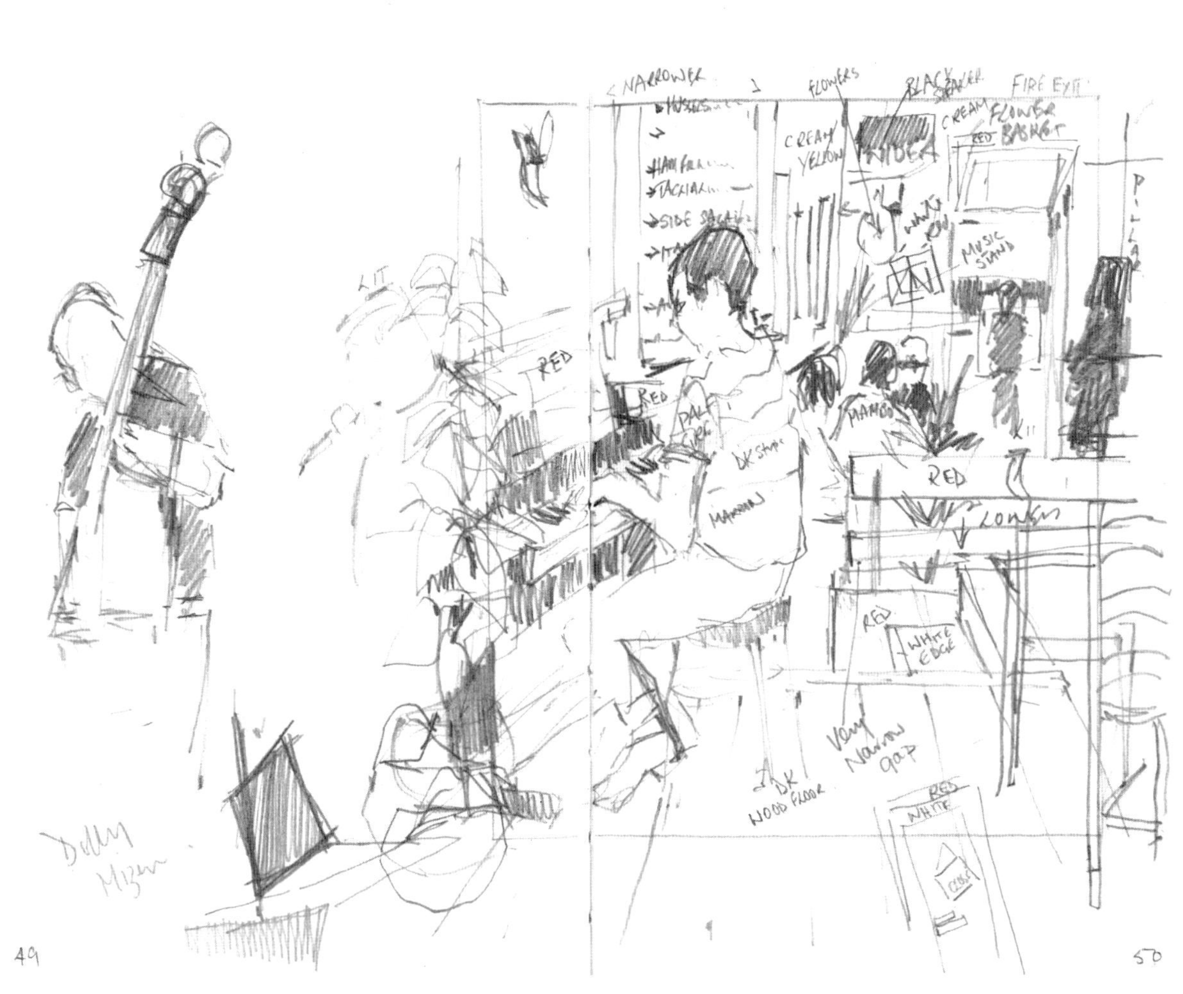

NARROWER
FLOWERS
BLACK SPEAKER
FIRE EXIT
HOUSES
CREAM YELLOW
CREAM
FLOWER BASKET
RED
HALL FRAMING
TACKLING
WHITE TOP
SIDE SAGA
MUSIC STAND
PILLAR
RED
RED
PALE PINK
DK SHAPE
MAROON
MAROON
RED
FLOWERS
RED
WHITE EDGE
DK WOOD FLOOR
Very Narrow gap
RED WHITE
Dolly Mizen

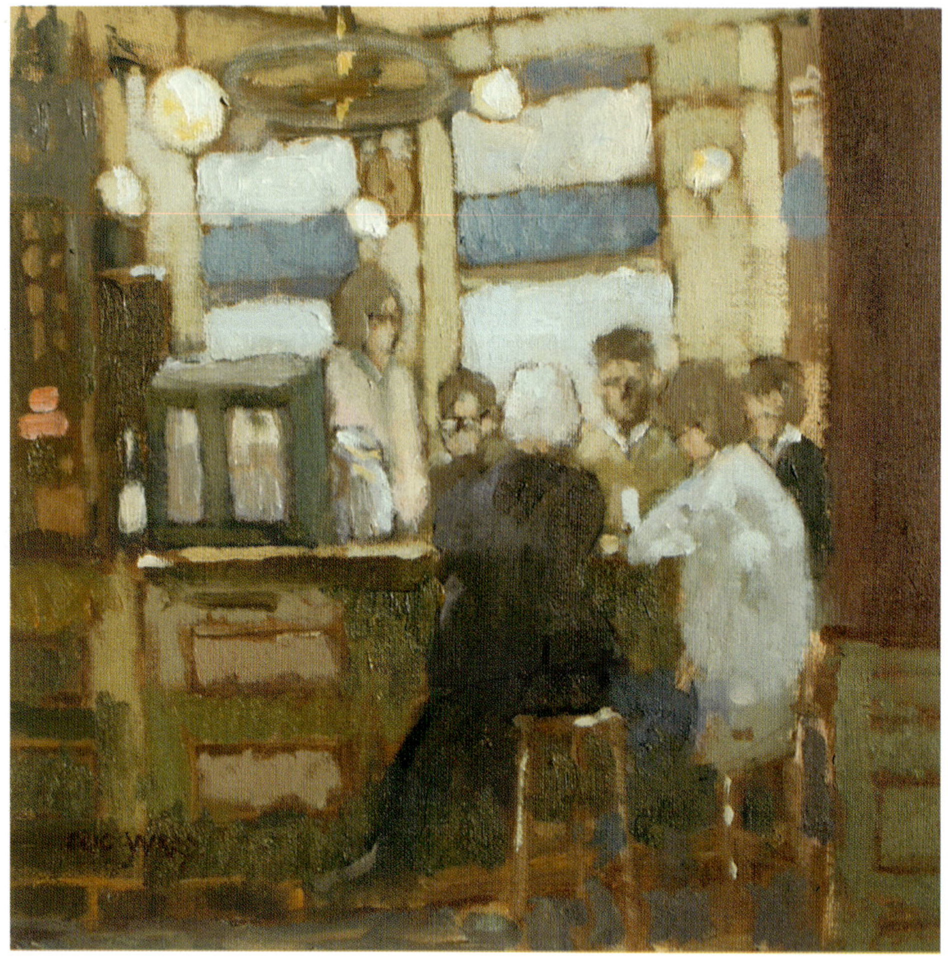

The French House, Soho, London
Oil on panel, 24 x 24cm

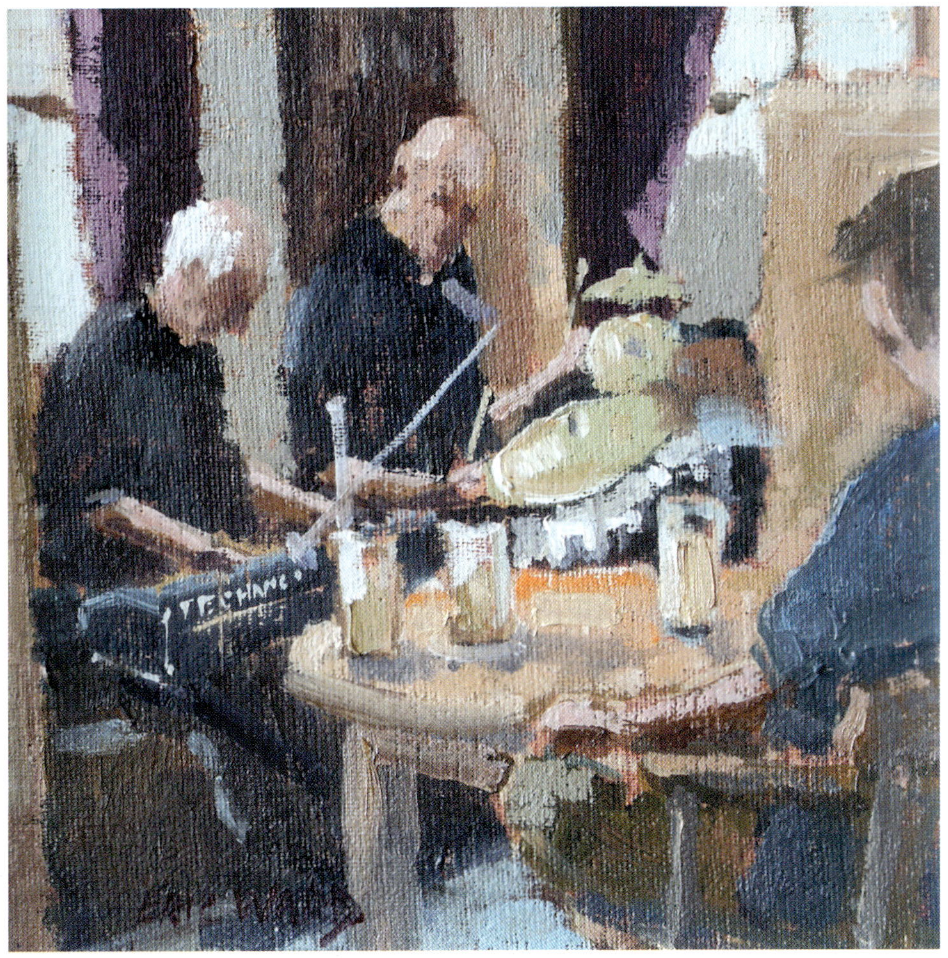

Jazz Trilogy, St Ives September Festival, Lifeboat Inn
Oil on panel, 15.2 x 15.2cm

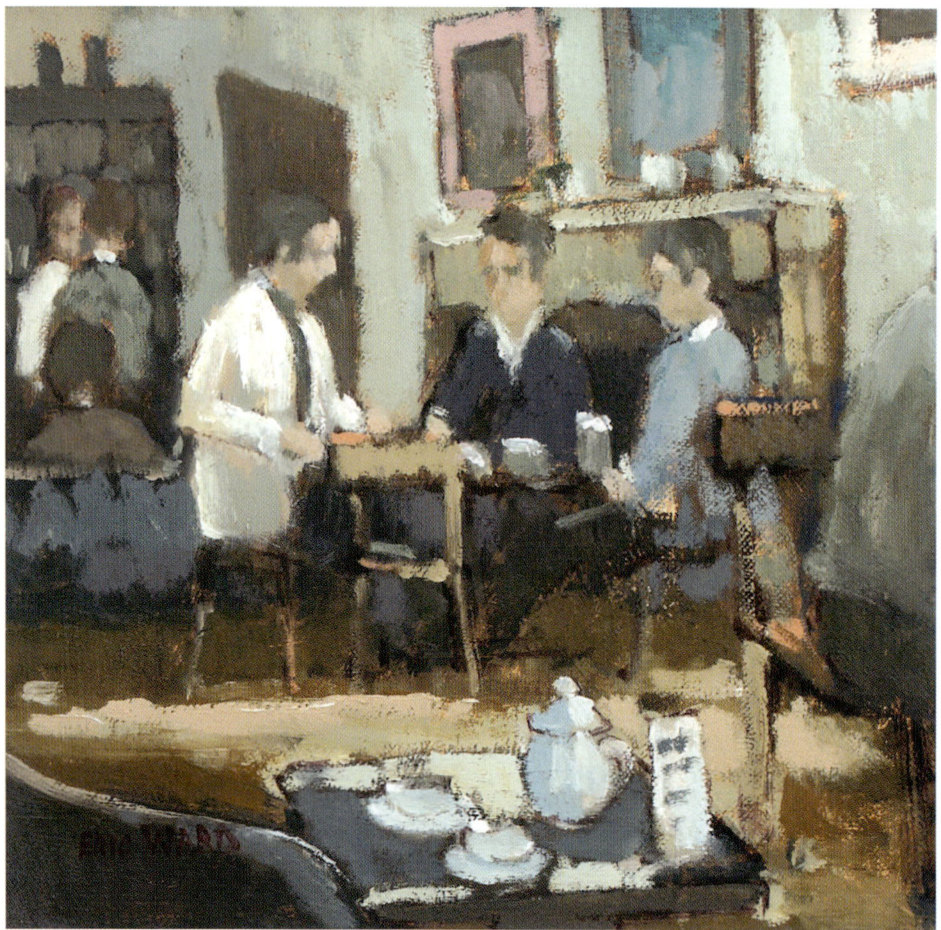

Friends' Room at the Royal Academy
Oil on panel, 20.3cm x 20.3cm

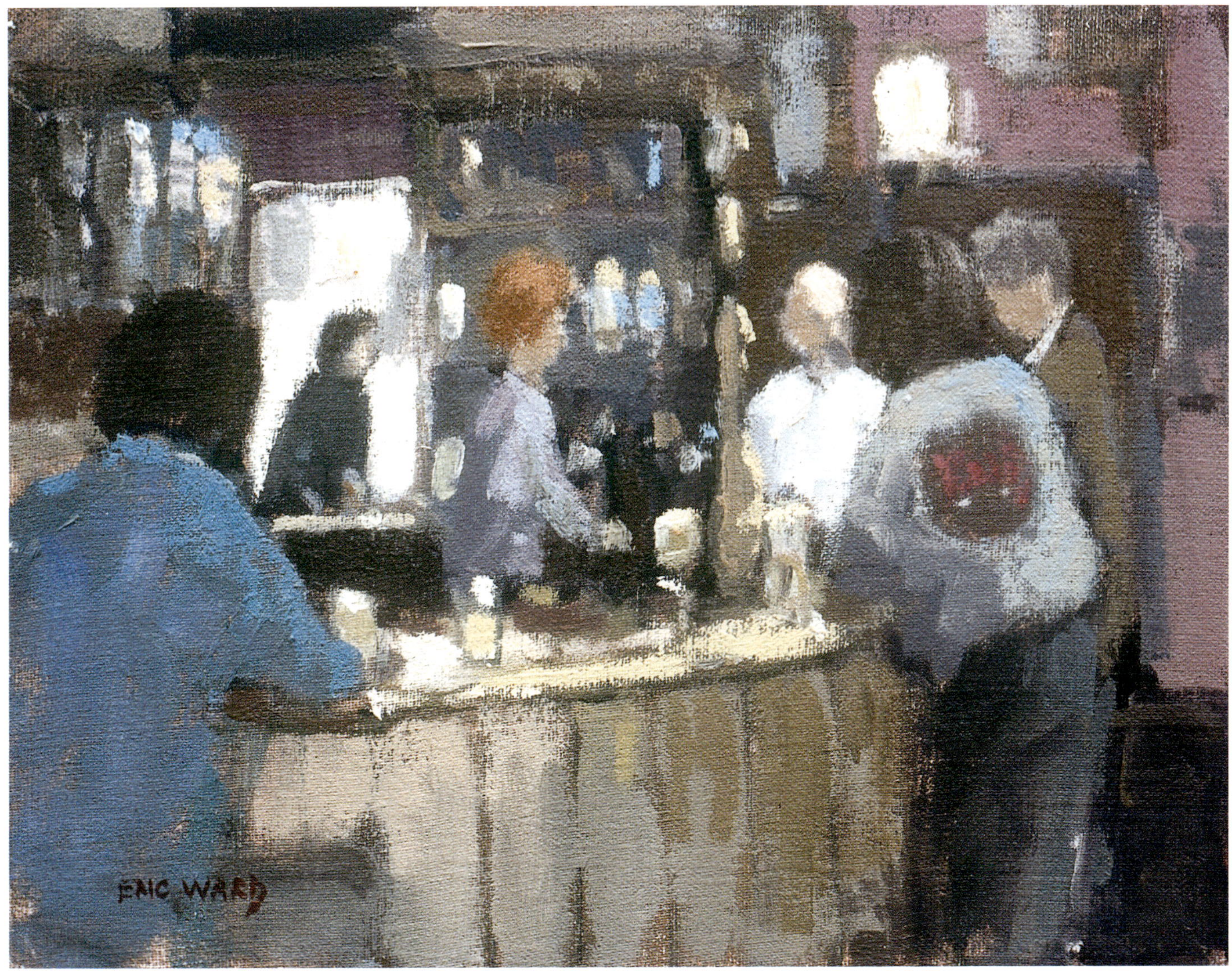

The Queen's Head, Chelsea
Oil on panel, 20.3 x 25.4cm

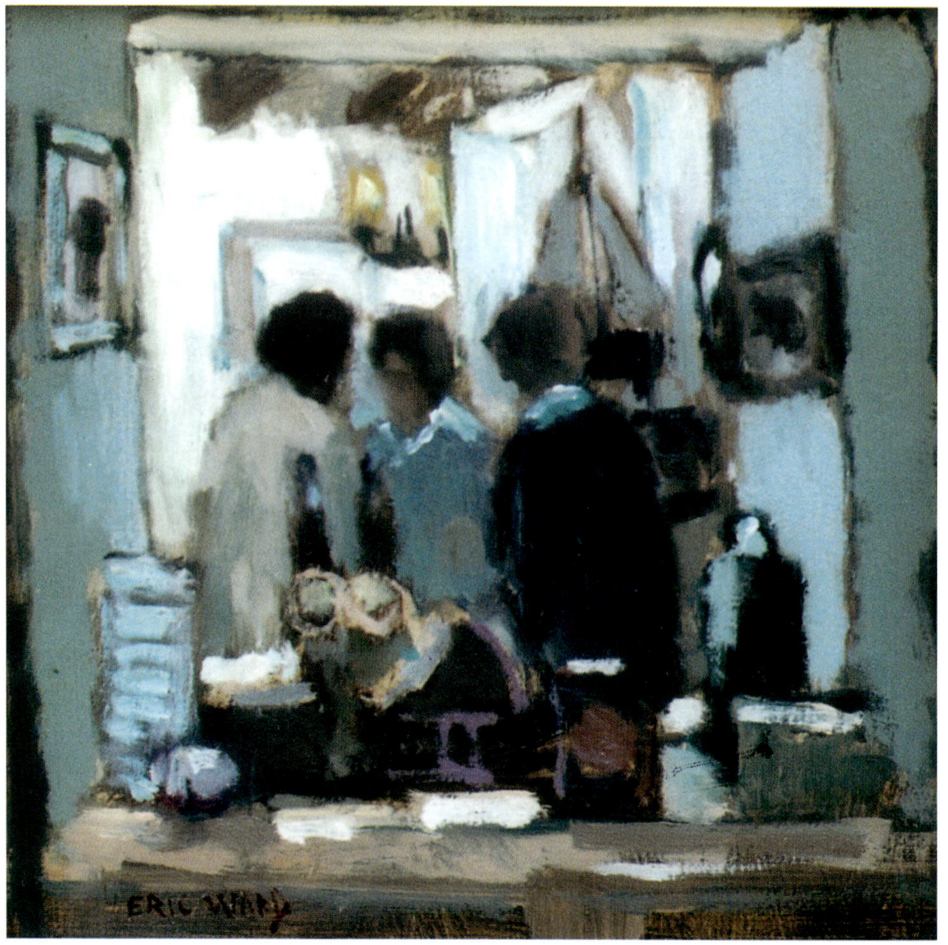

The Plume of Feathers, Portscatho
Oil, 17.8 x 17.8cm

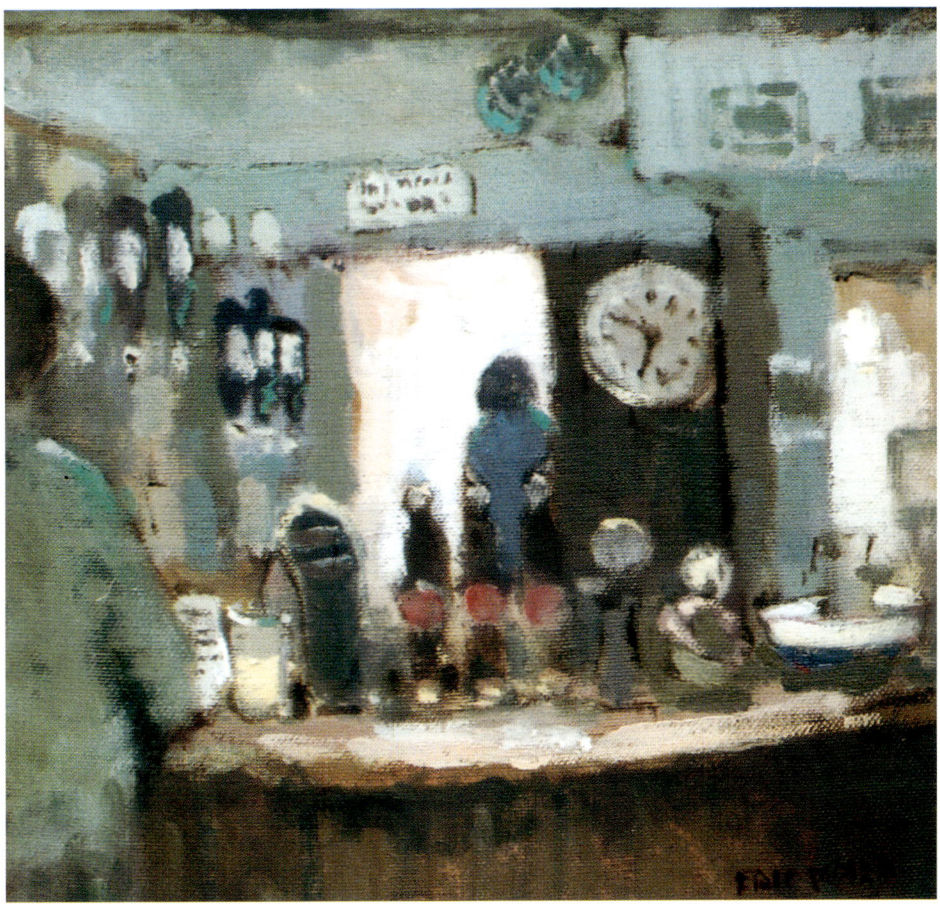

The Plume of Feathers, Portscatho
Oil, 20.3 x 20.3cm

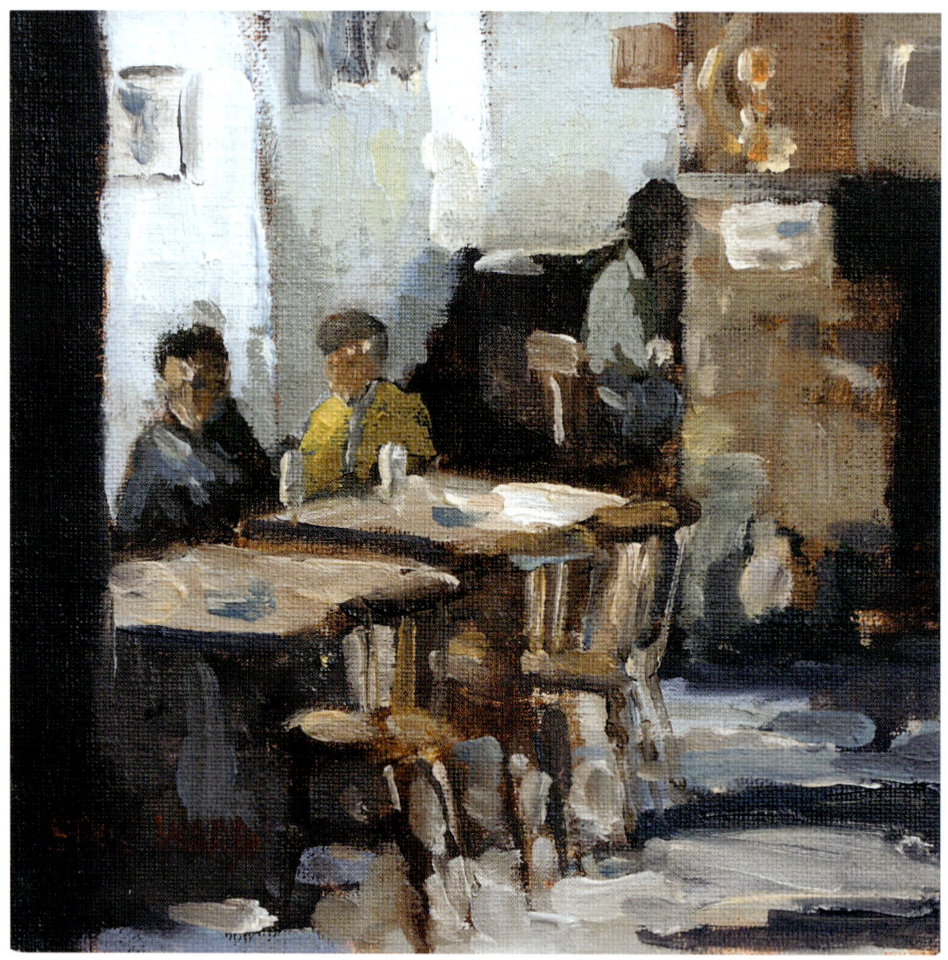

Lunchtime Drinks at the Fort, Salcombe
Oil on panel, 17.8 x 17.8cm

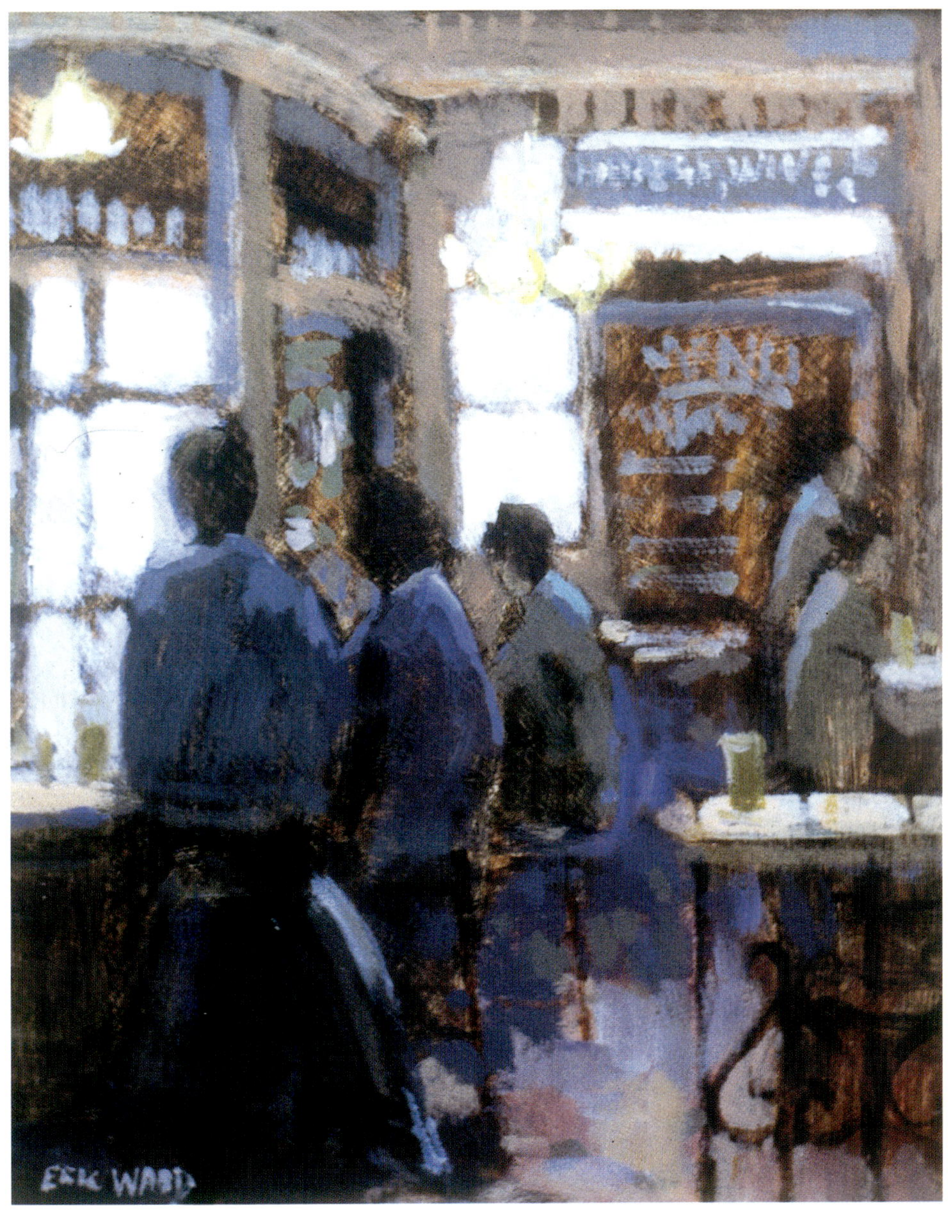

Paxton's Head, Knightsbridge, London
Acrylic on panel, 25.4 x 20.3cm

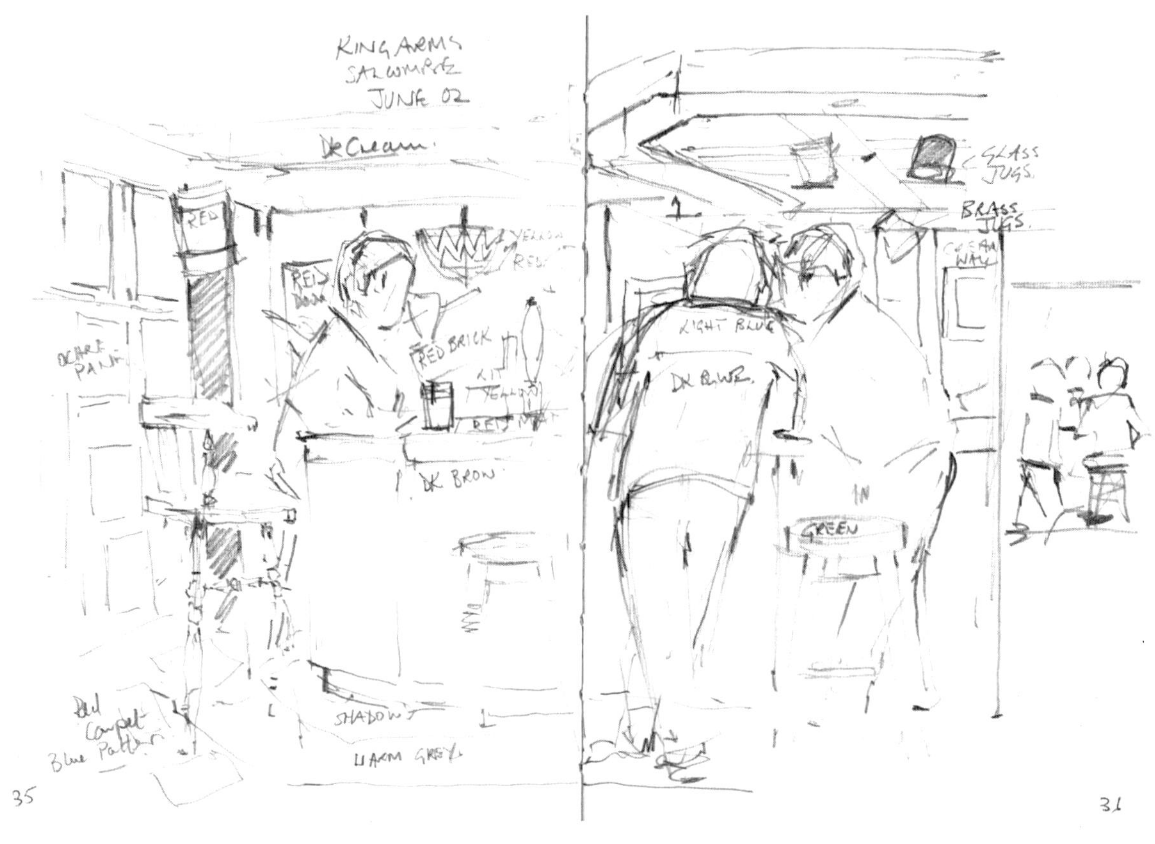
KING ARMS
SALISBURY
JUNE 02
DK CREAM.
RED
RED
DOOR
OCHRE
PAINT
YELLOW
RED
RED BRICK
LIT
YEALLA
RED
DK BROW
SHADOWS
WARM GREY.
Red
Carpet
Blue Pattern
GLASS
JUGS.
BRASS
JUGS.
CREAM
WALL
LIGHT BLUE
DK BLUE.
IN
GREEN
35
31

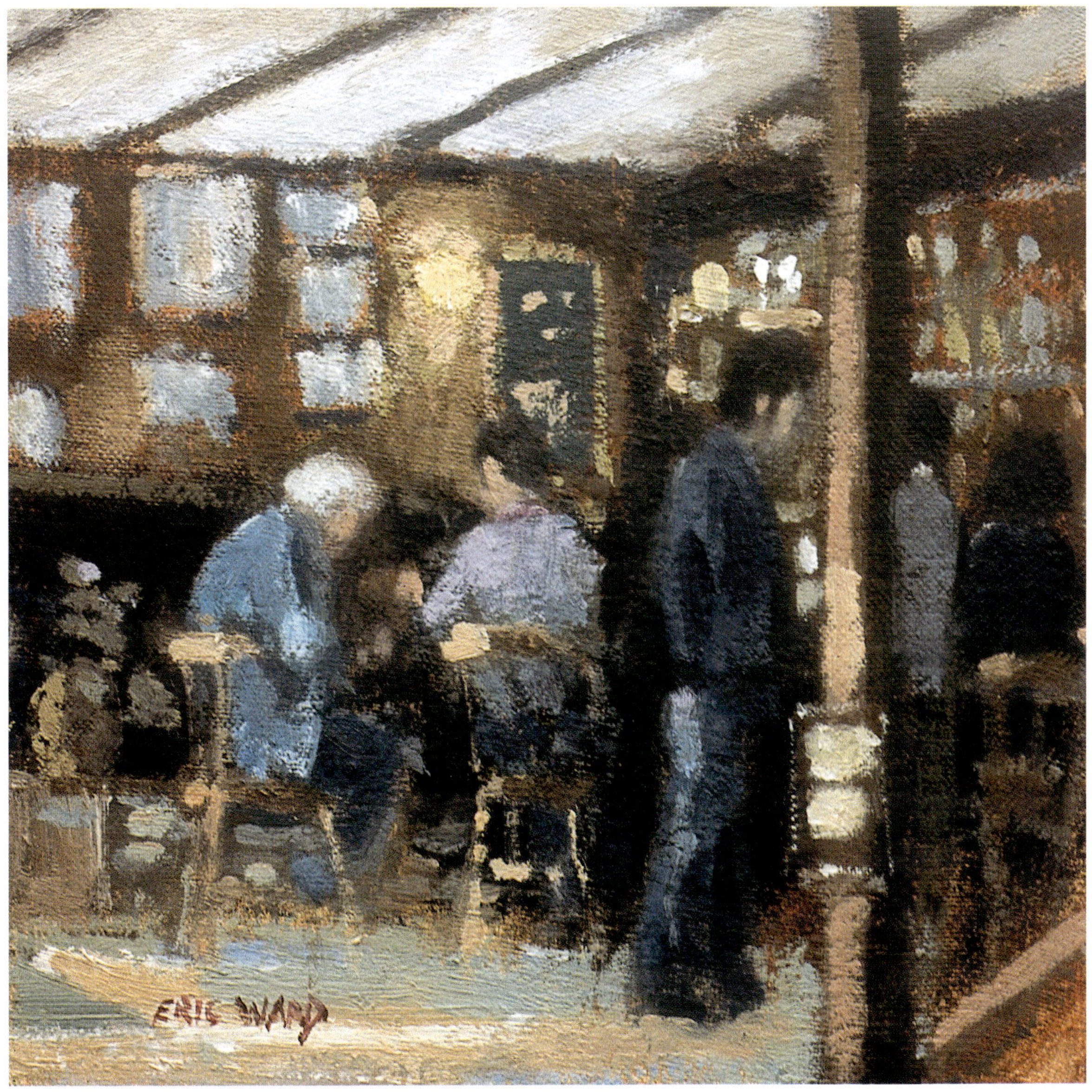

Fortesque Arms, Salcombe
Oil on panel, 17.8 x 17.8cm

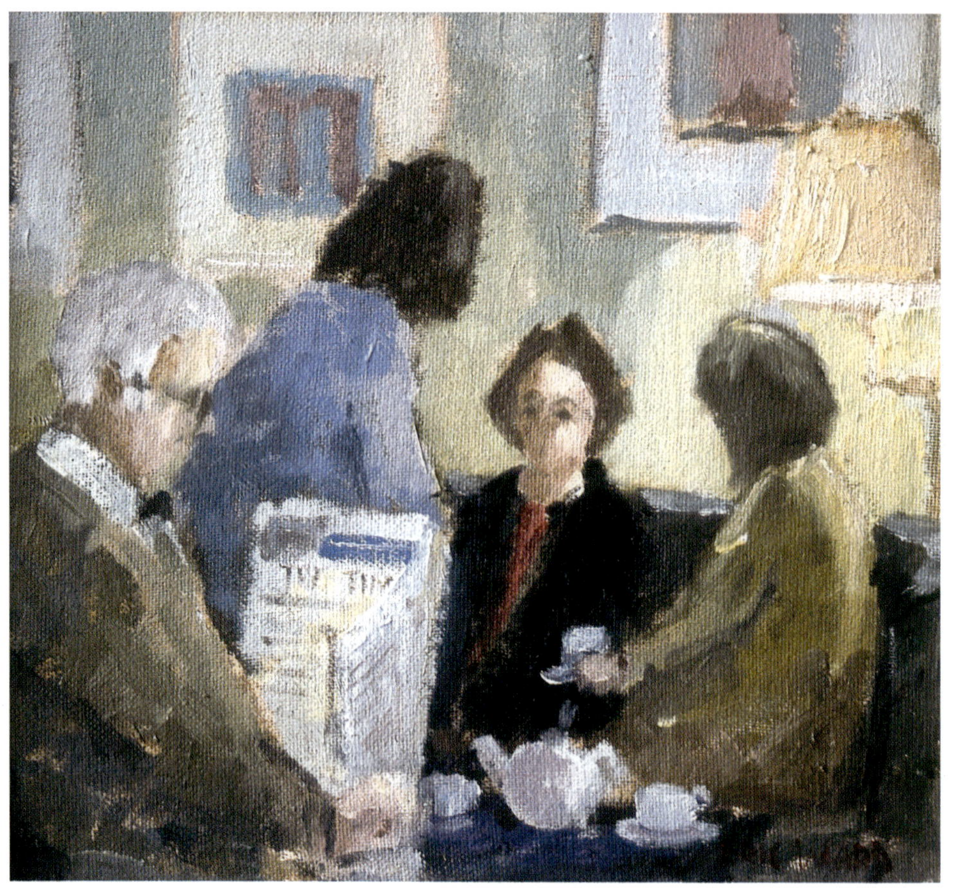

Tea in the Friends' Room, Royal Academy
Oil on panel, 19 x 20.3cm

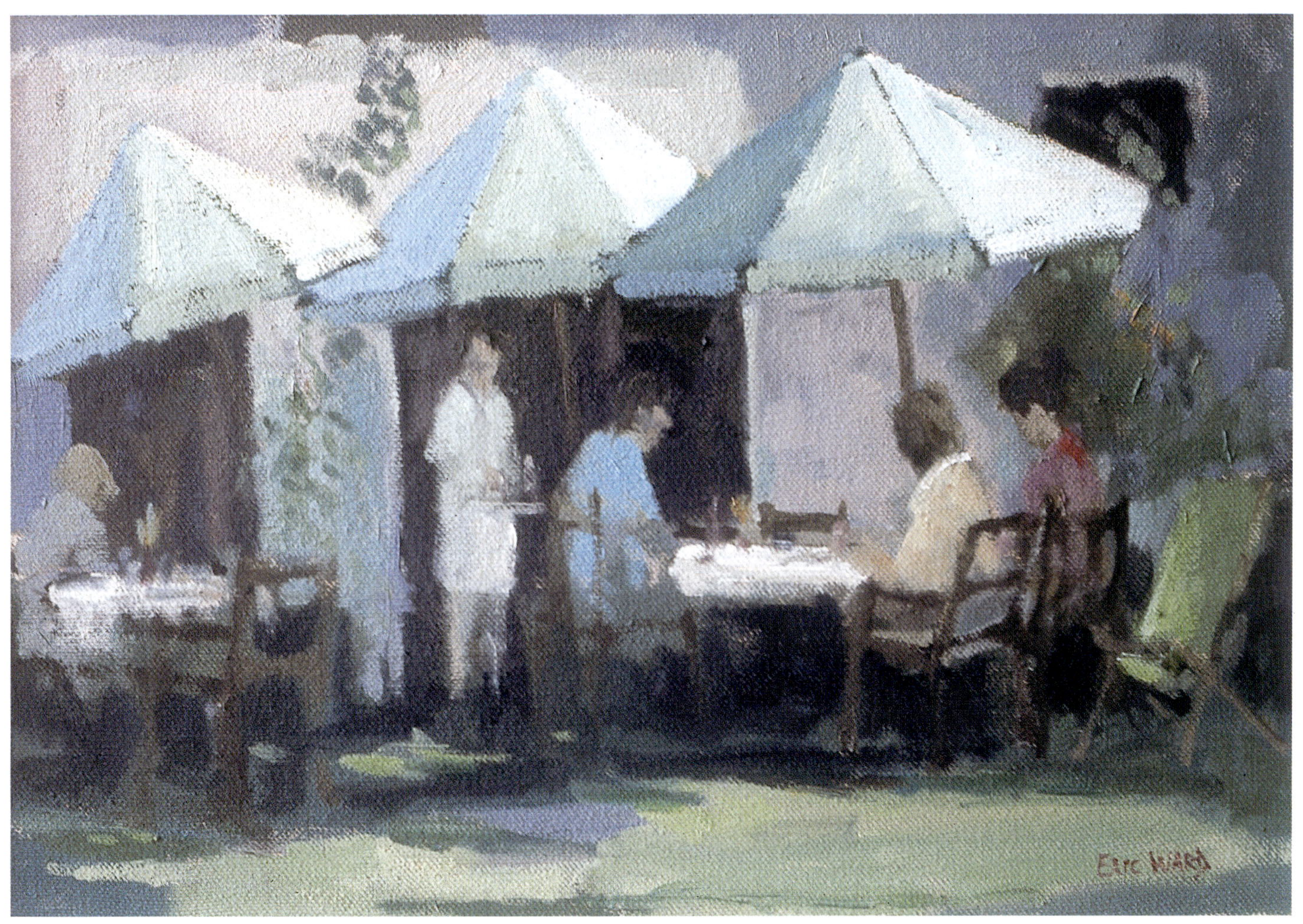

Lunch, Chelsea Arts Club
Oil on canvas, 25.4 x 35.5cm

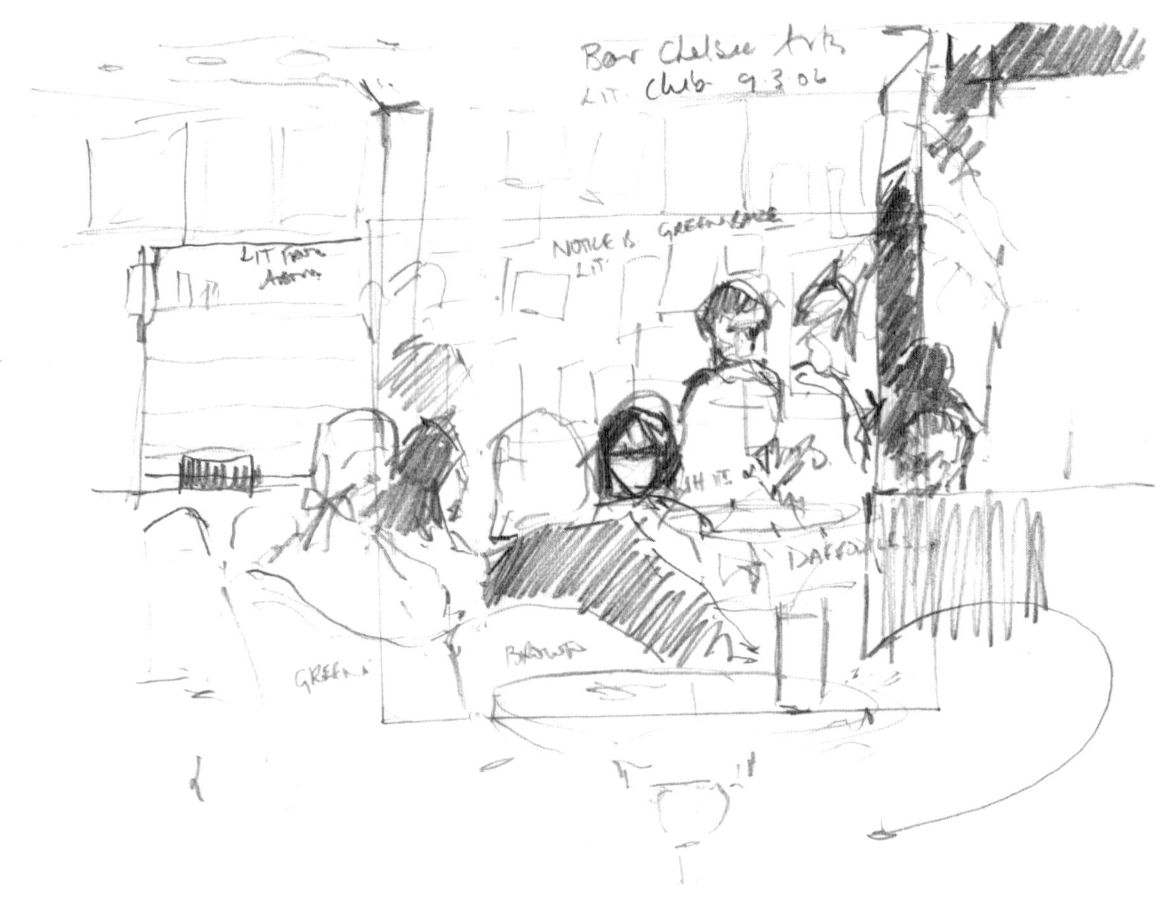

Bar Chelsea Arts
LIT Club 9.3.06
LIT Frame
Astern
NOTICE IS GREEN/BLUE
LIT.
GREEN
BROWN
DAFFODIL

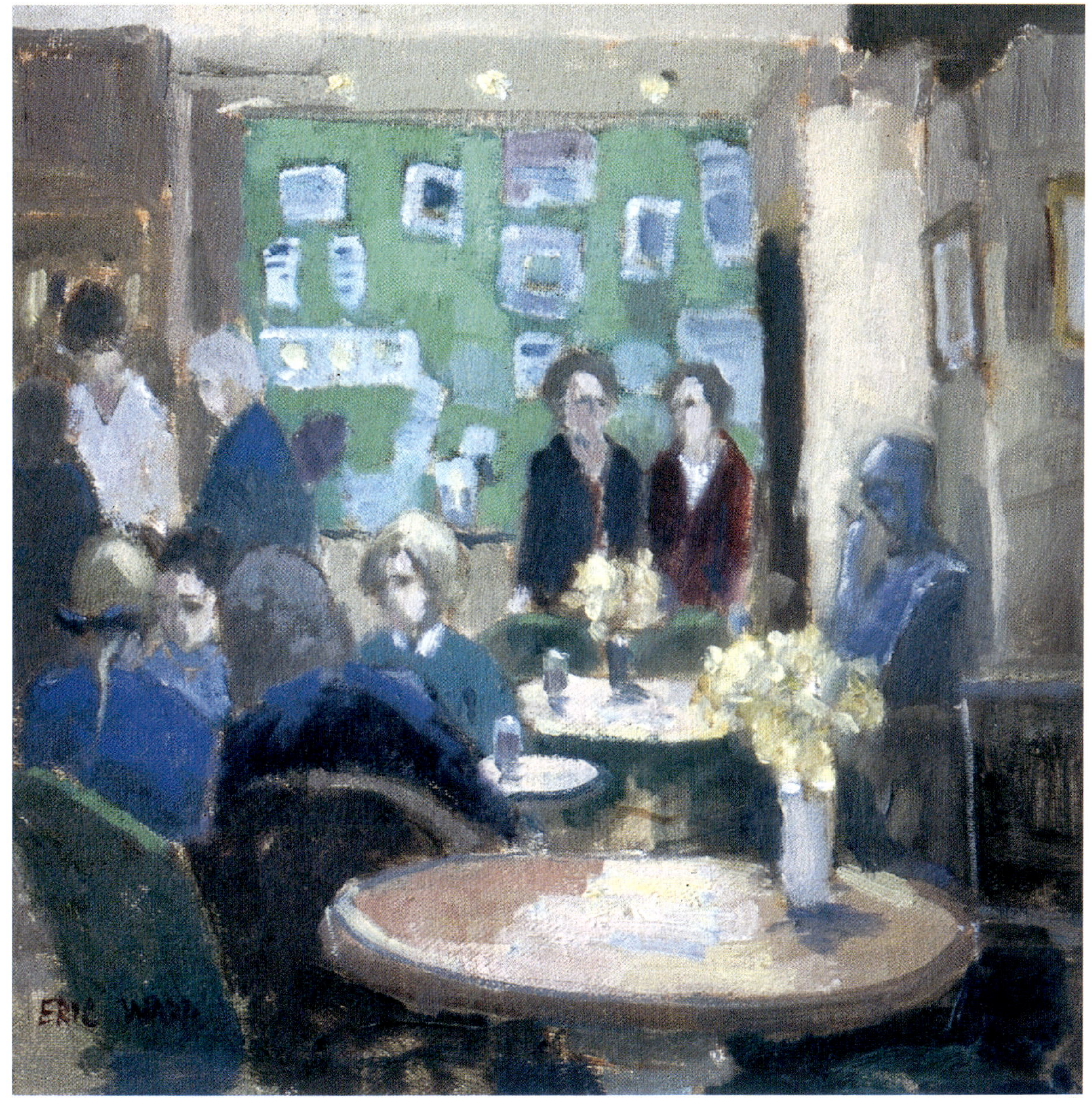

Early Evening at the Bar of the Chelsea Arts Club
Oil on panel, 25.4 x 25.4cm

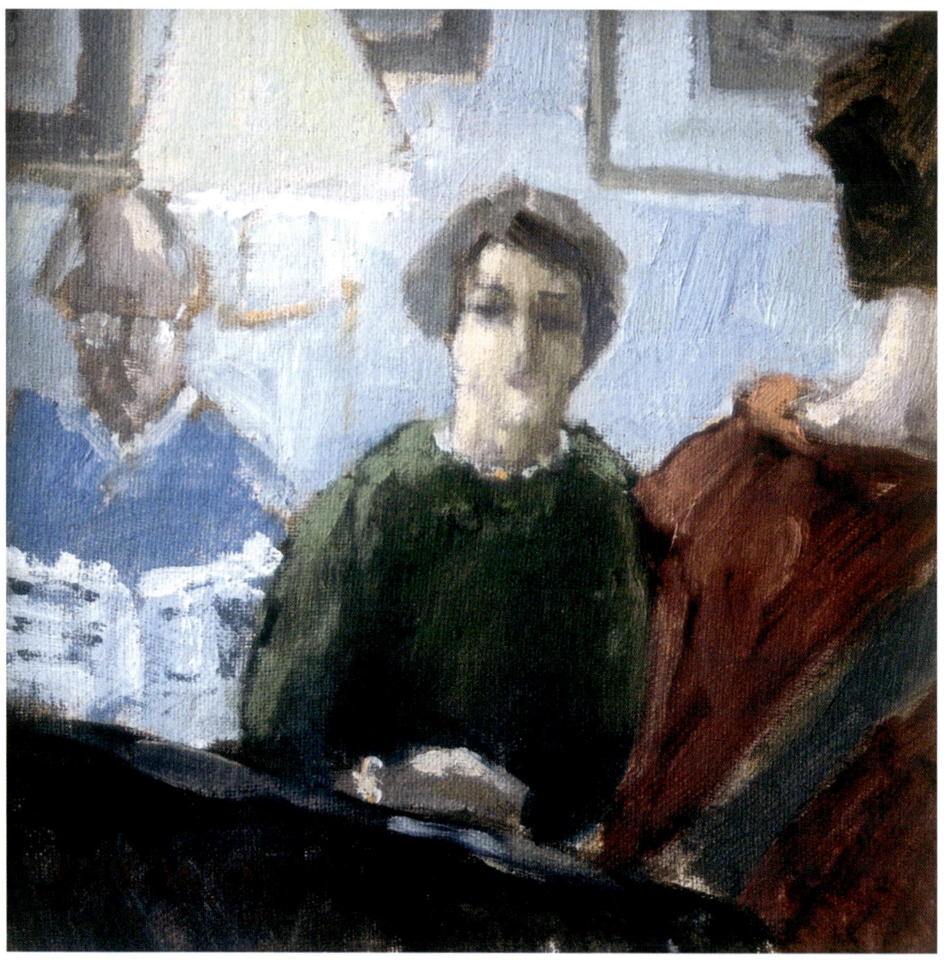

Ladies' Chat, Friends' Room, Royal Academy
Oil on panel, 17.8 x 17.8cm

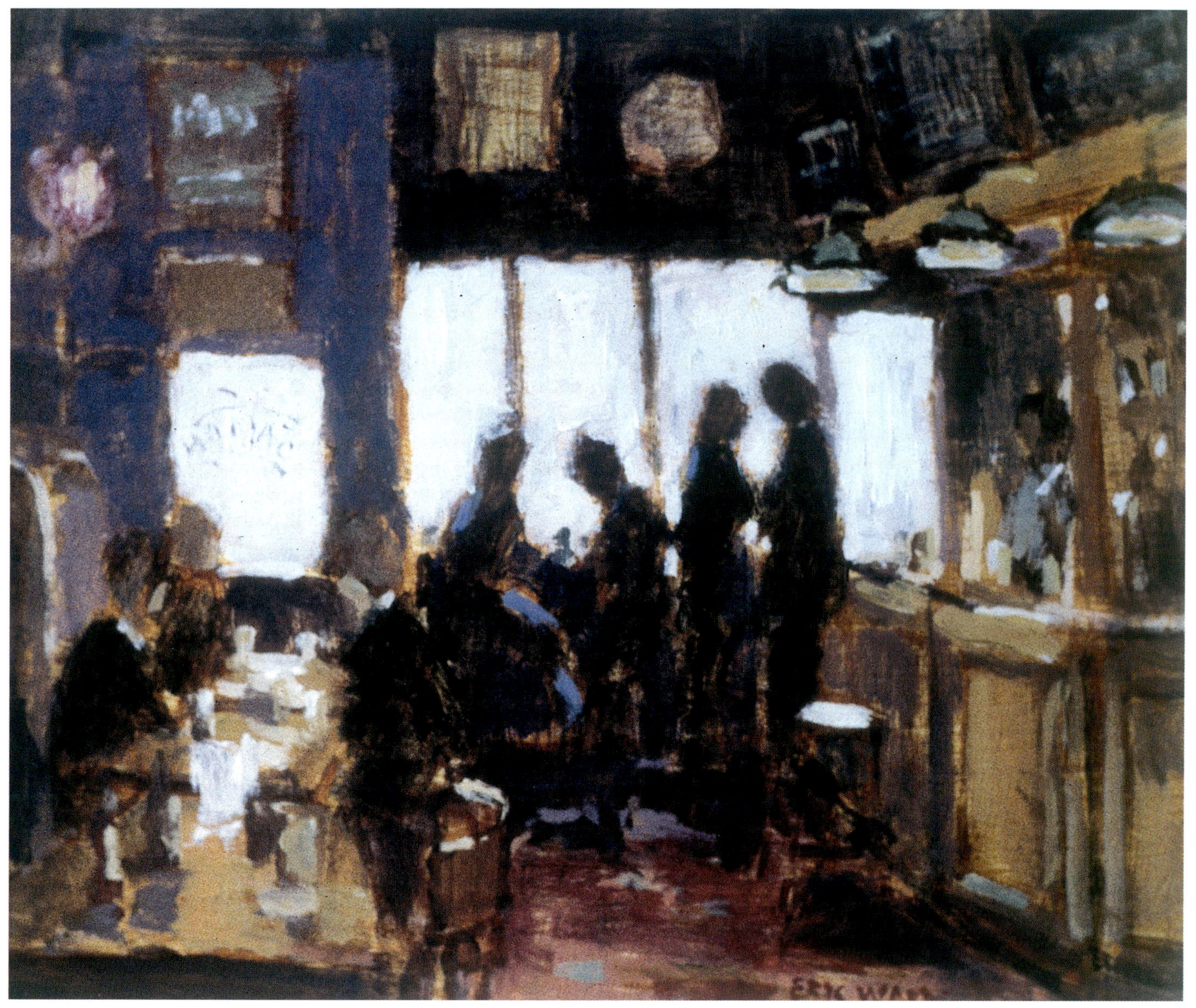

The Tottenham Public House, Oxford Street, London
Acrylic on panel, 20.3 x 25.4cm

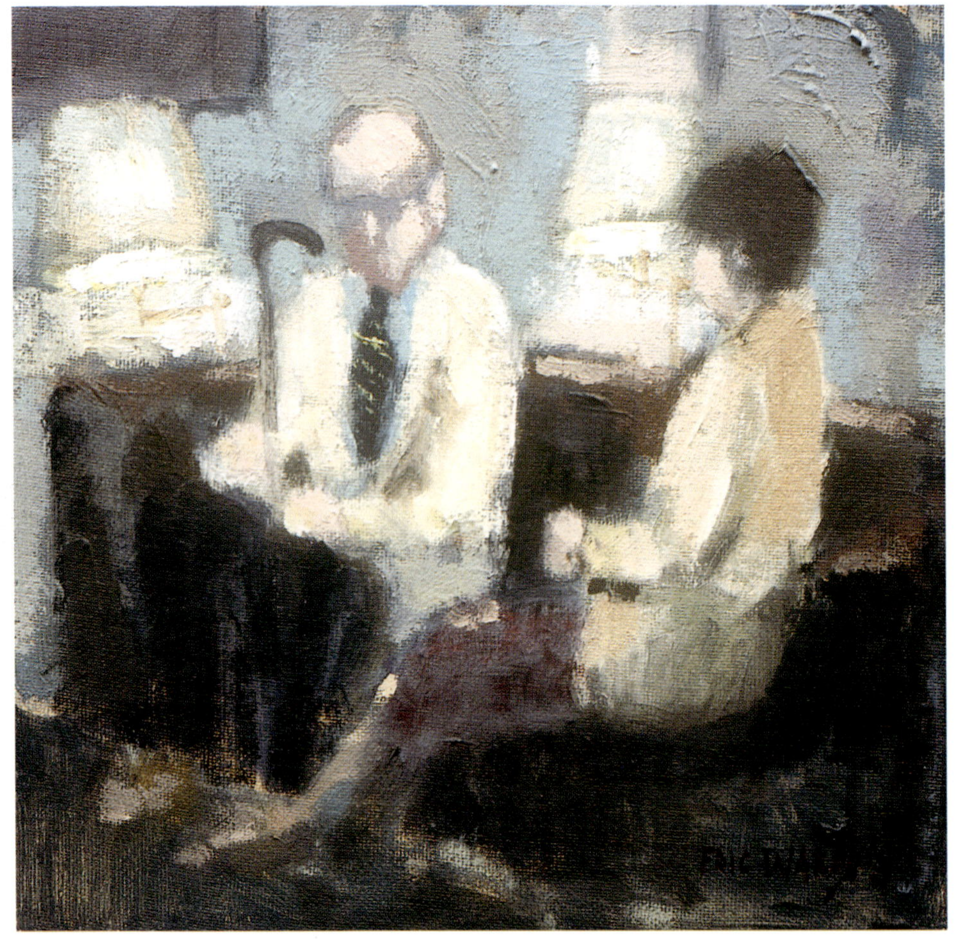

Friends' Room at the Royal Academy (2)
Oil on panel, 17.8 x 17.8cm

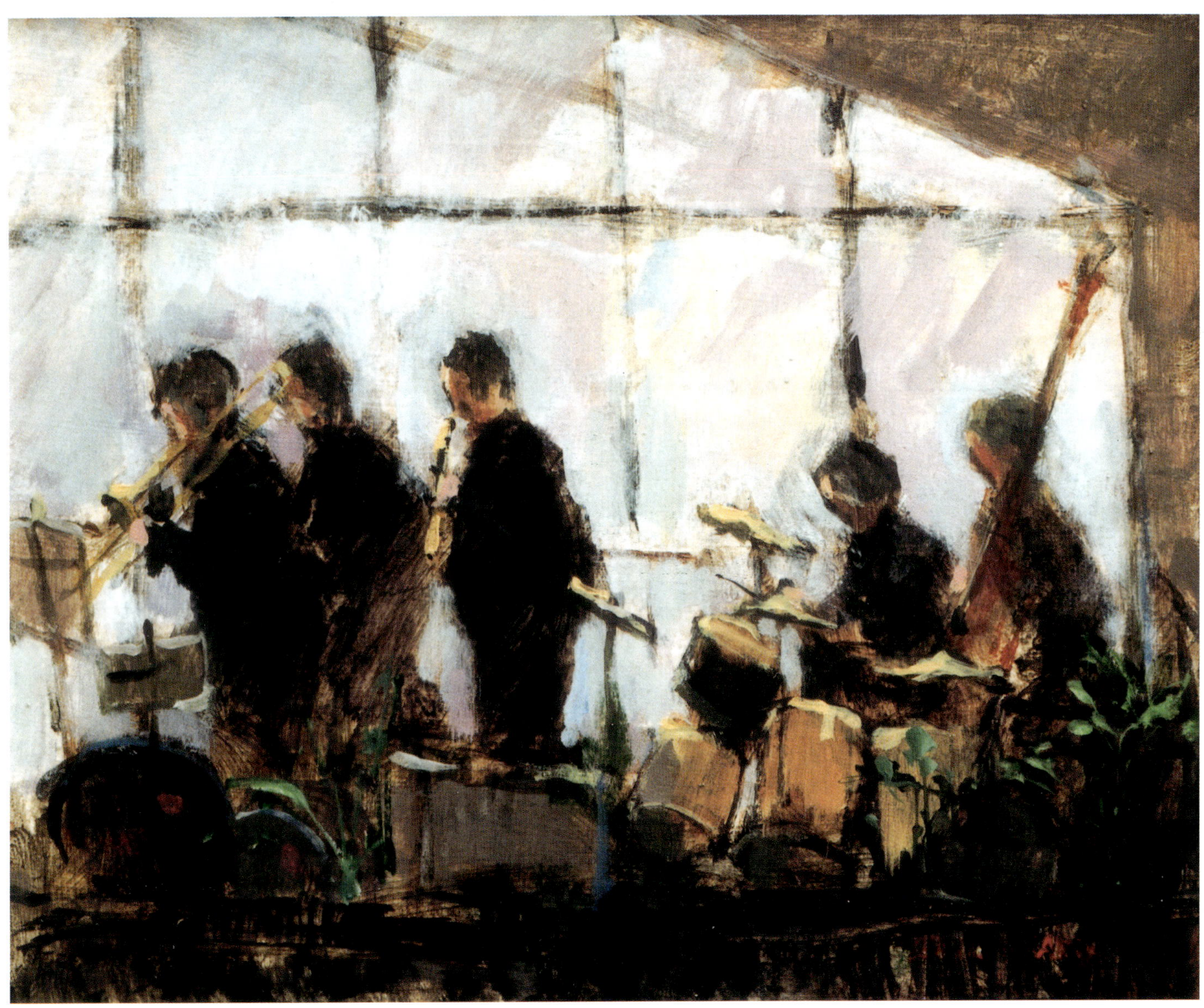

Festival Hall 1
Acrylic

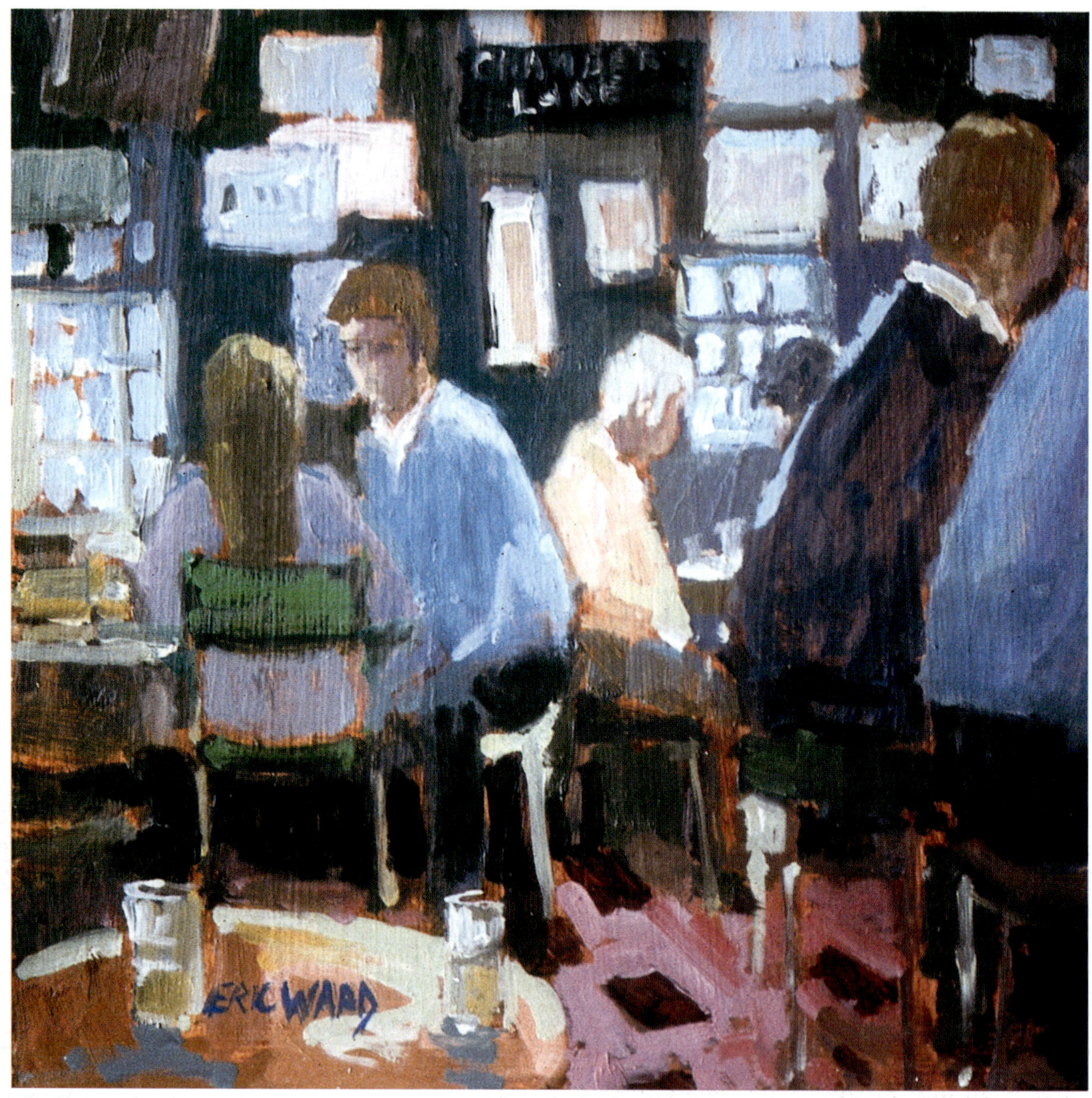

The Churchill Arms, Kensington Church Street
Oil on panel, 20.3 x 20.3cm

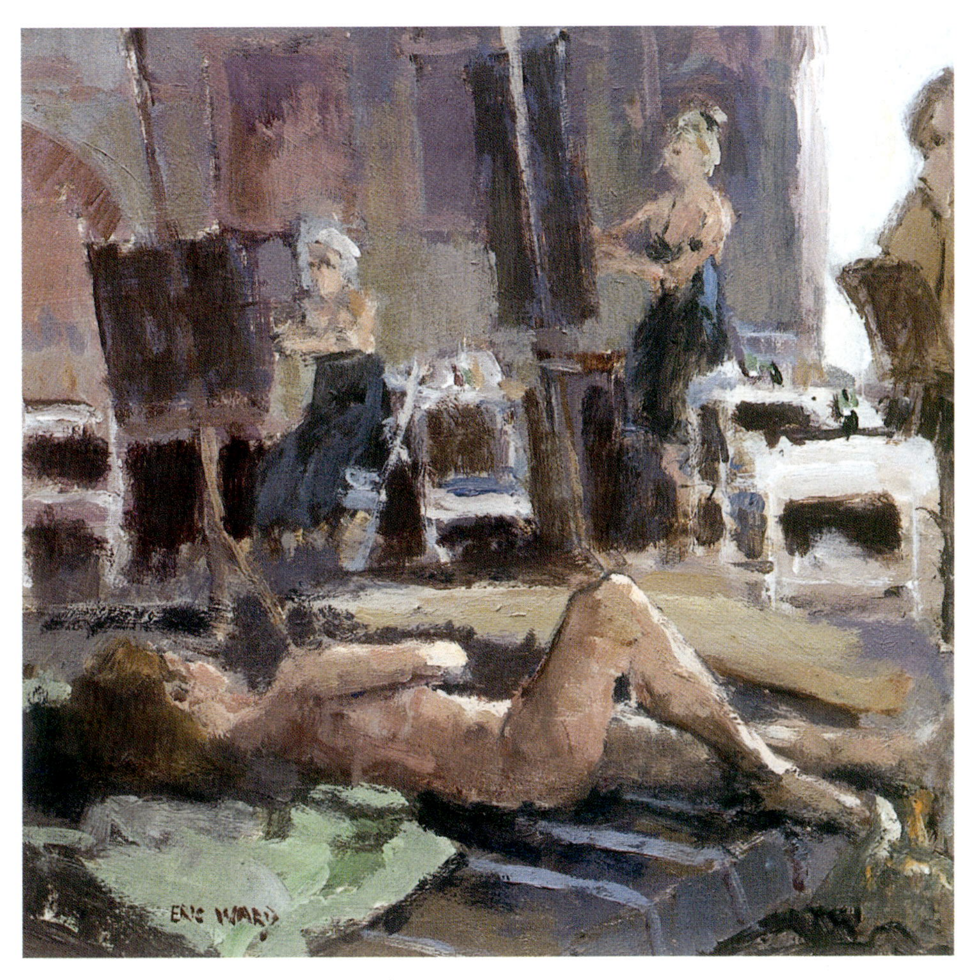

LIFE, STILL LIFE
& INTERIORS

Life painting is where I developed my initial skills; thank goodness for the St Ives School of Painting. I am lucky that in my life it seems no two days have been the same, and that applies with art. Every subject fascinates me, as does tackling the many problems that occur and different ways of using light in order to bring a subject alive. The joy of endless subjects to be inspired and challenged by – what more would any artist want?

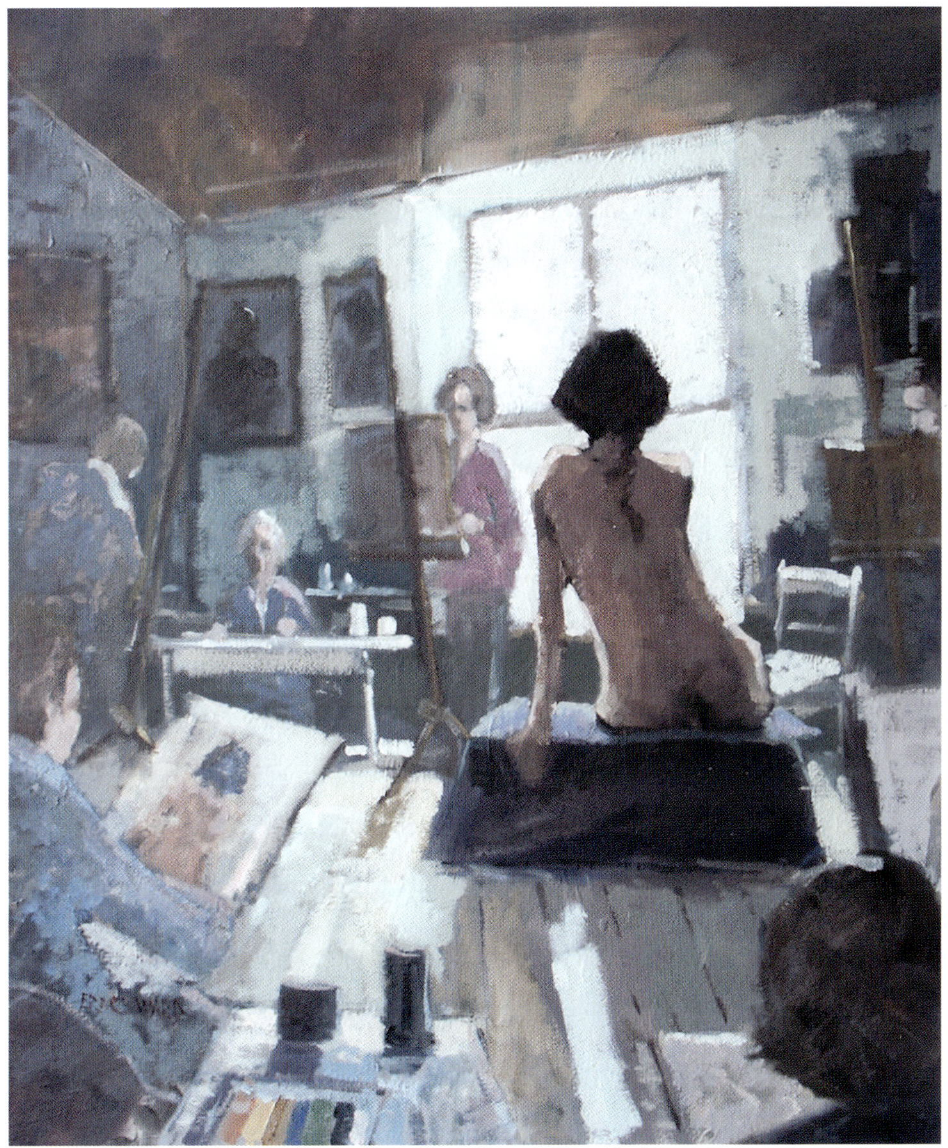

Life Room, St Ives School of Painting
Oil on canvas, 60.8 x 50.8cm

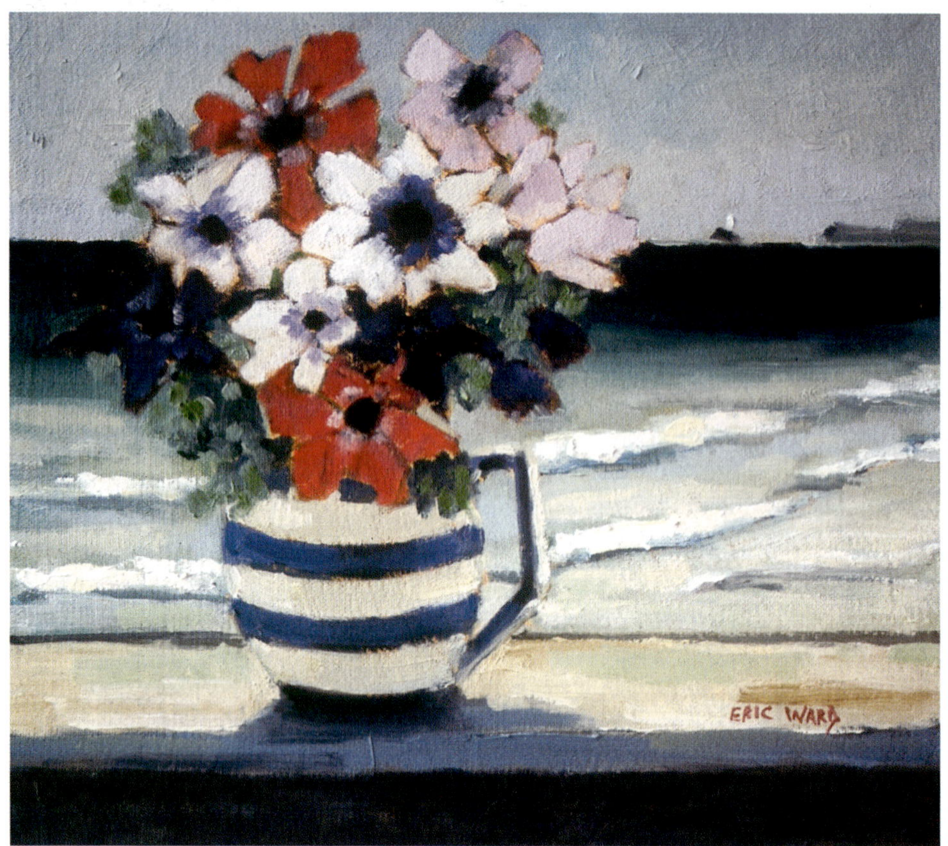

Anemones in the Window
Oil on panel, 22.9 x 25.4cm

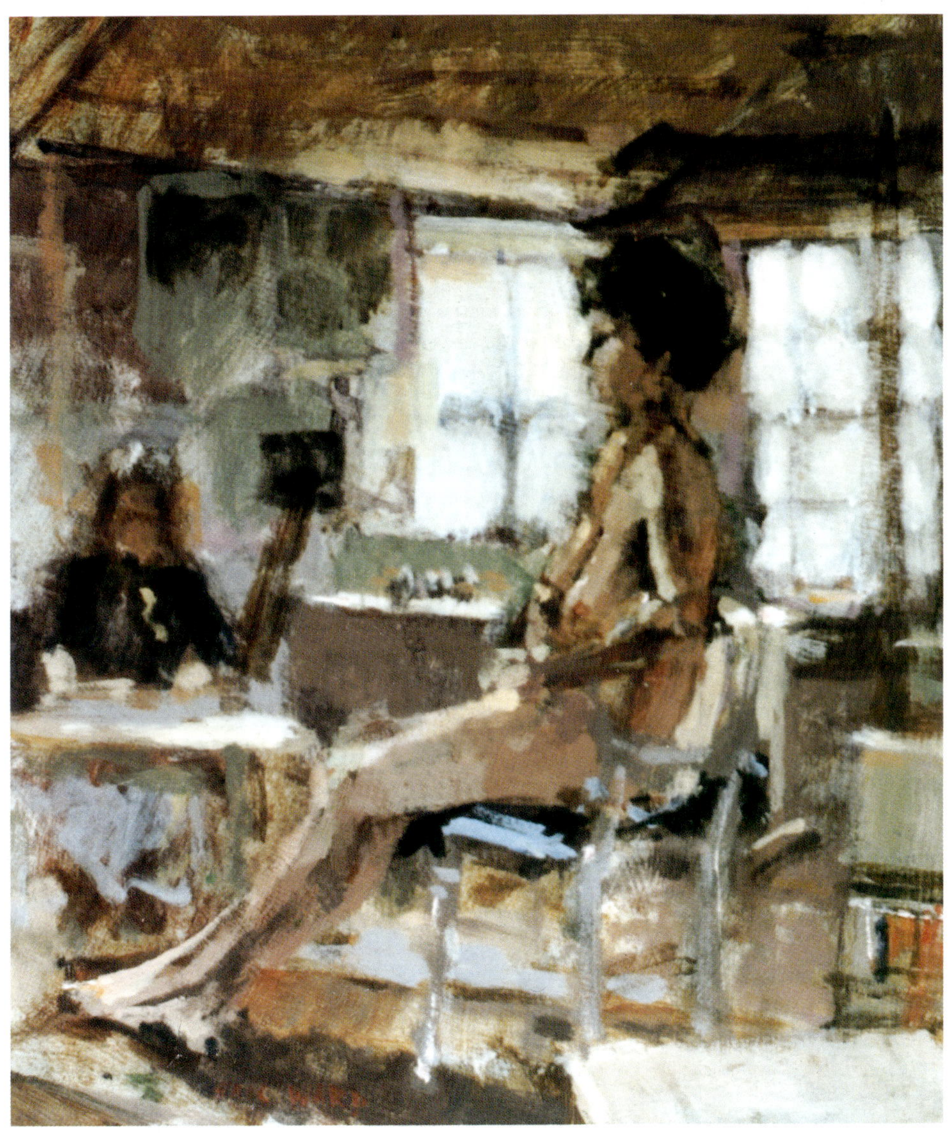

The St Ives School of Painting
Acrylic, 30.5 x 25.4cm

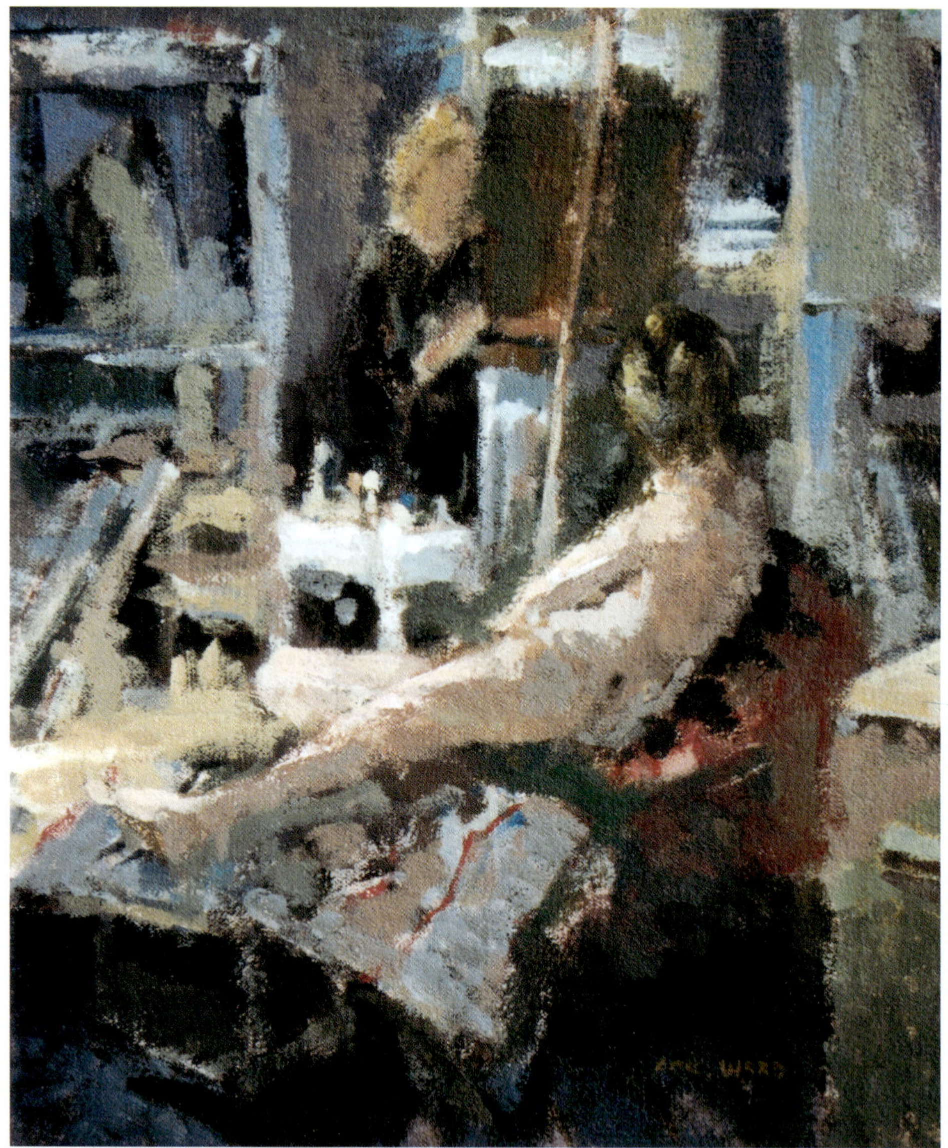

The St Ives School of Painting, Life Room
Acrylic, 30.5 x 25.4cm

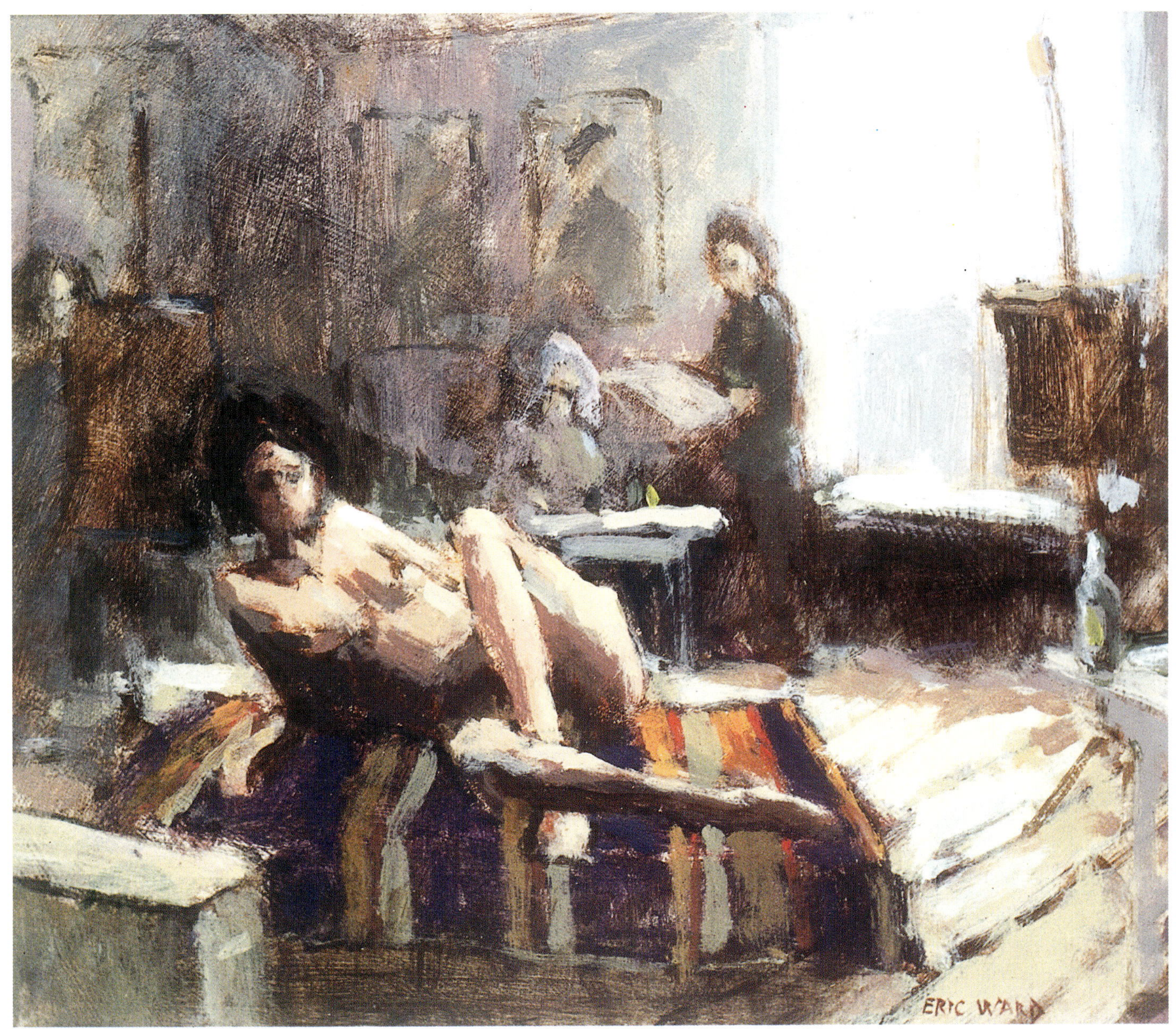

Jane in the Life Room
Acrylic on panel, 22.9 x 27.9cm

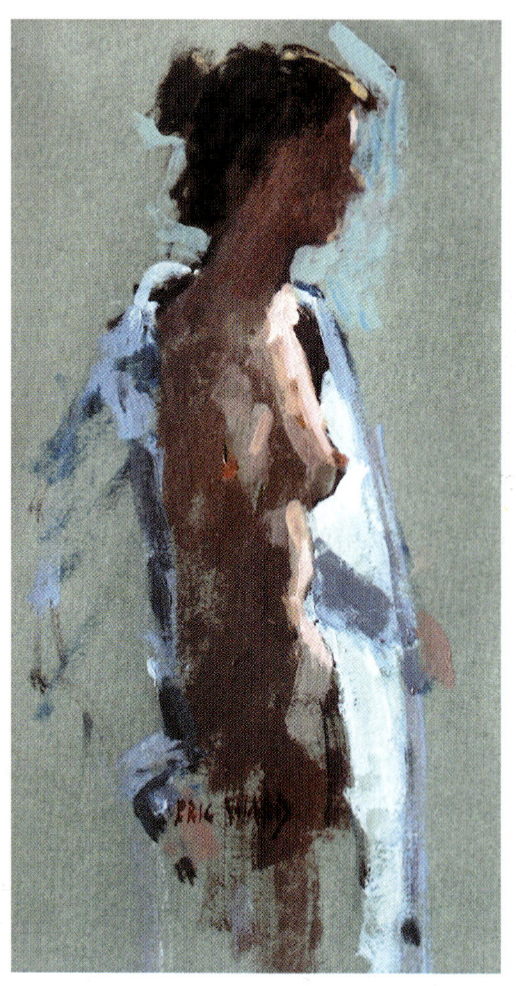

Christine
Acrylic on paper, 21.6 x 12.7cm

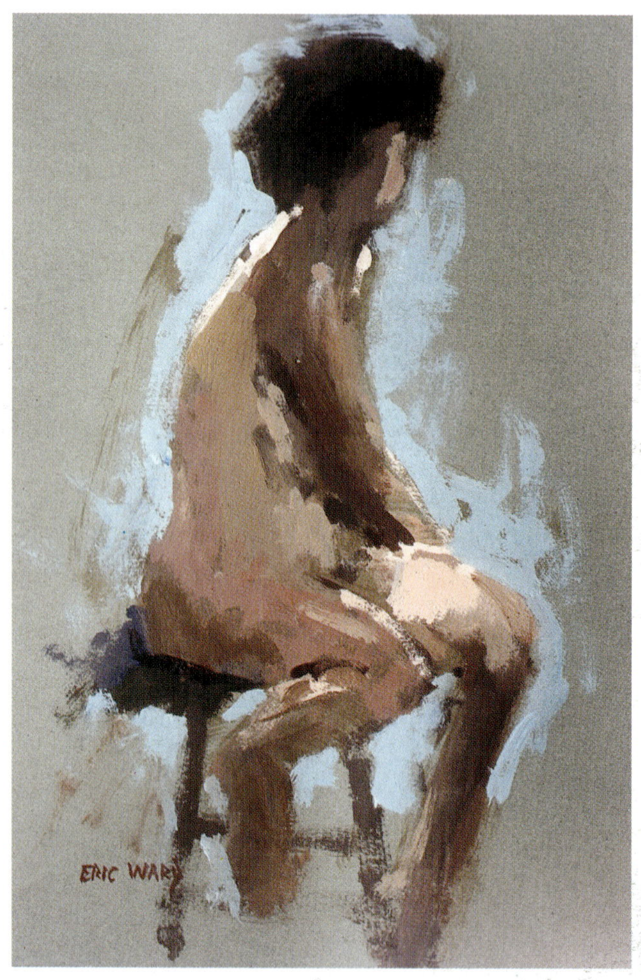

Nina
Acrylic on paper, 22.2 x 16.5cm

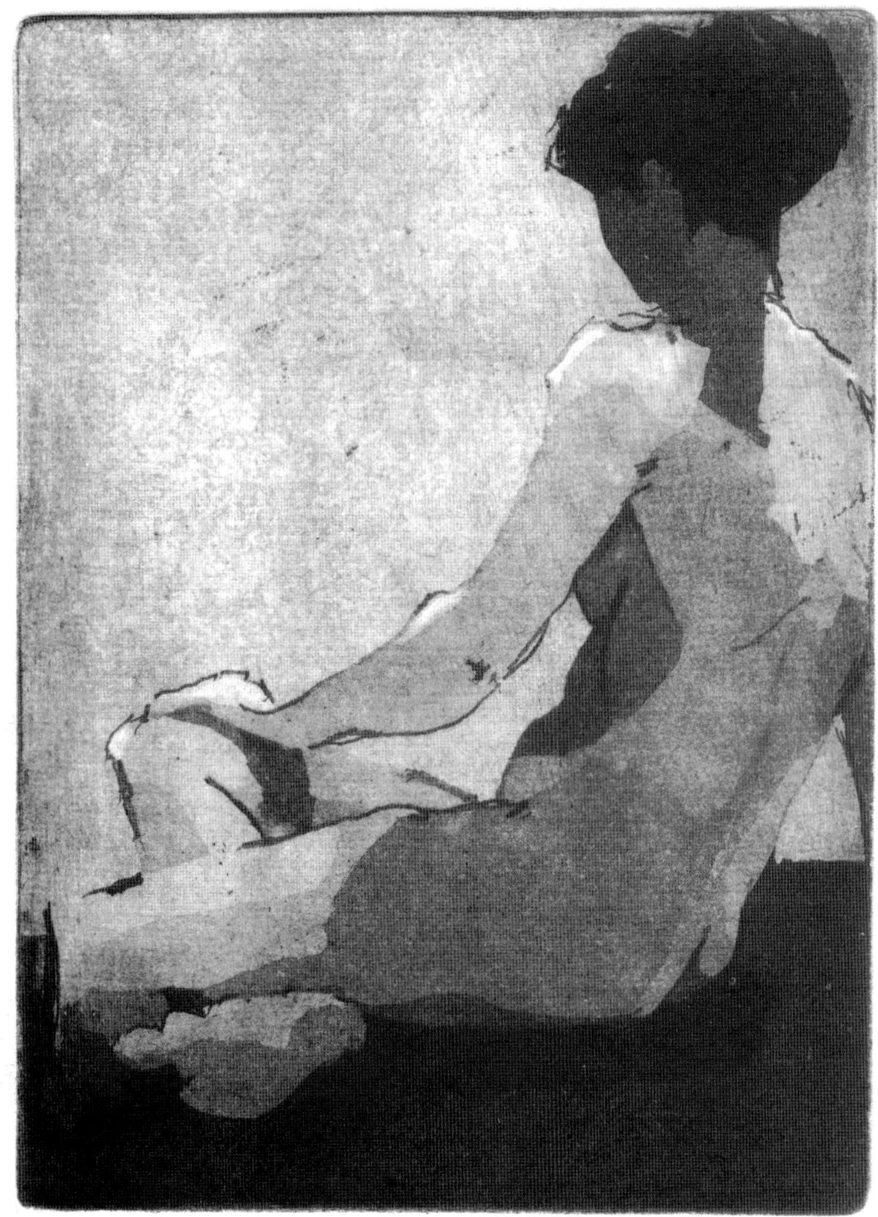

Lois
Etching, copper plate

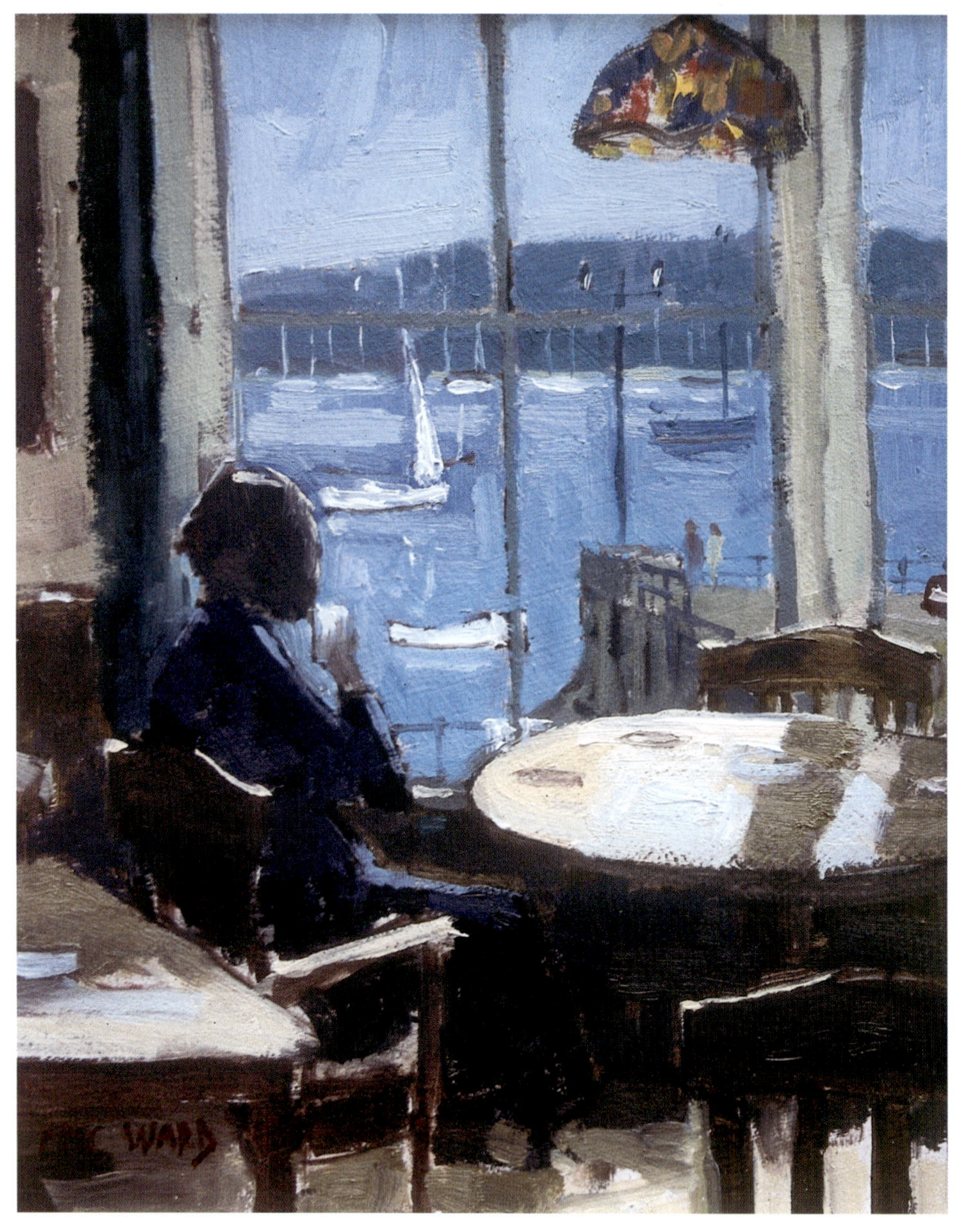

The View from the King of Prussia
Oil on panel, 25.4 x 20.3cm

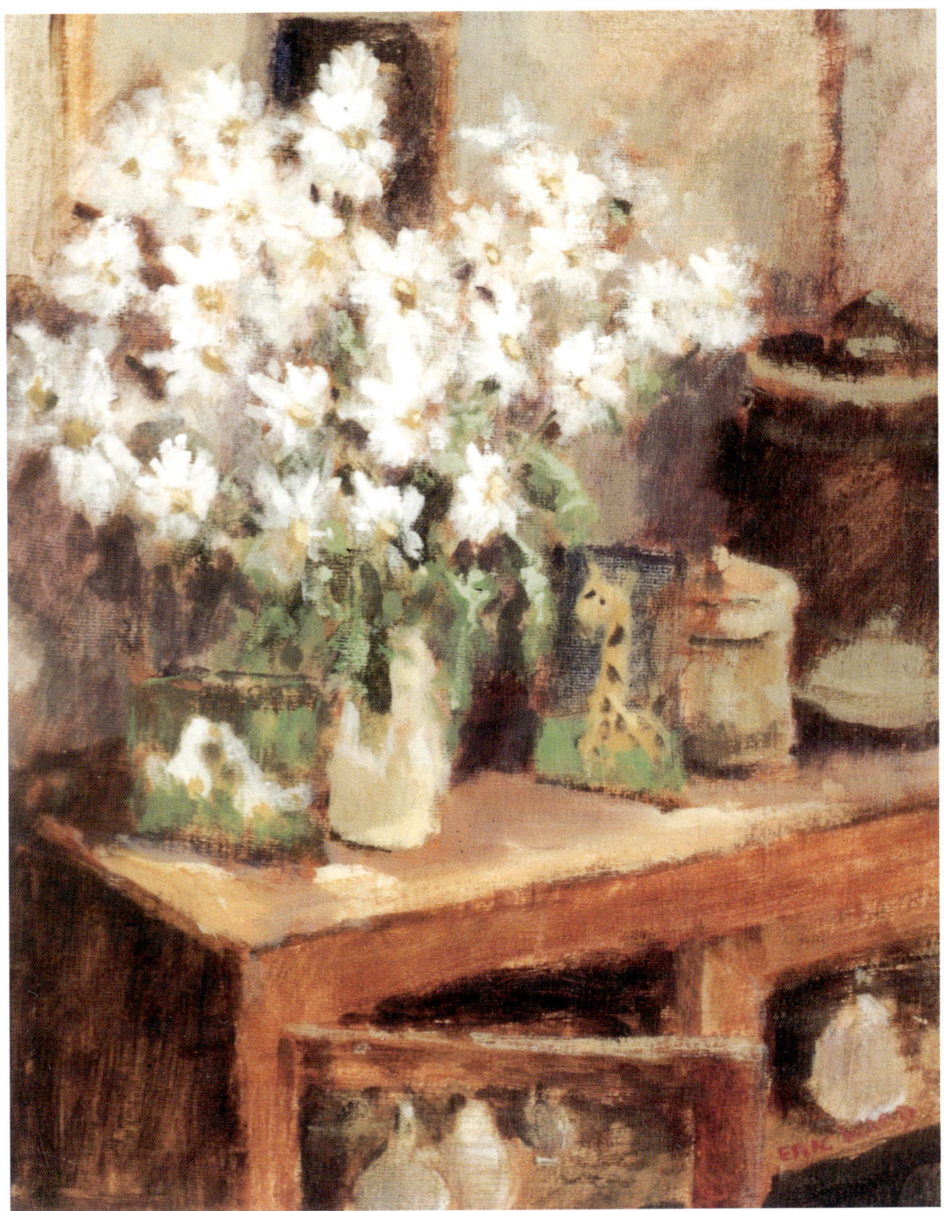

White Daisies
Acrylic, 30.5 x 25.4cm

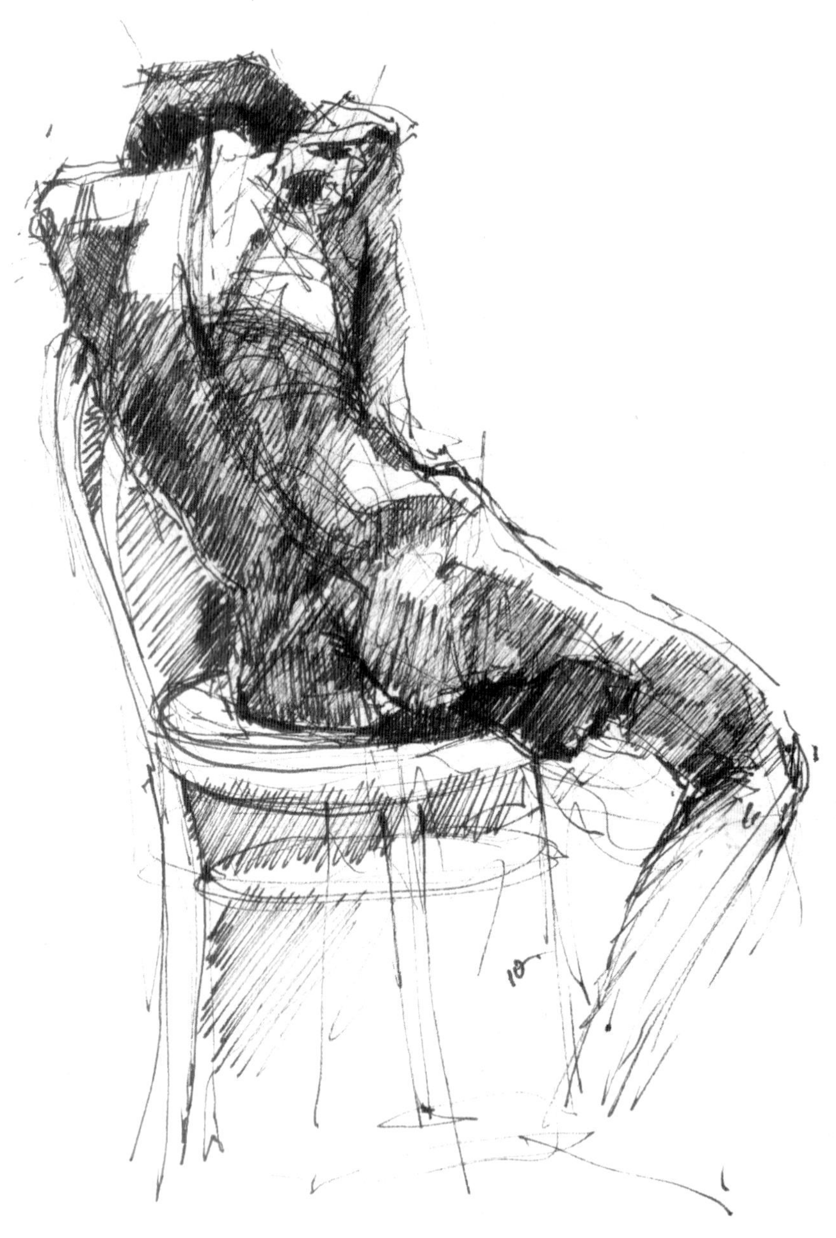

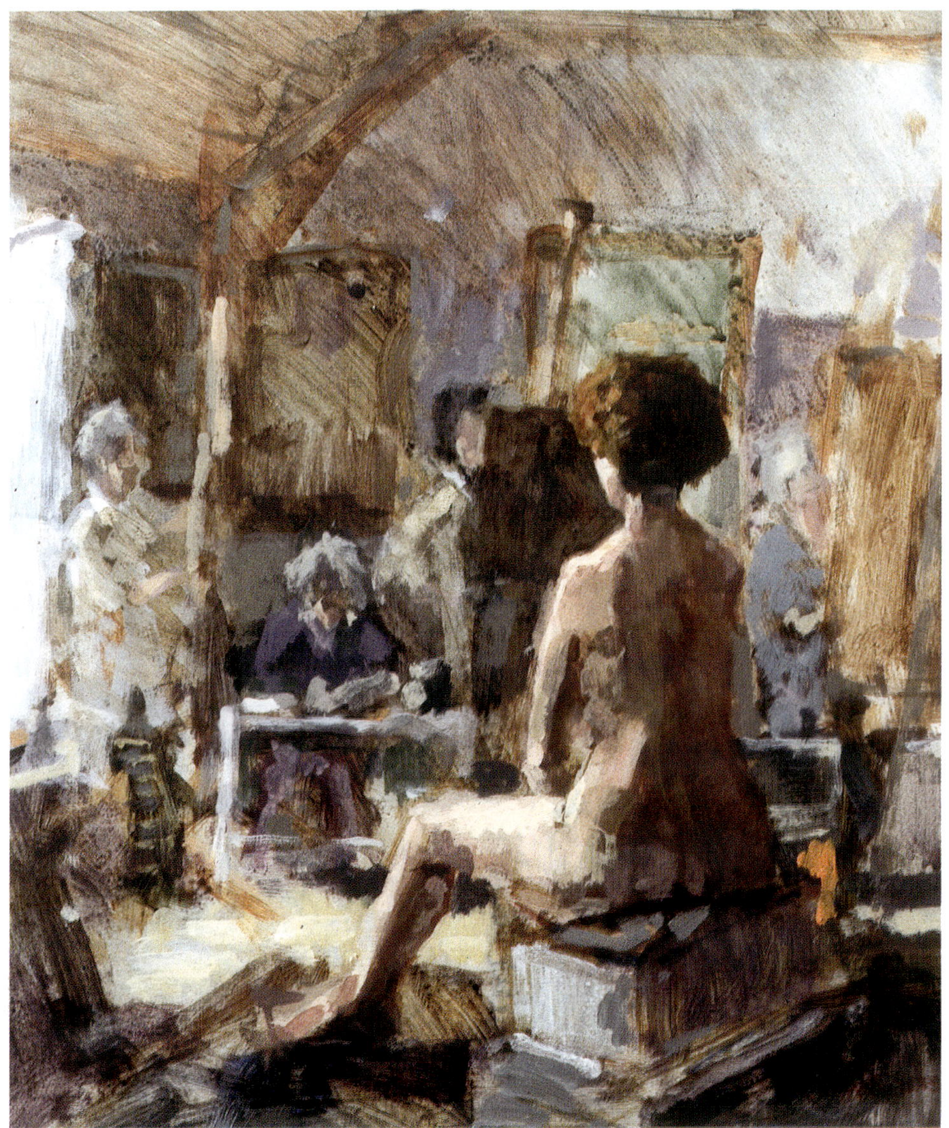

Elizabeth
Acrylic on panel, 30.5 x 25.4cm

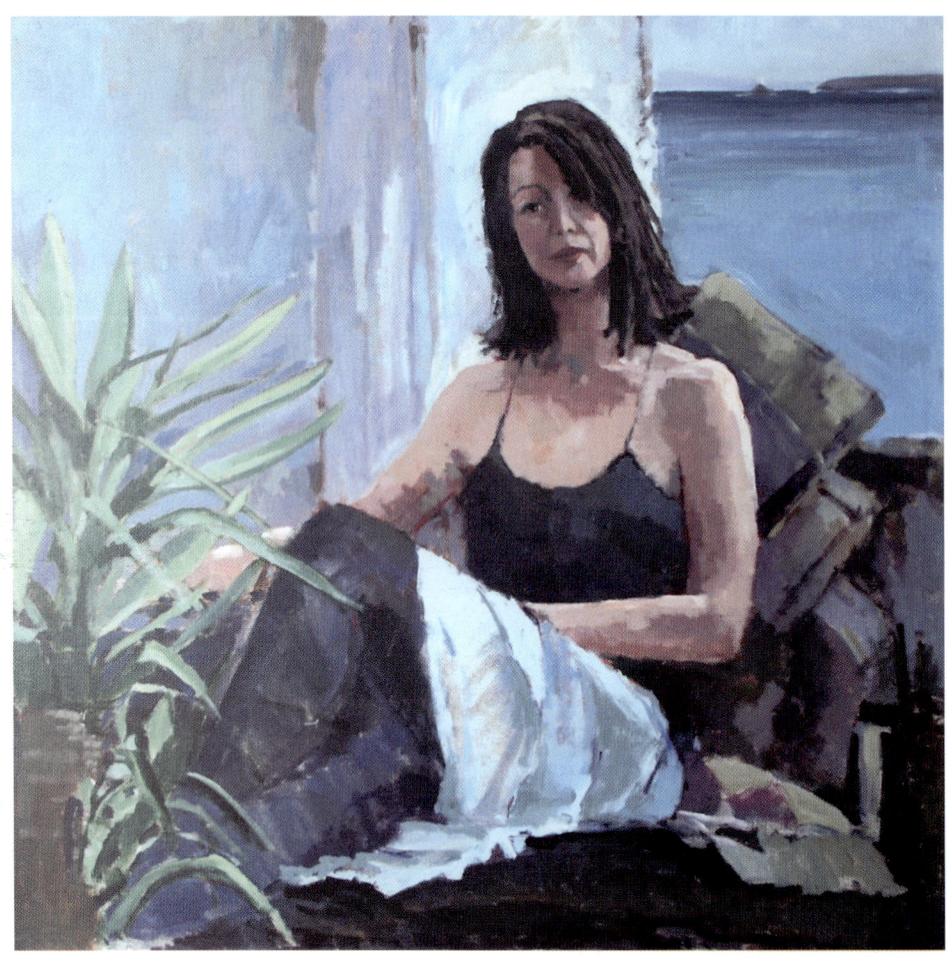

Yvonne
Acrylic on canvas, 76.2 x 76.2cm

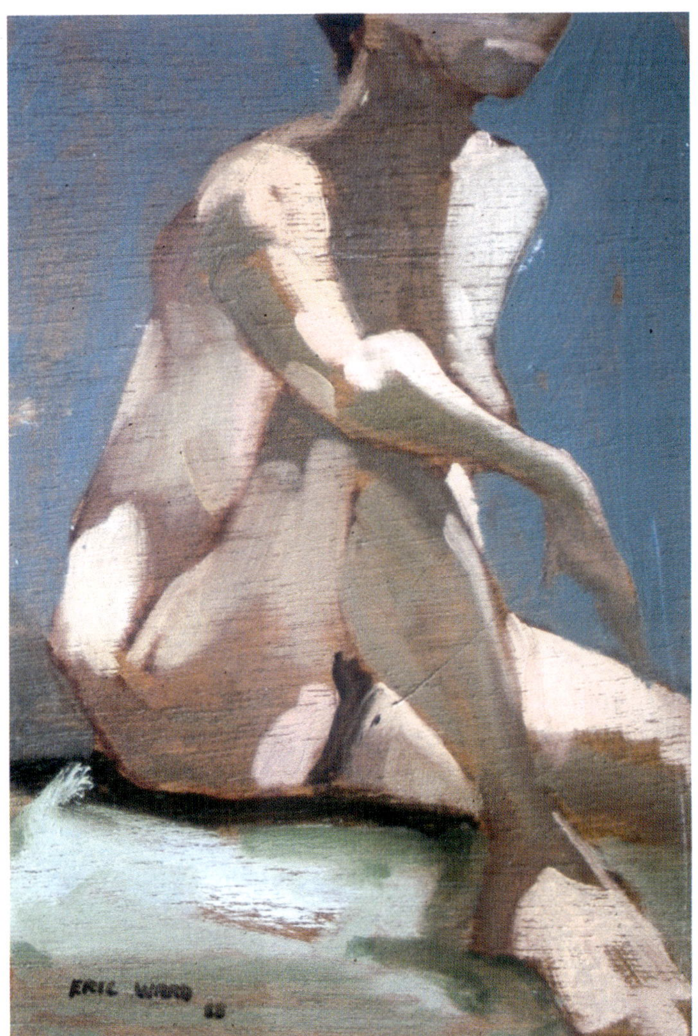

Figure Study
Oil on panel, 20.3 x 15.2cm

The first painting sold by the artist – for £5.

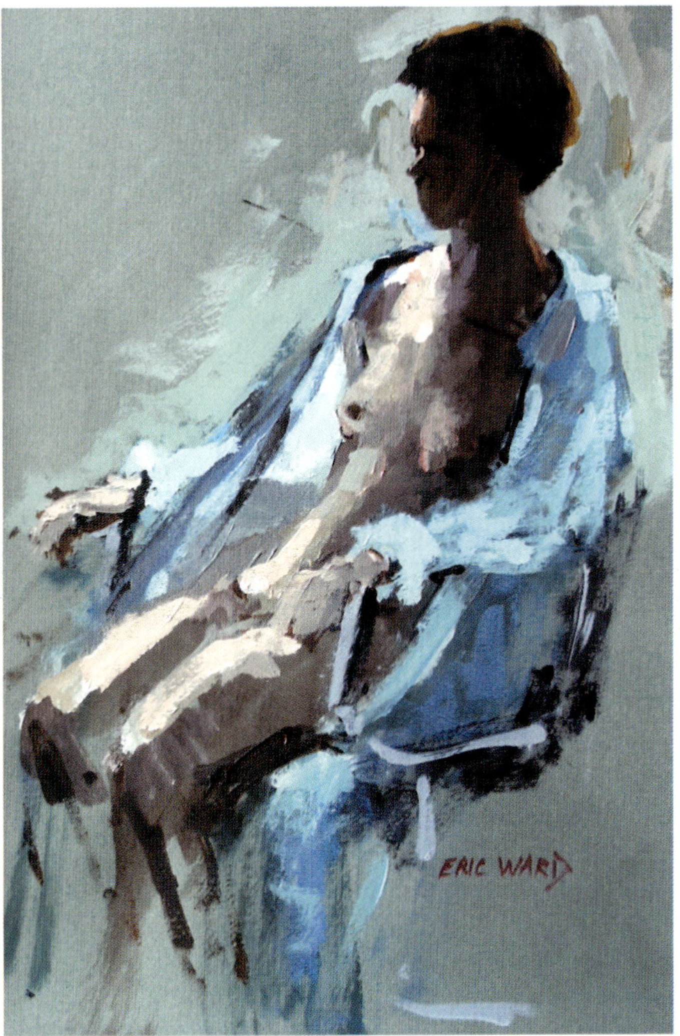

Christine (4)
Acrylic on paper, 26.7 x 19.1cm

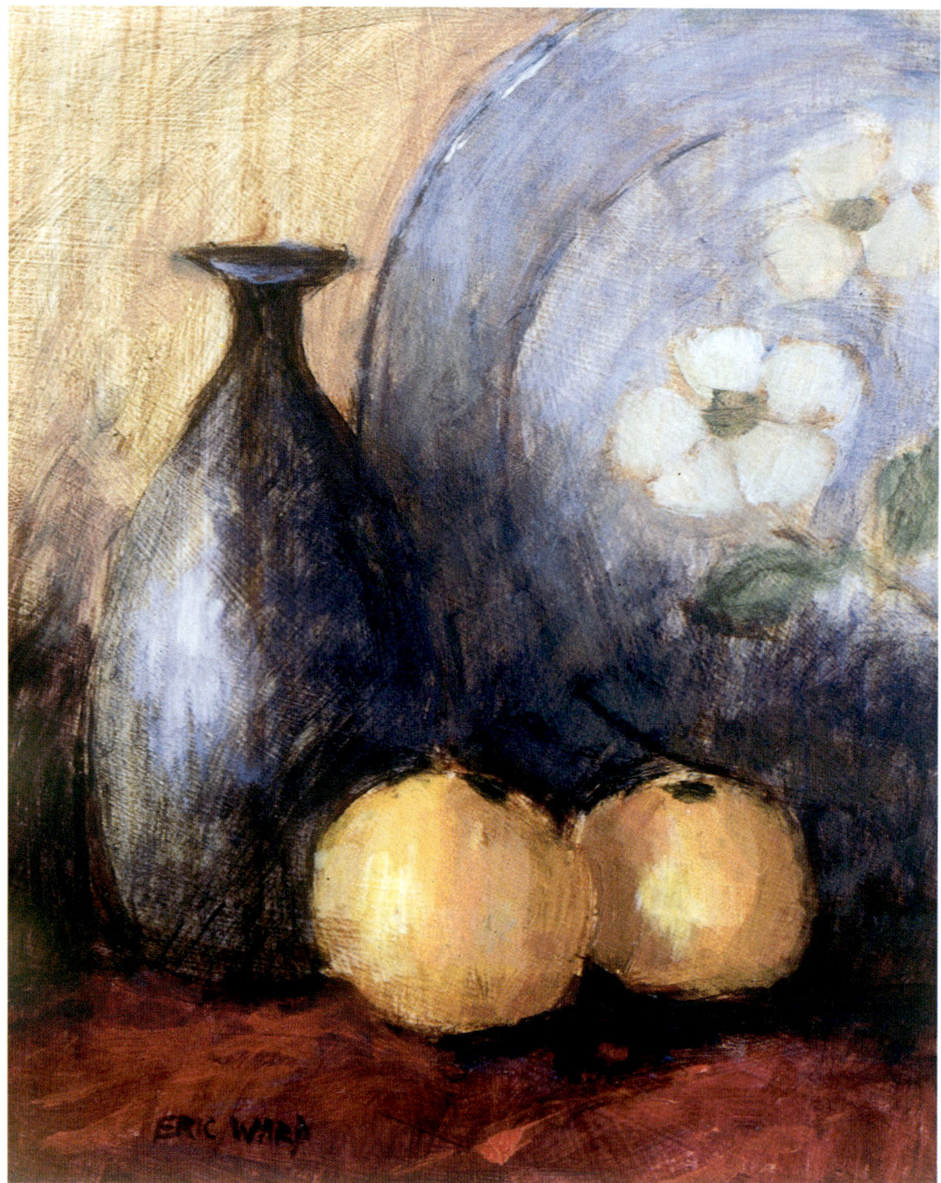

Oranges
Acrylic on panel, 25.4 x 20.3cm

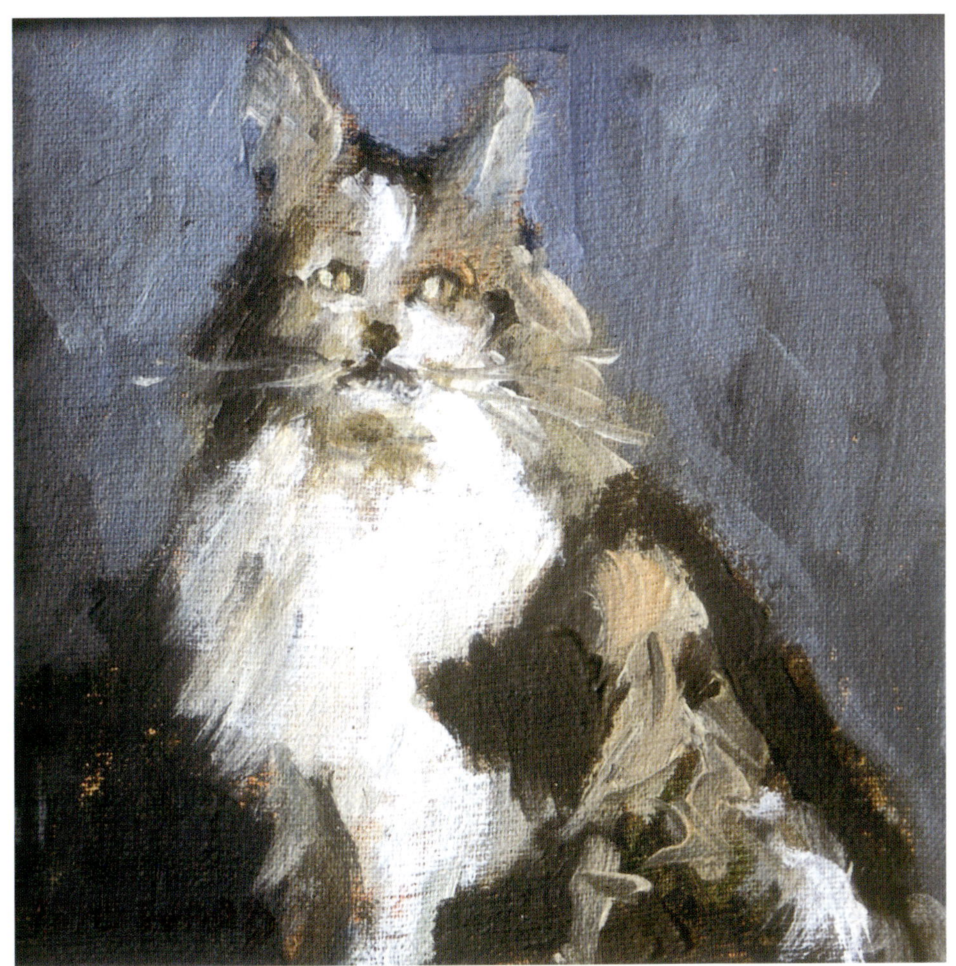

Vimmie (aka T.C.) – The Cat who comes for his Holidays
Oil on panel, 15.2 x 15.2cm

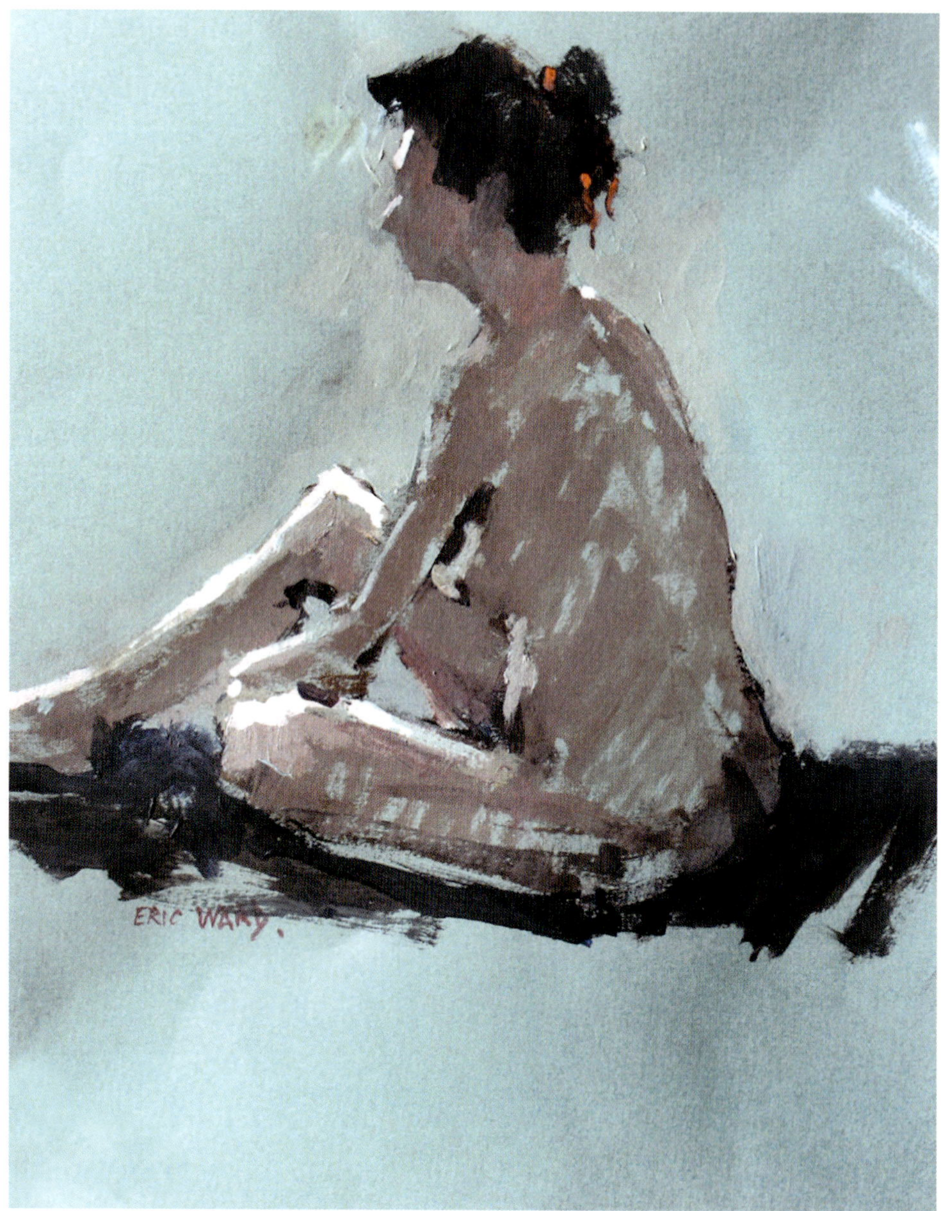

Figure
Acrylic on paper, 22.9 x 20.3cm

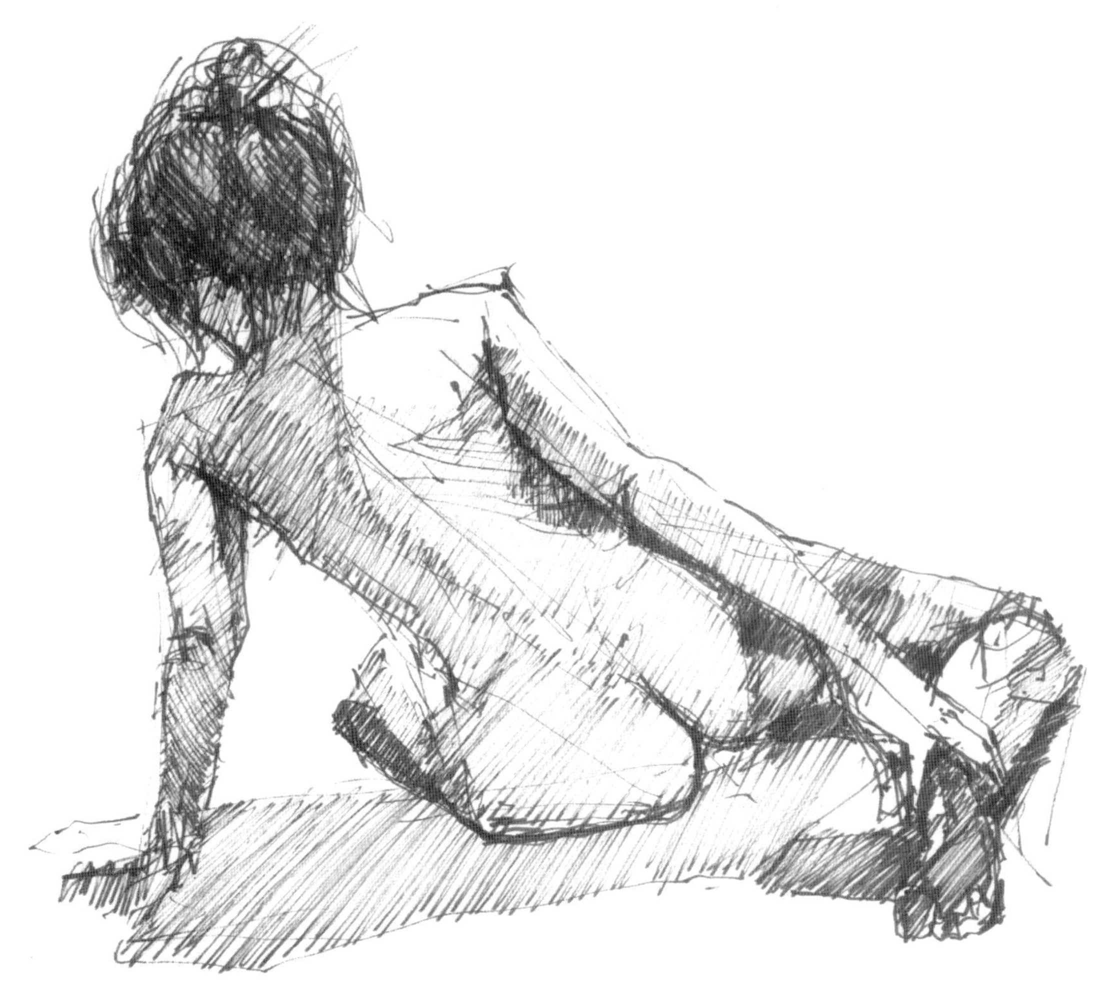

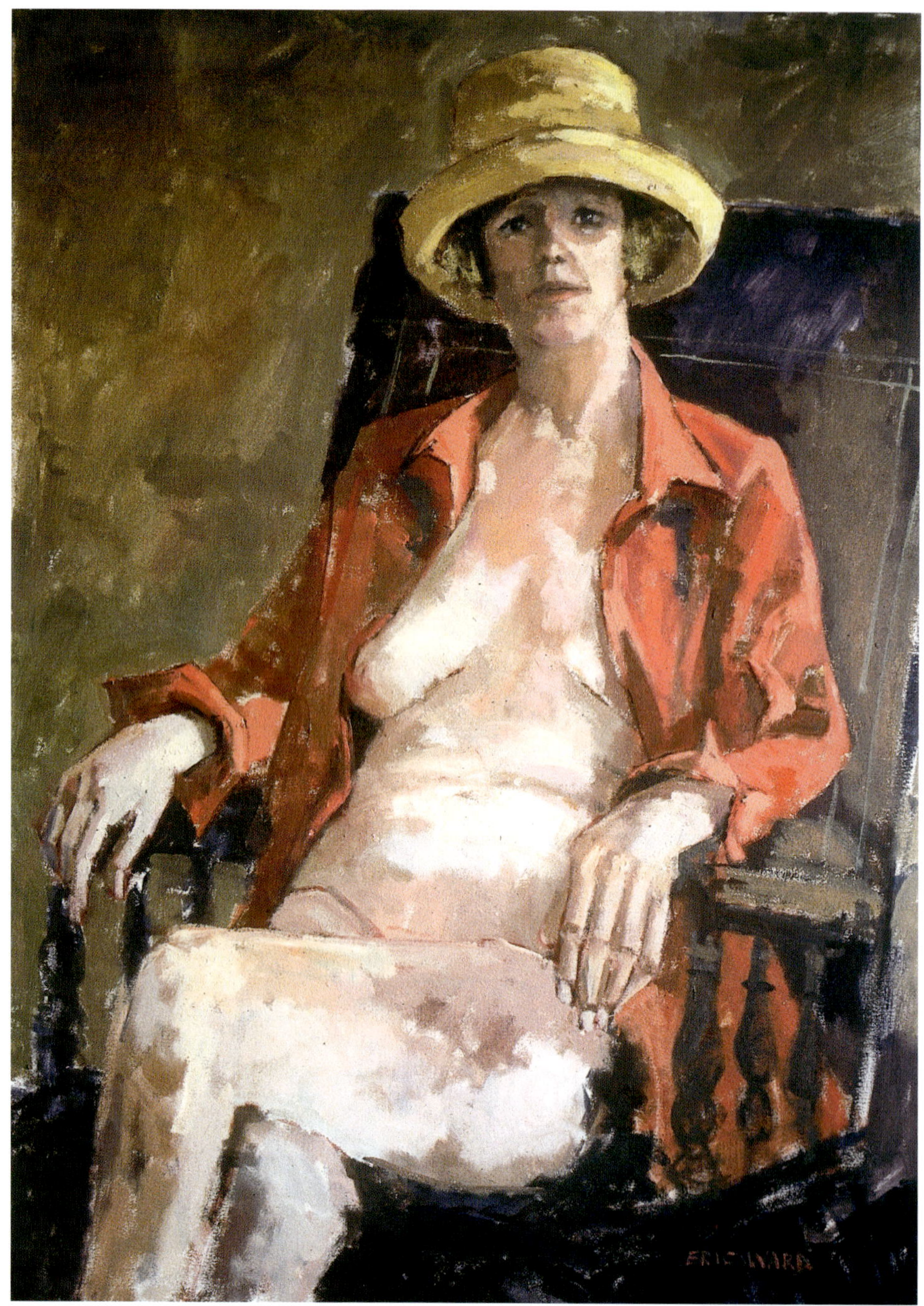

Karen
Oil on canvas, 91.6 x 66cm

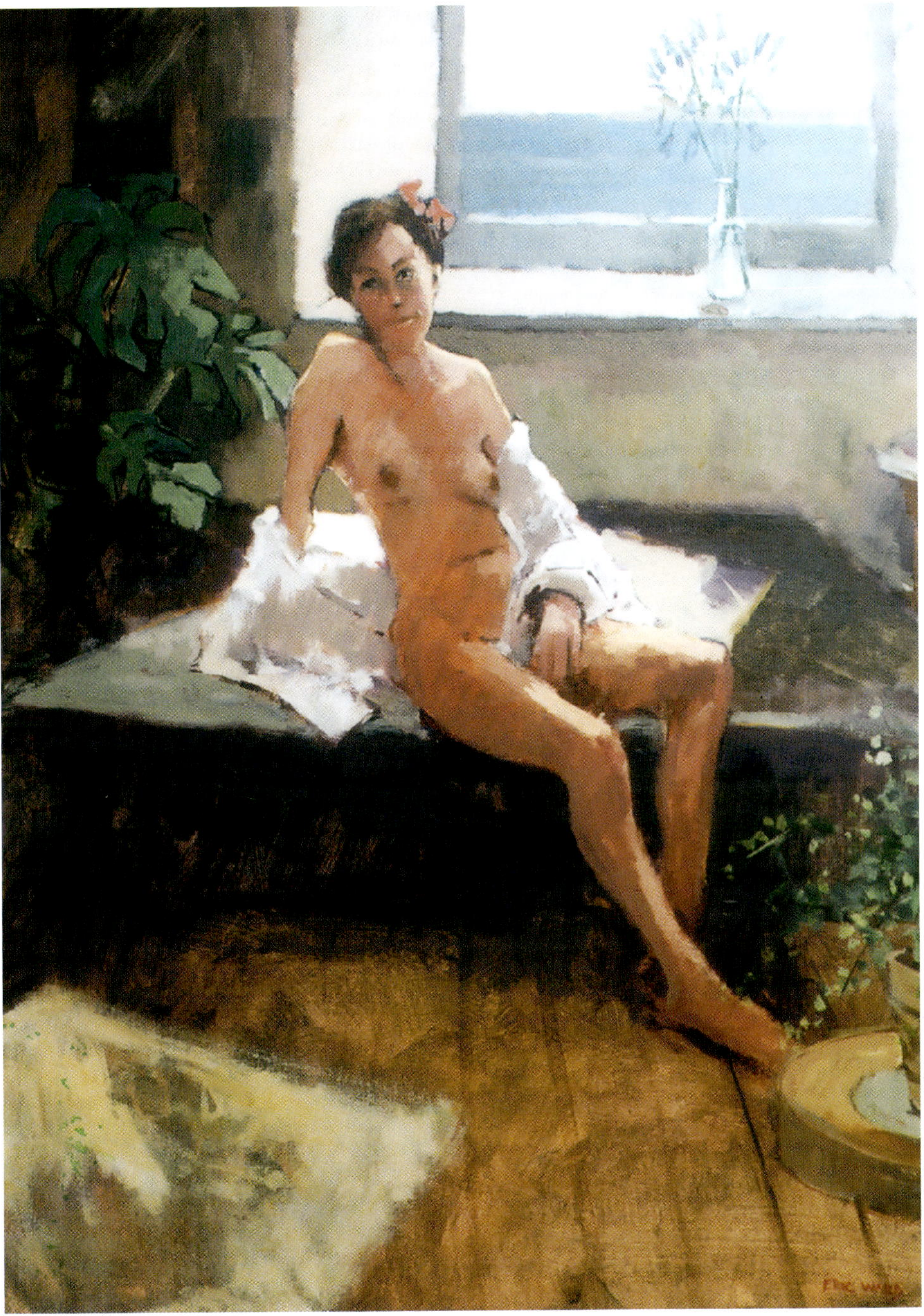

Paula
Acrylic, 91.6 x 76.2cm

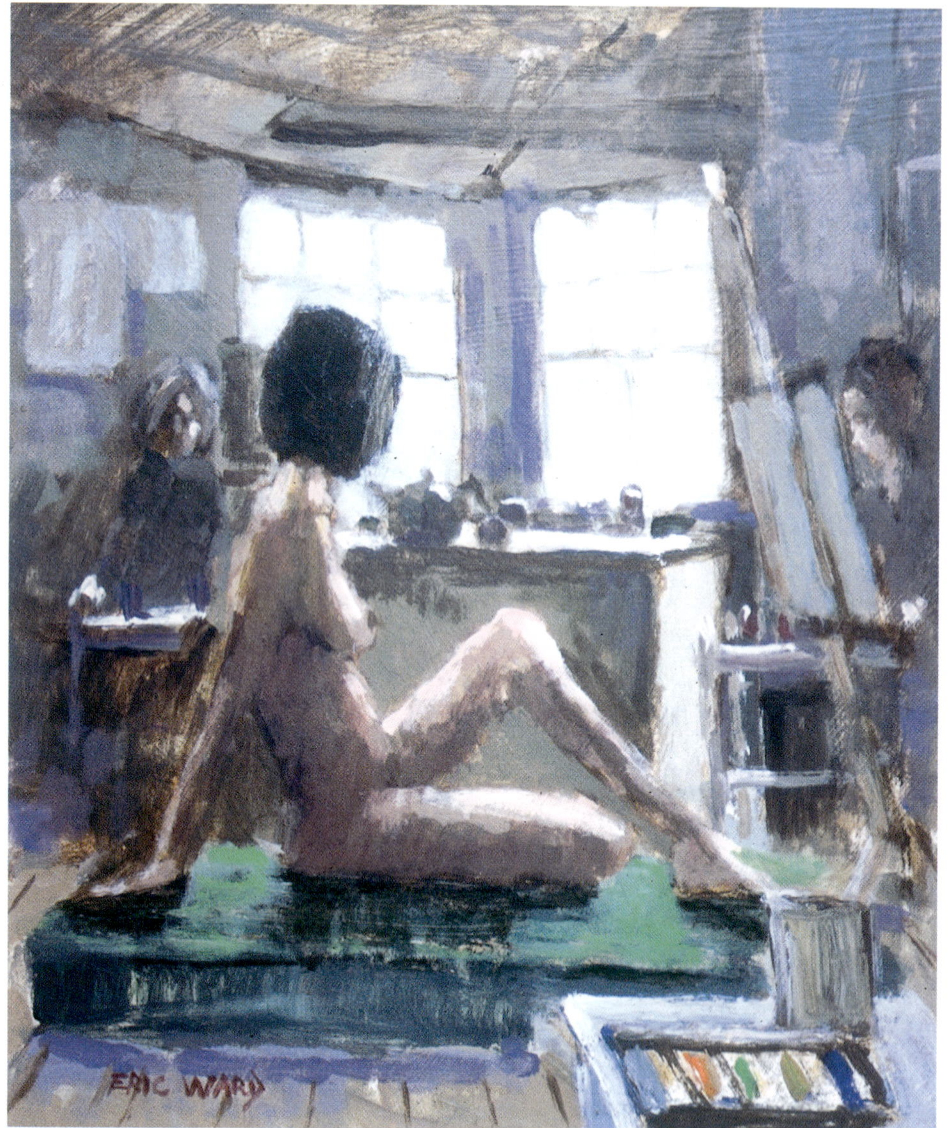

Mary
Acrylic on panel, 30.5 x 25.4cm

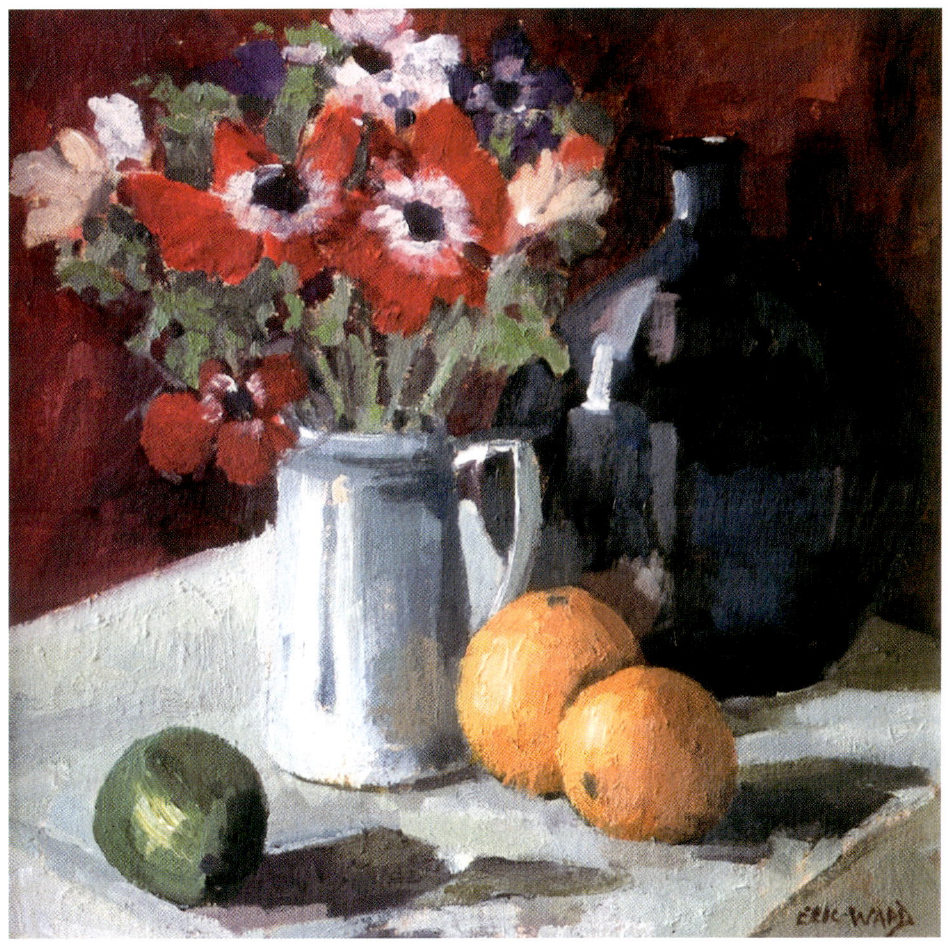

Still Life with Anemones
Oil on panel, 28 x 28cm

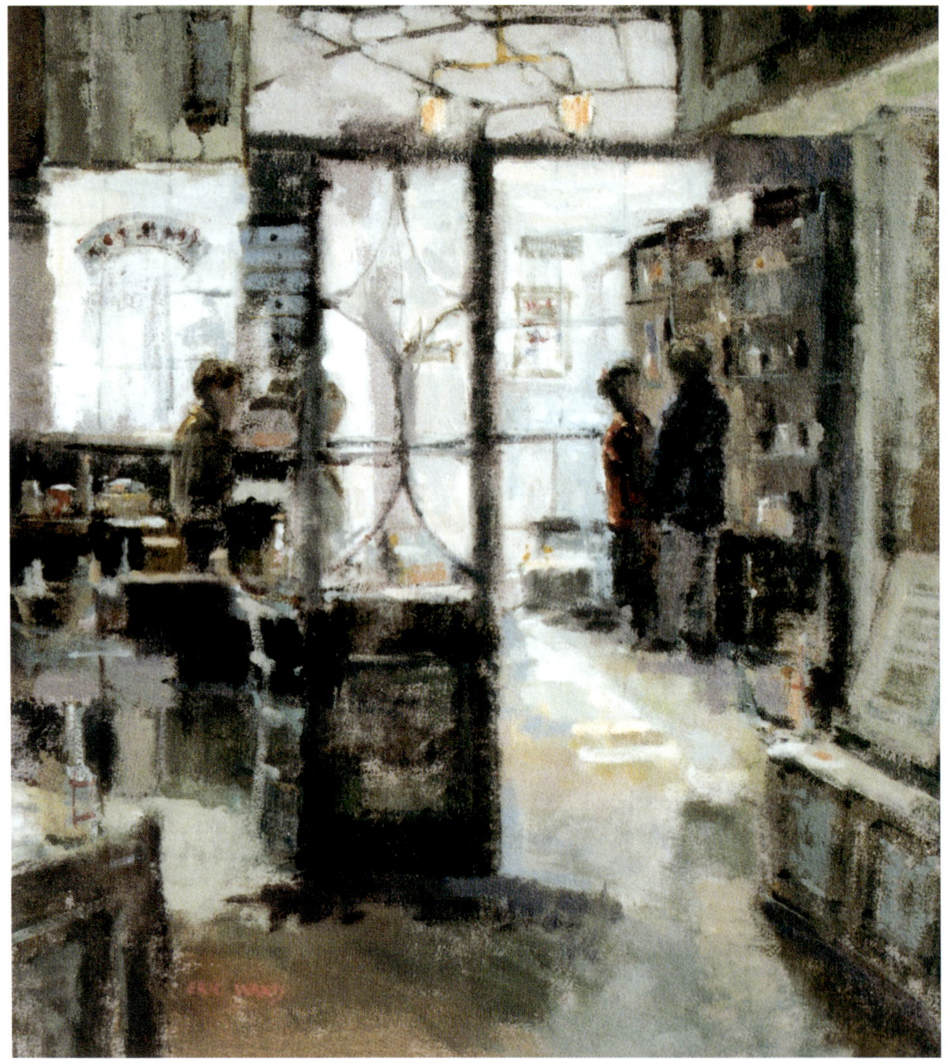

Shop in the Haymarket, London
Acrylic, 45.8 x 40.6cm

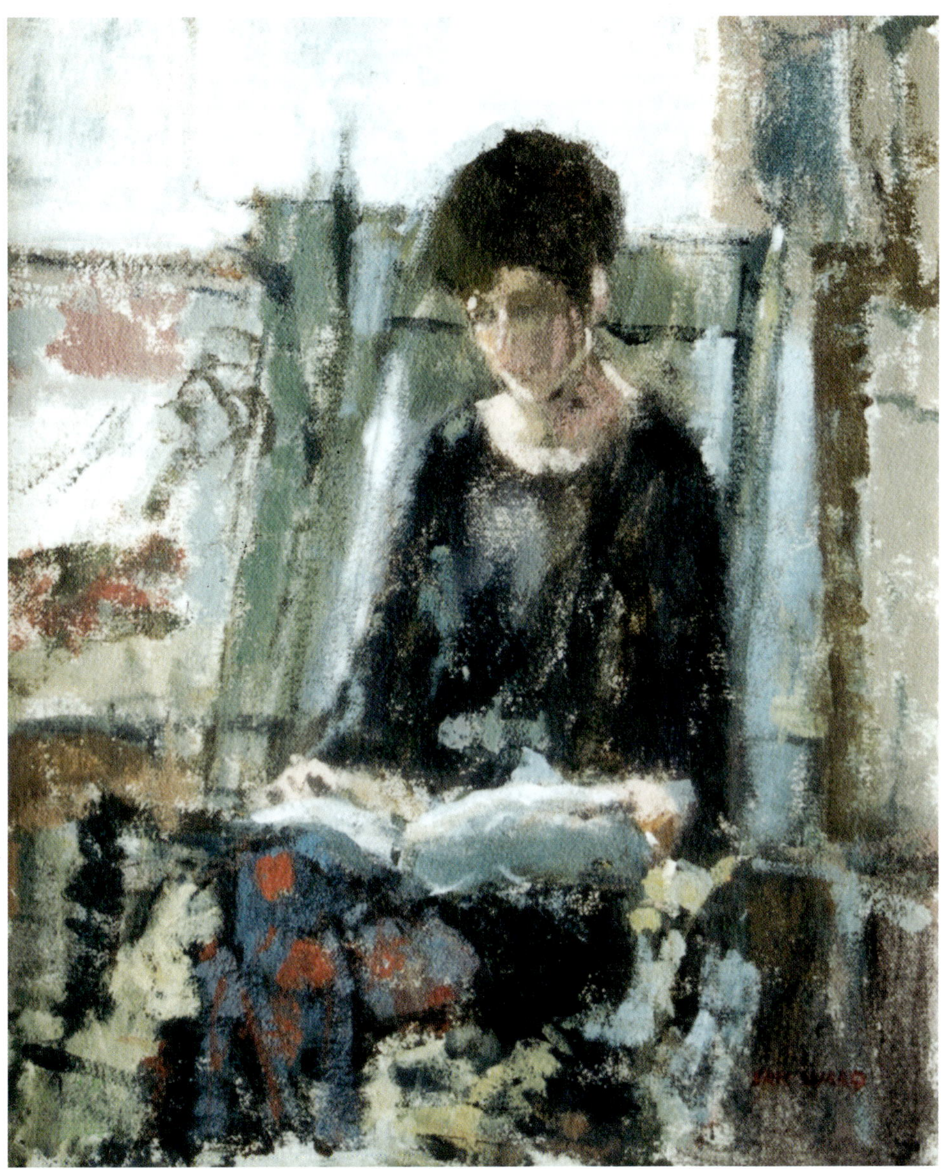

Lynne
Acrylic, 30.5 x 25.4cm

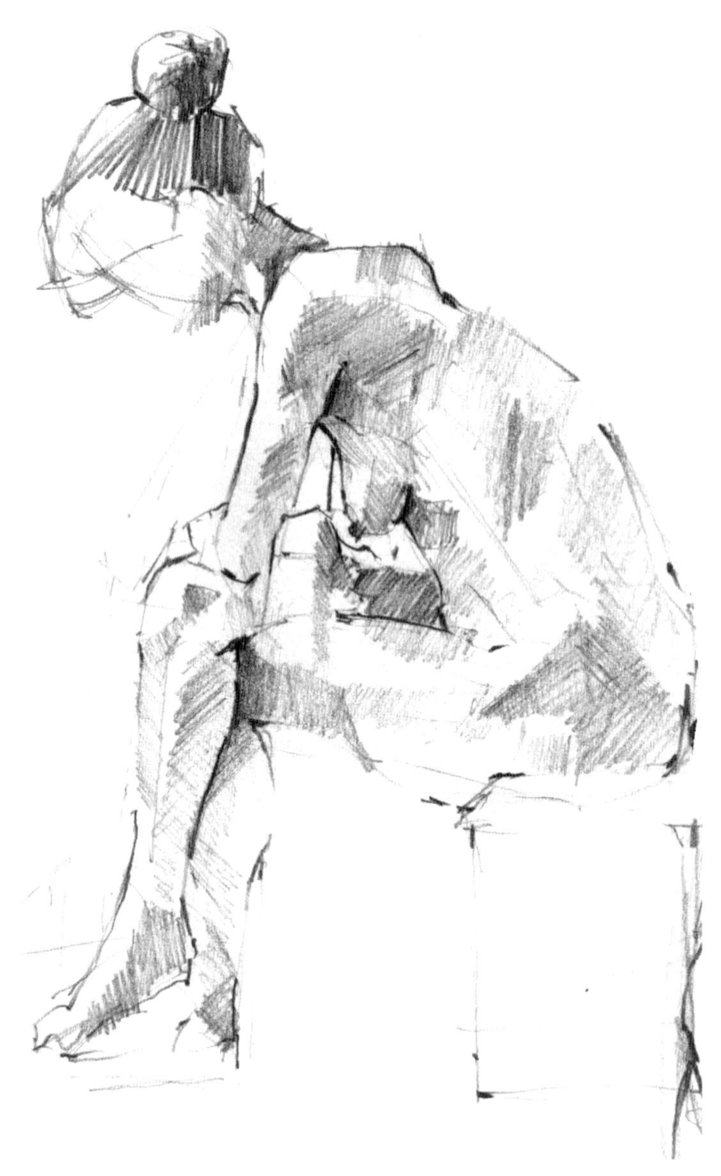

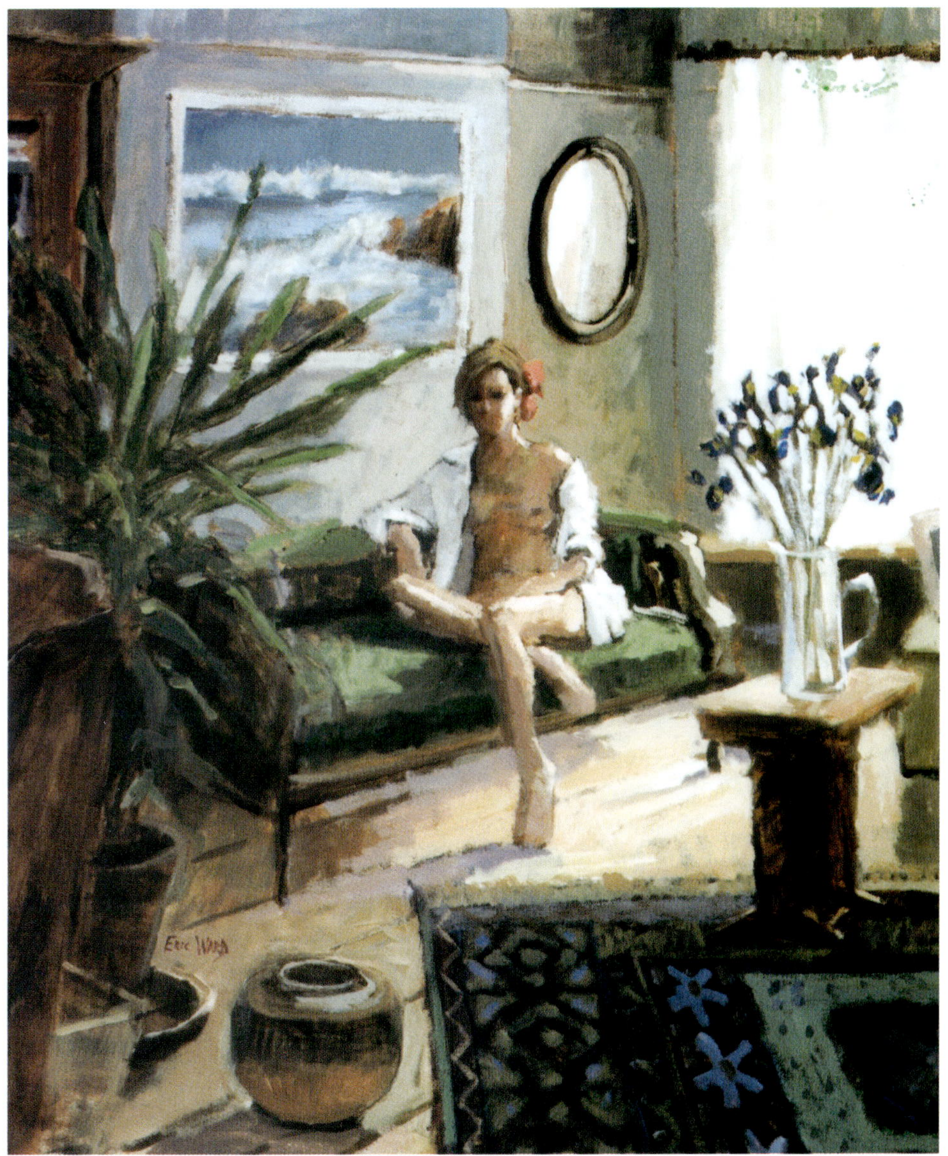

The Red Ribbon
Acrylic, 91.6 x 81.2cm

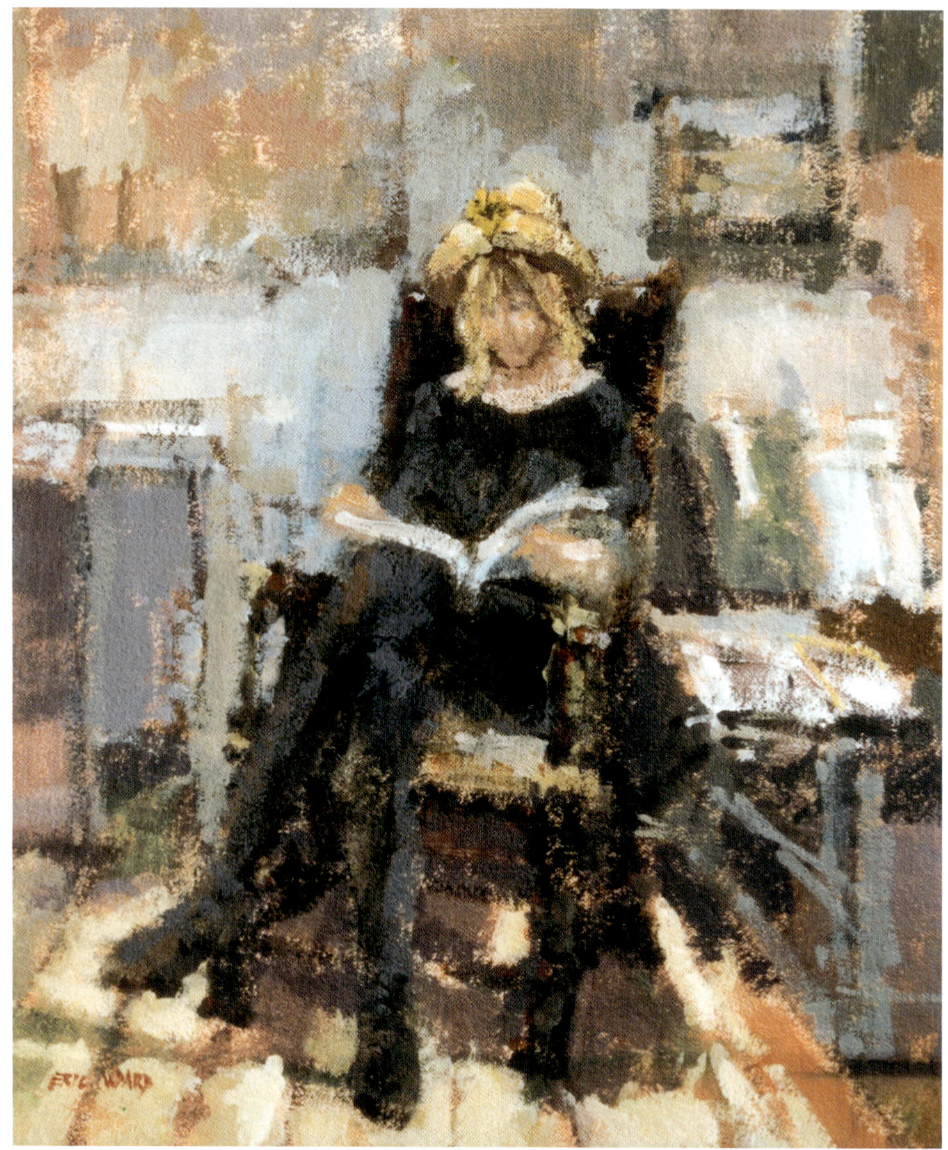

Susie
Acrylic, 30.5 x 25.4cm

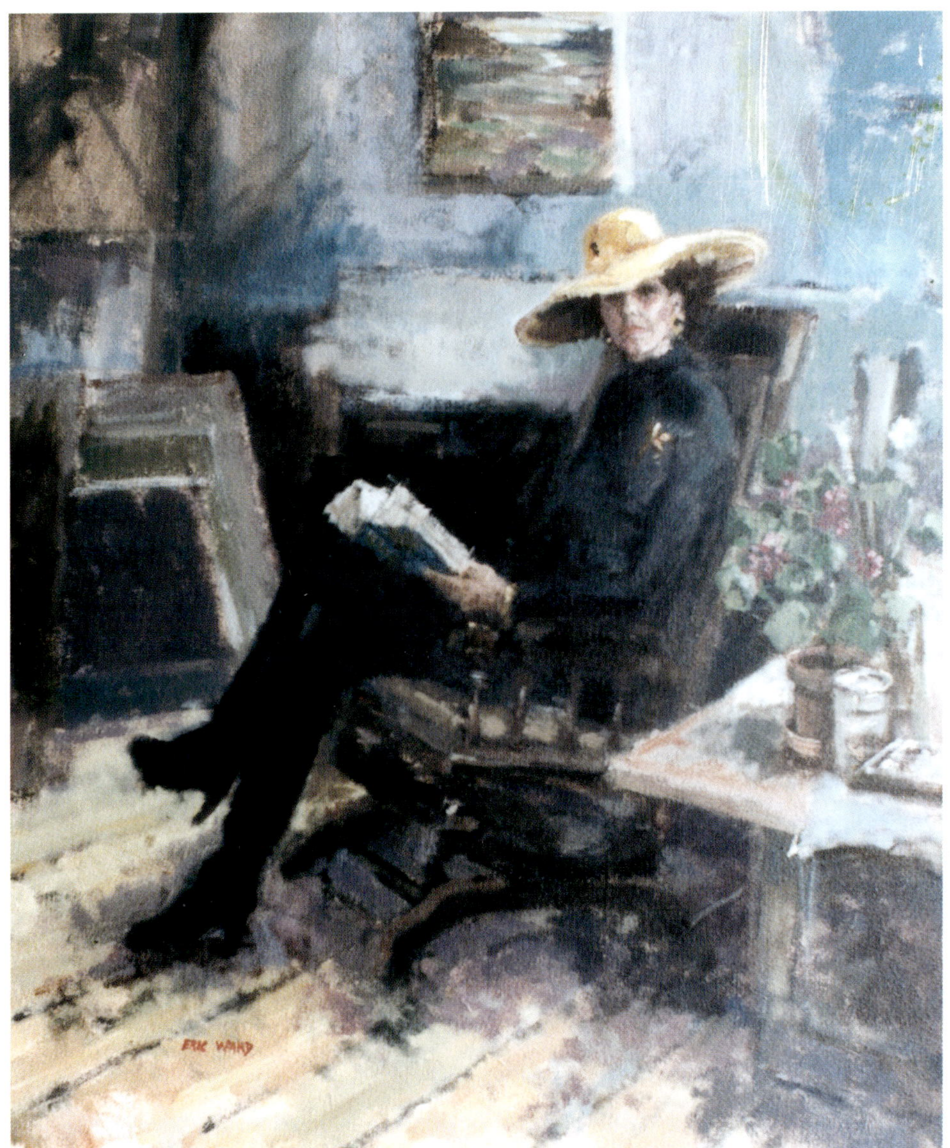

The Yellow Hat
Acrylic, 60.8 x 50.8cm

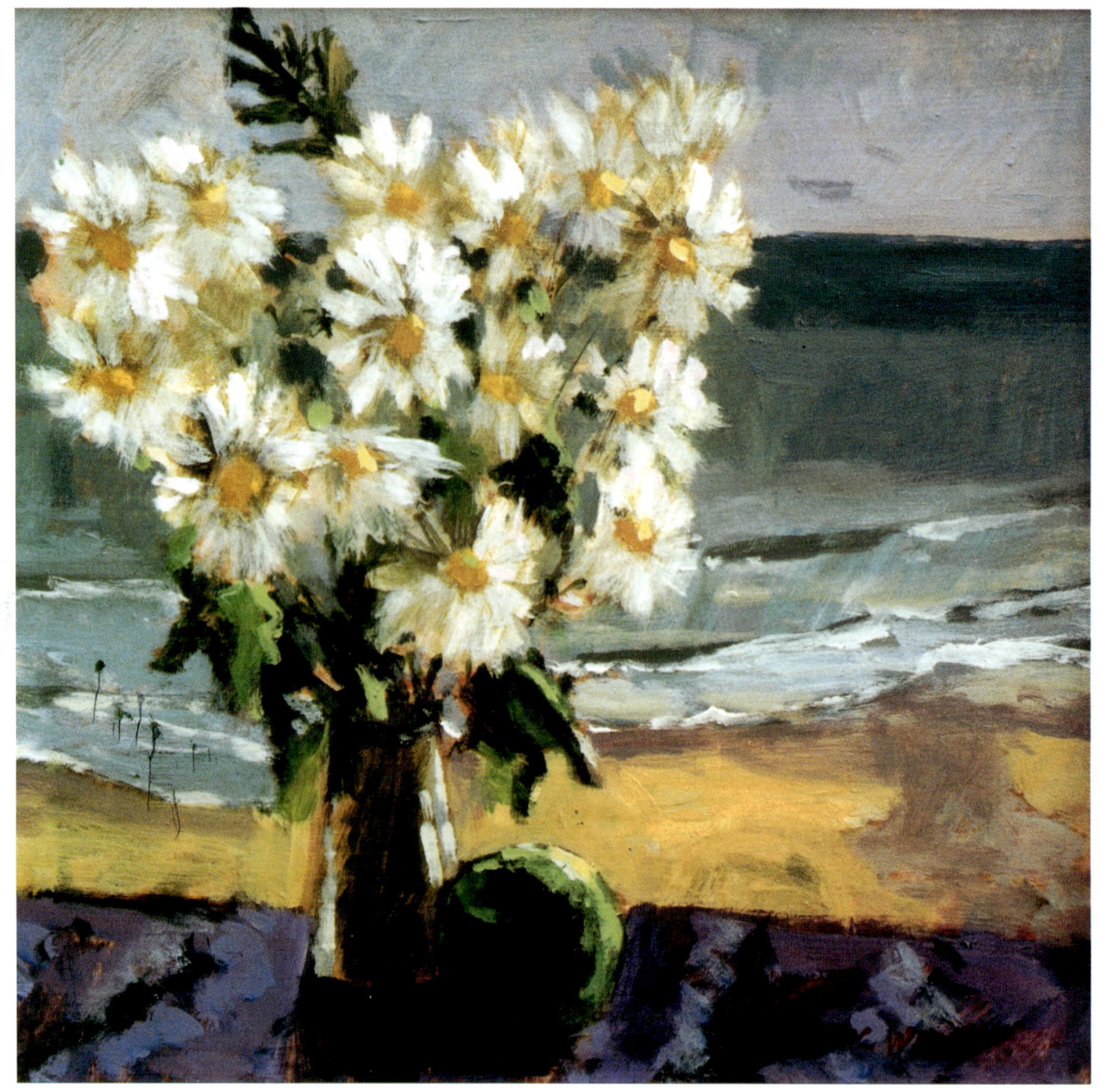

Daisies
Acrylic, 25.4 x 25.4cm

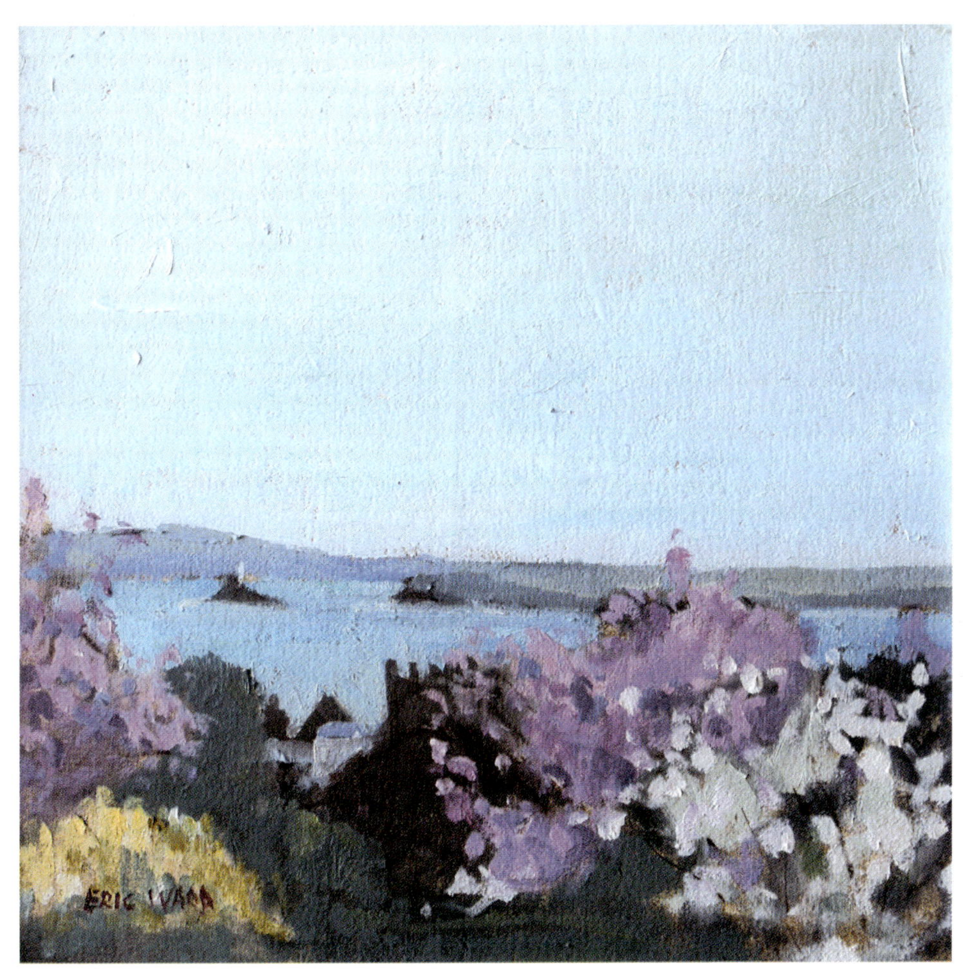

SEA & LANDSCAPES

Looking through this section I am suddenly aware that few of my landscapes do not feature water in some form. It perhaps also serves to remind one that in Cornwall and Devon you are never far away from the sea and it becomes an ongoing experience. Observing the sea's ever-changing moods is fascinating. From glassy calms to raging waves, there is always something different, always something new, always the unexpected.

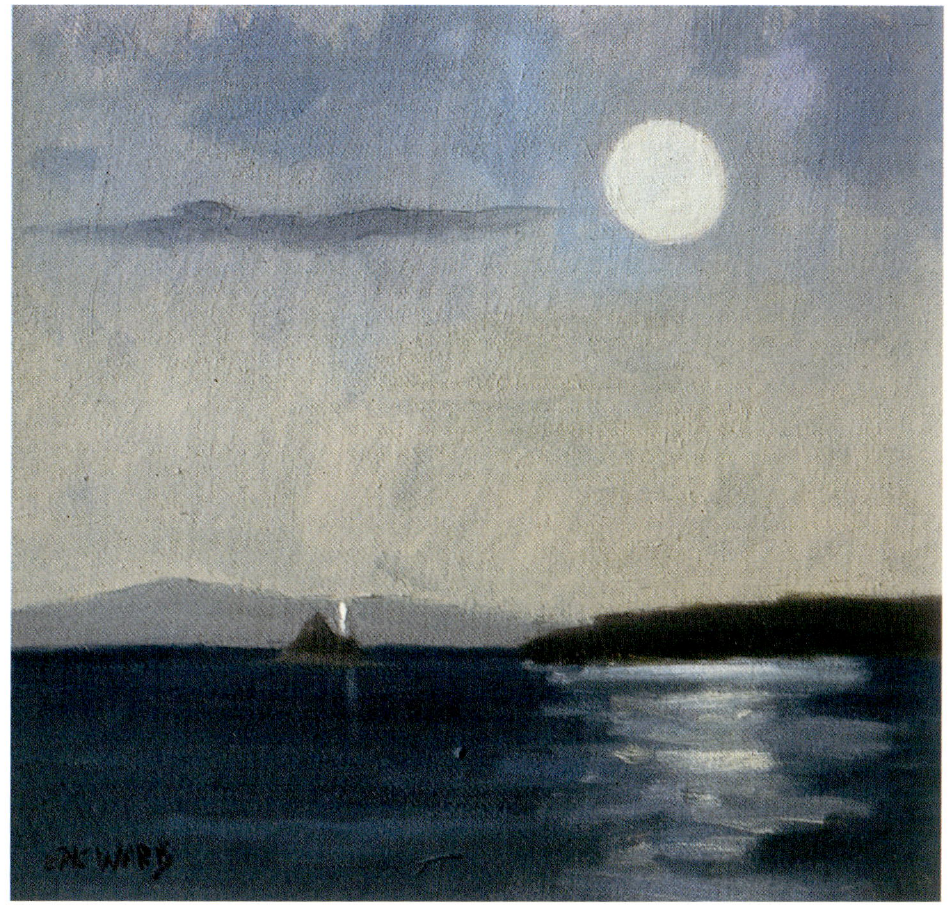

January Moon over Godrevy Lighthouse
Oil on panel, 20.3 x 20.3cm

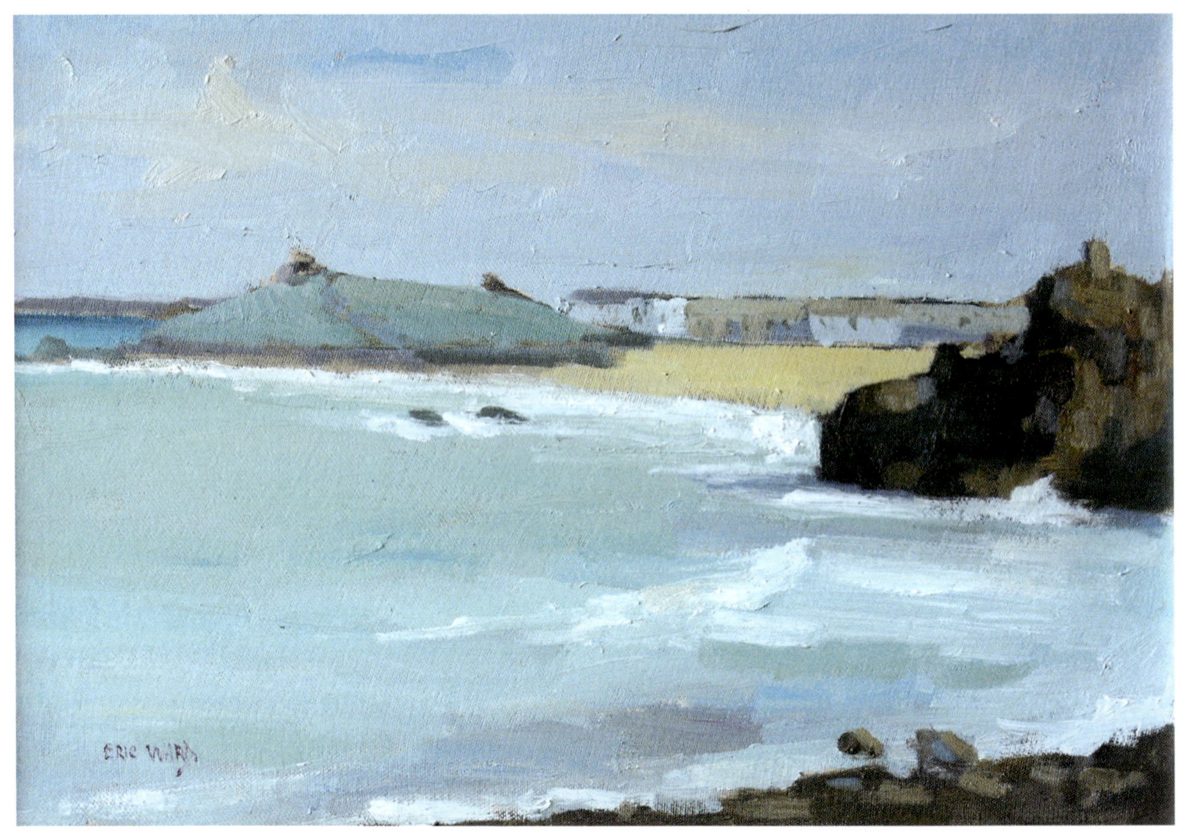

Porthmeor Beach and St Ives Island
Oil on panel, 25.4 x 35.5cm

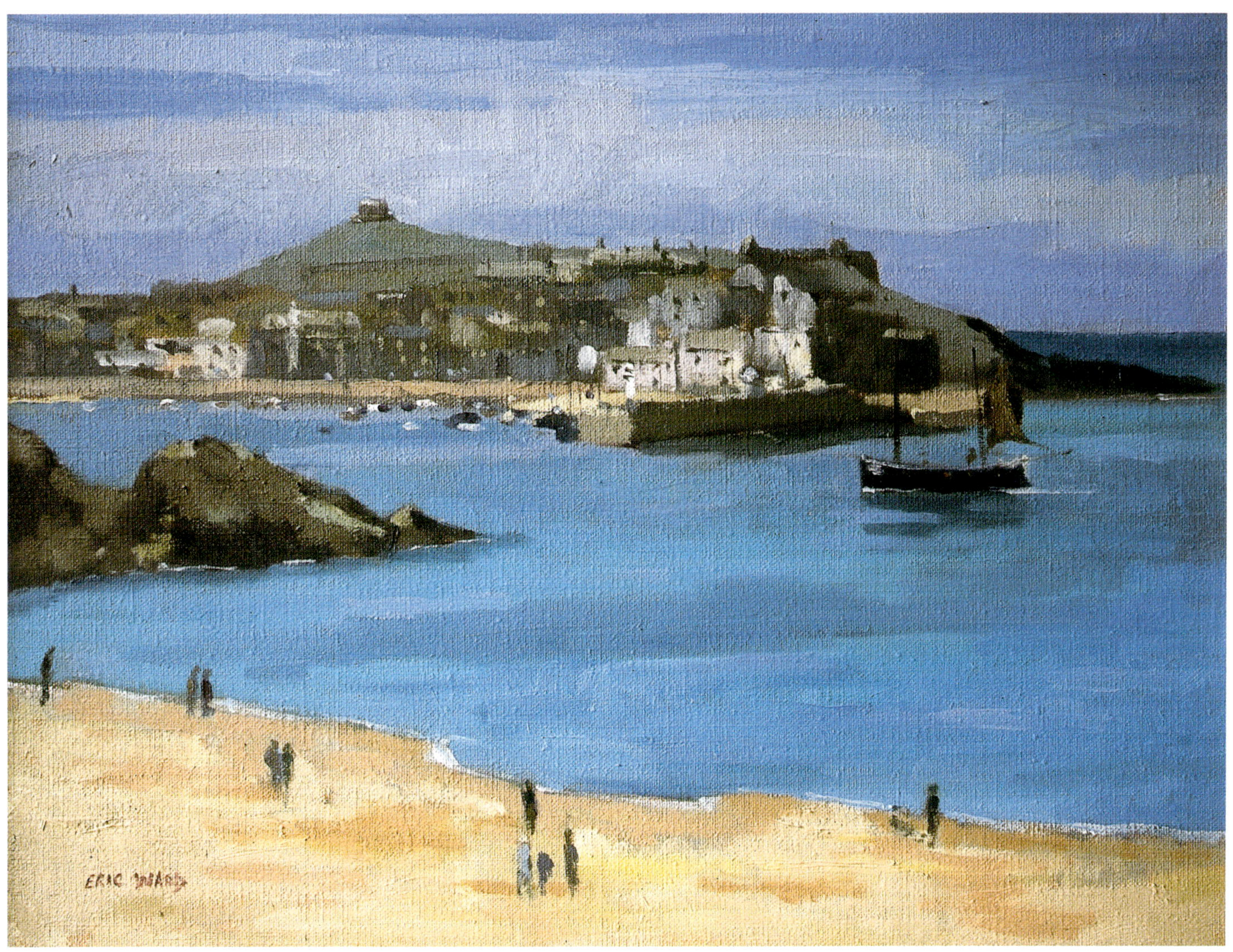

St Ives Harbour from Porthminster
Oil on linen, 35.5 x 45.8cm

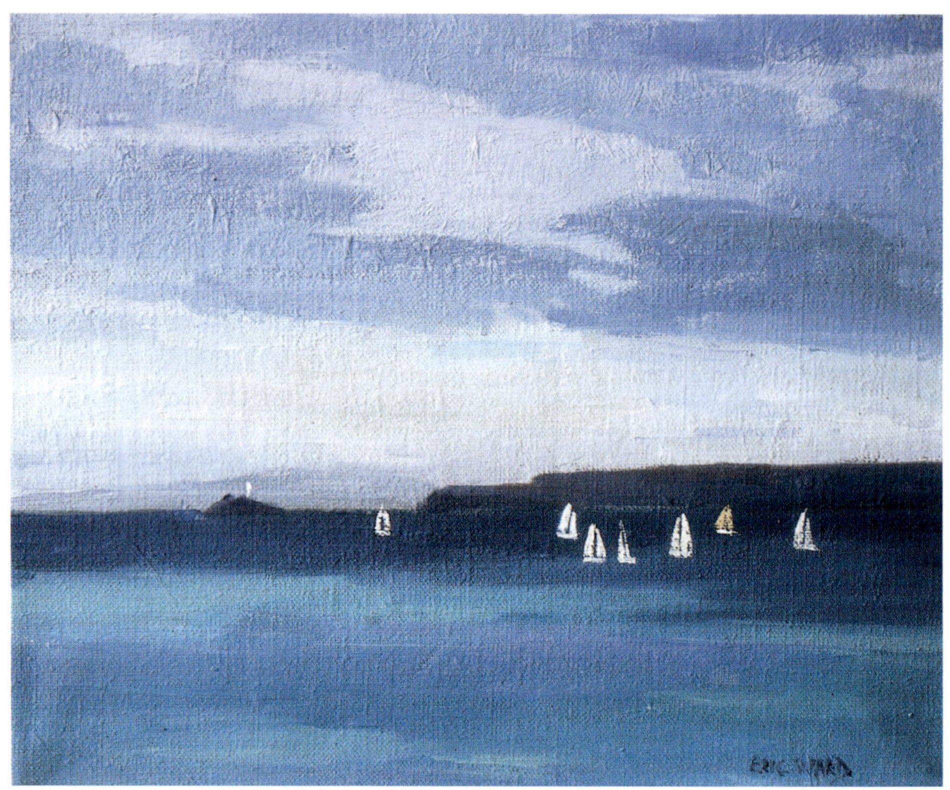

Yachts off Godrevy
Oil on linen, 25.4 x 30.5cm

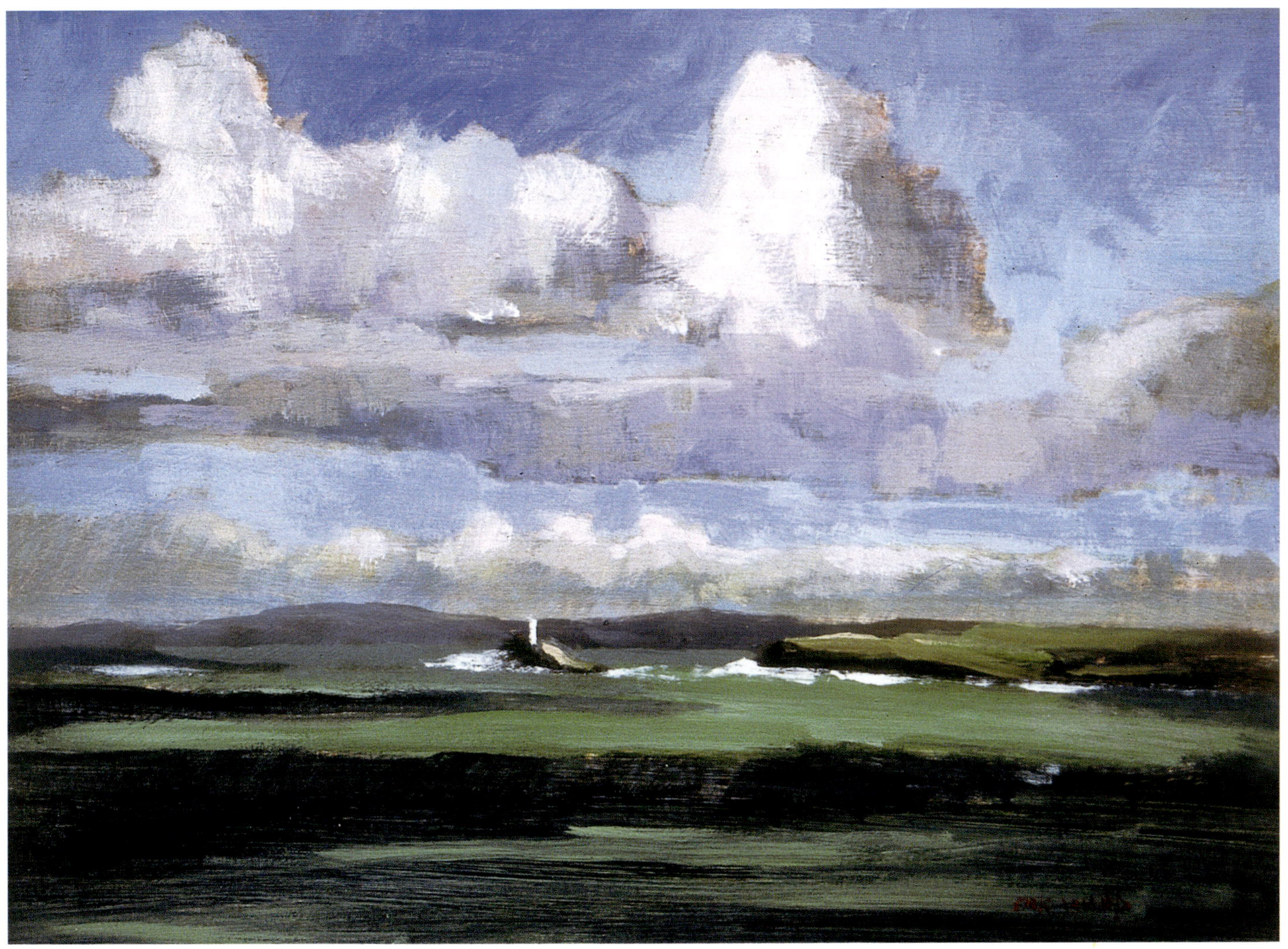

Godrevy Point, St Ives
Acrylic on panel, 25.4 x 33cm

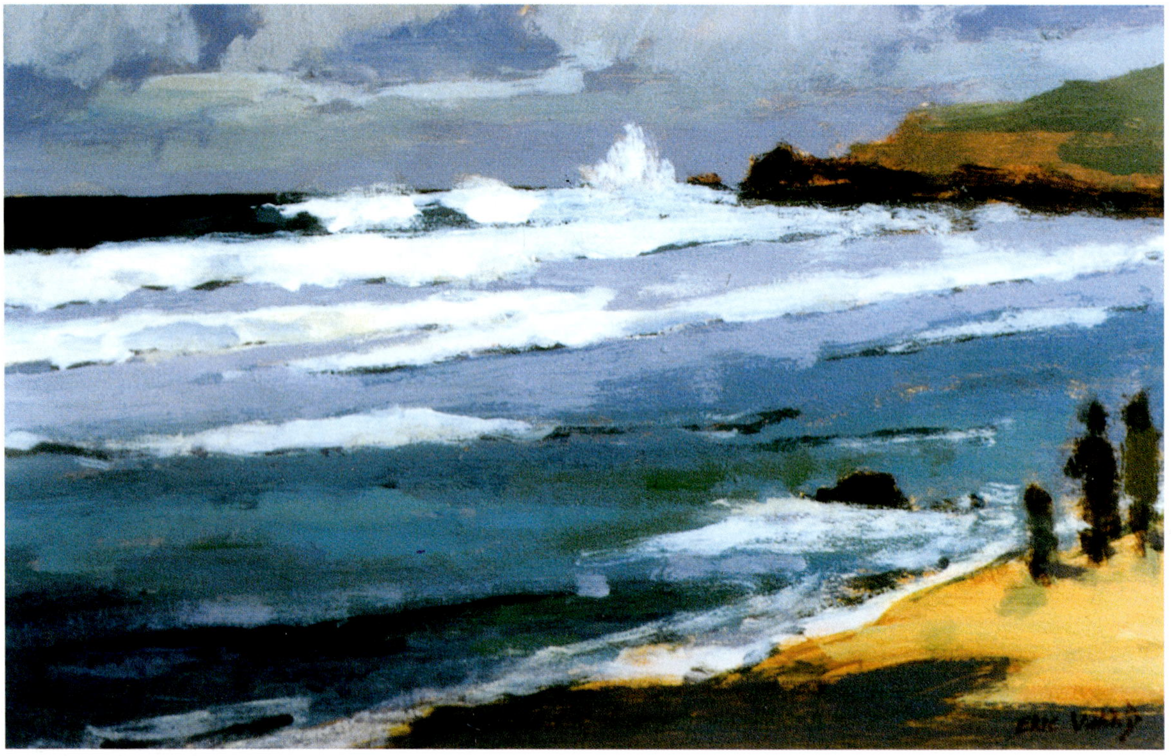

Porthmeor Beach, St Ives
Acrylic on panel, 25.4 x 35.5cm

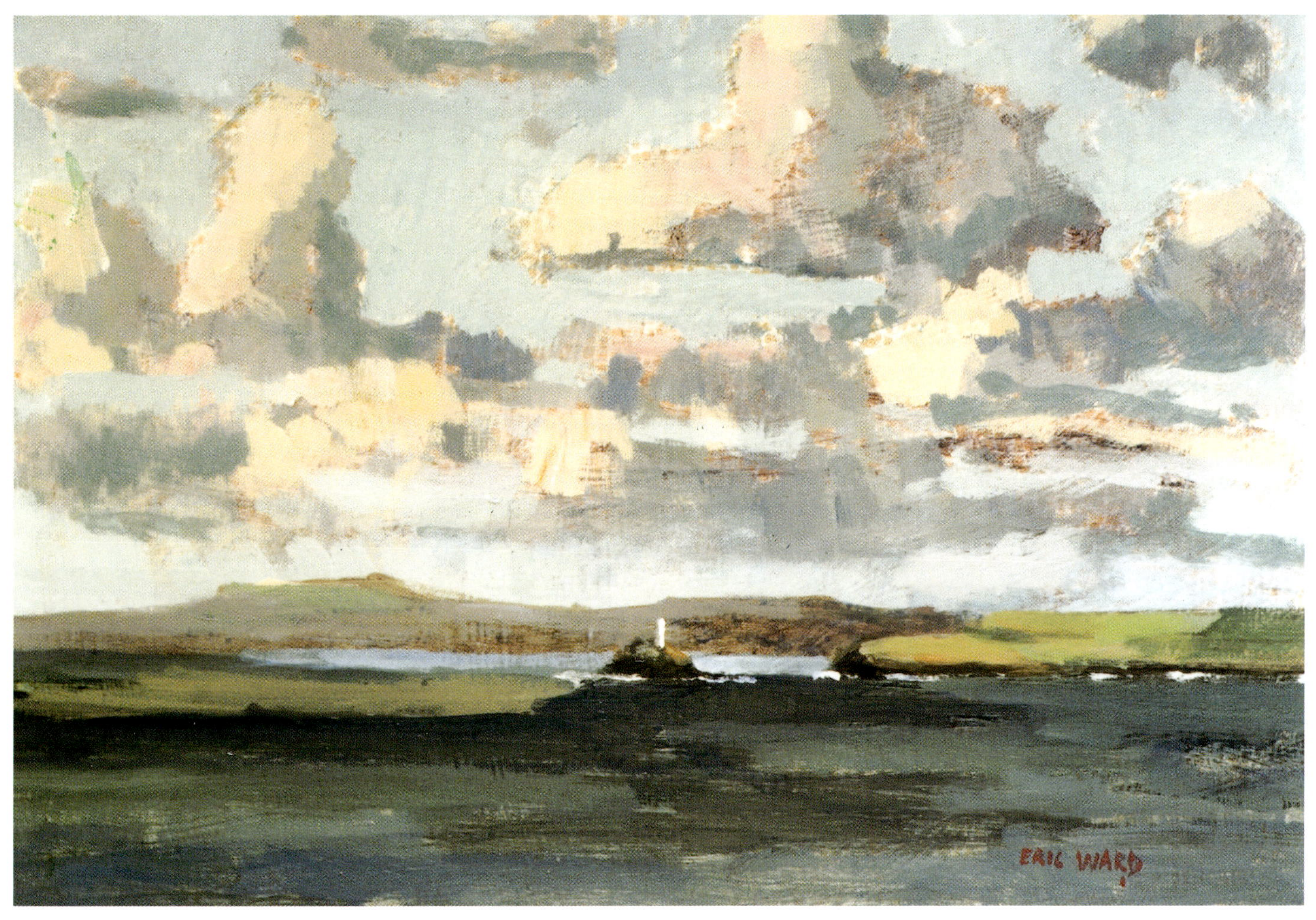

Godrevy Lighthouse on a Windy Day
Acrylic, 25.4 x 35.5cm

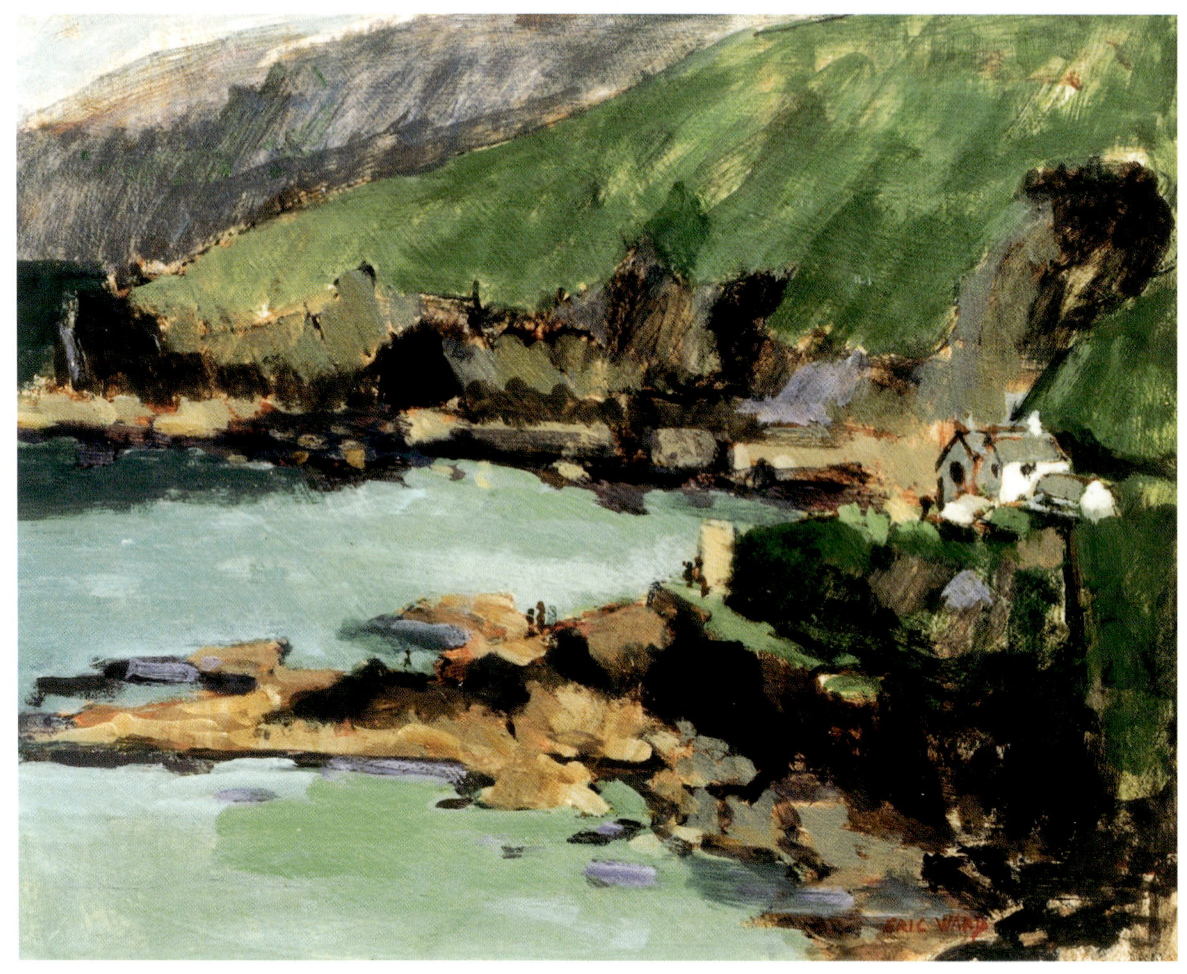

Cottages at Gurnard's Head
Acrylic, 25.4 x 30.5cm

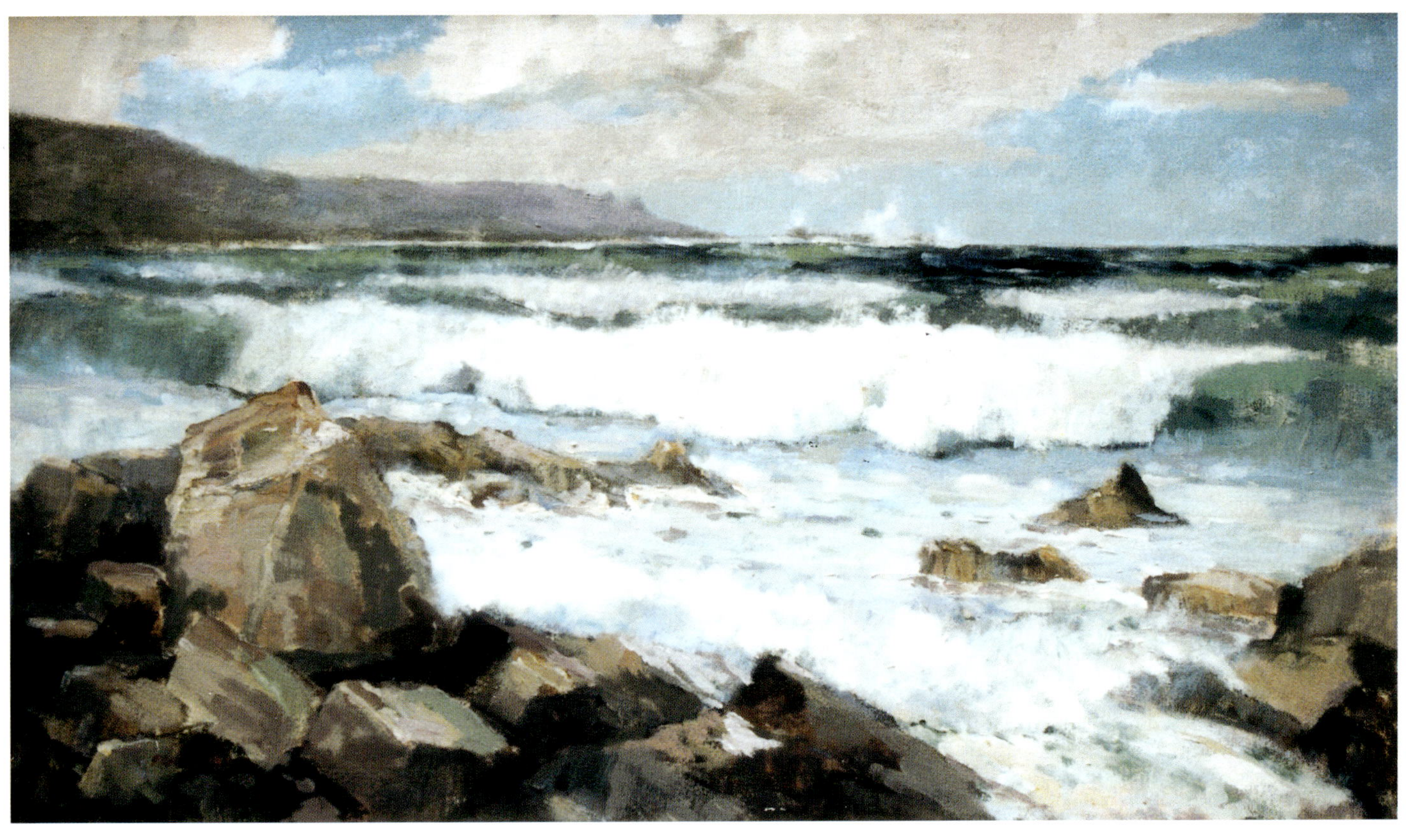

Towards Clodgy Point
Acrylic, 45.8 x 76.2cm

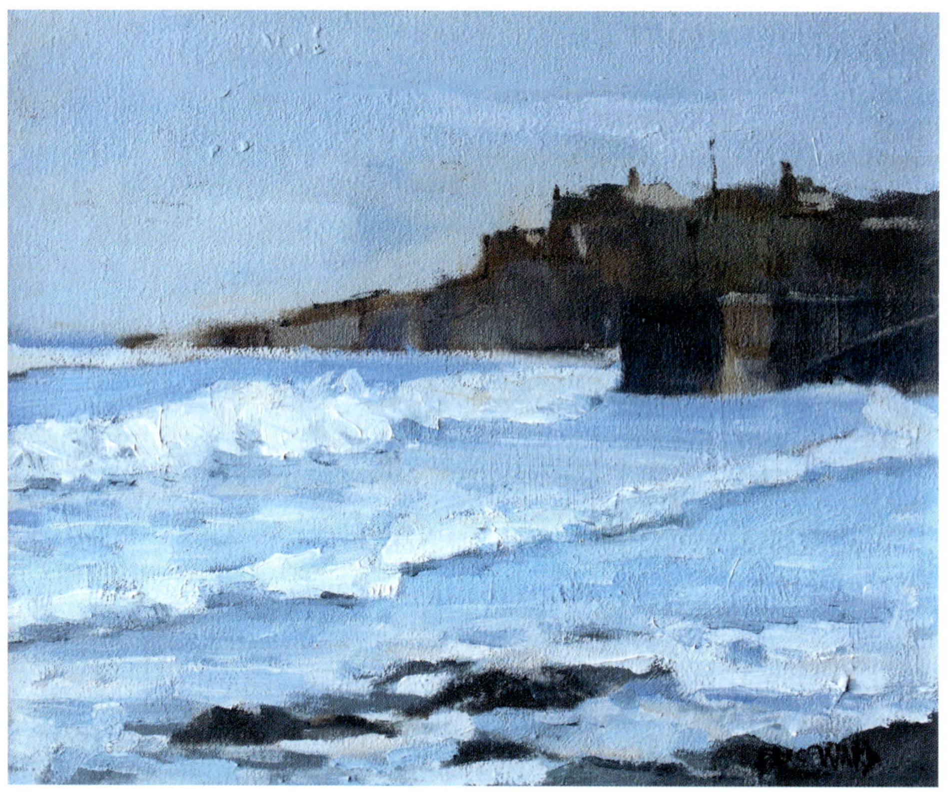

Rough Seas at Portscatho
Oil on panel, 25.4 x 30.5cm

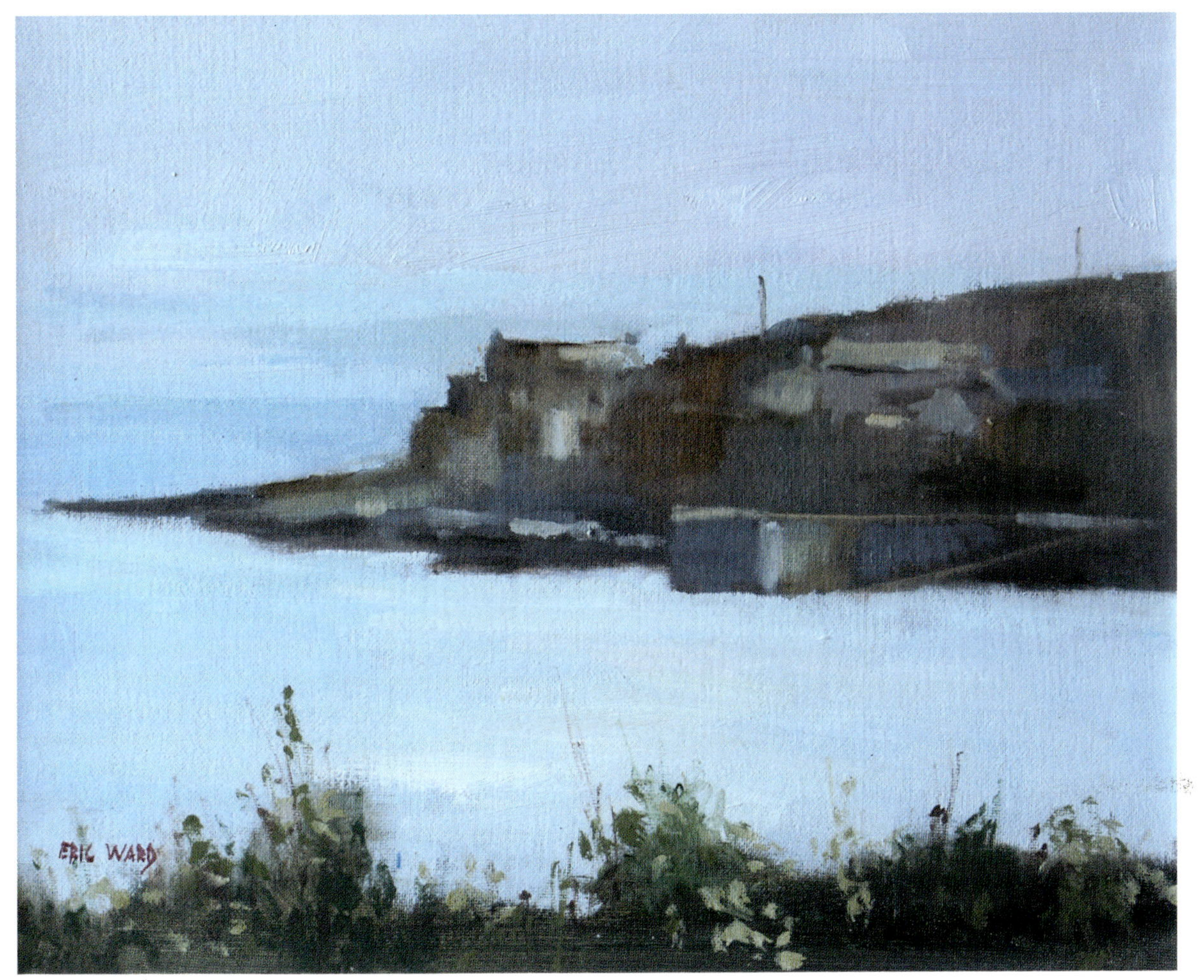

Hazy Days, Portscatho
Oil on panel, 25.4 x 30.5cm

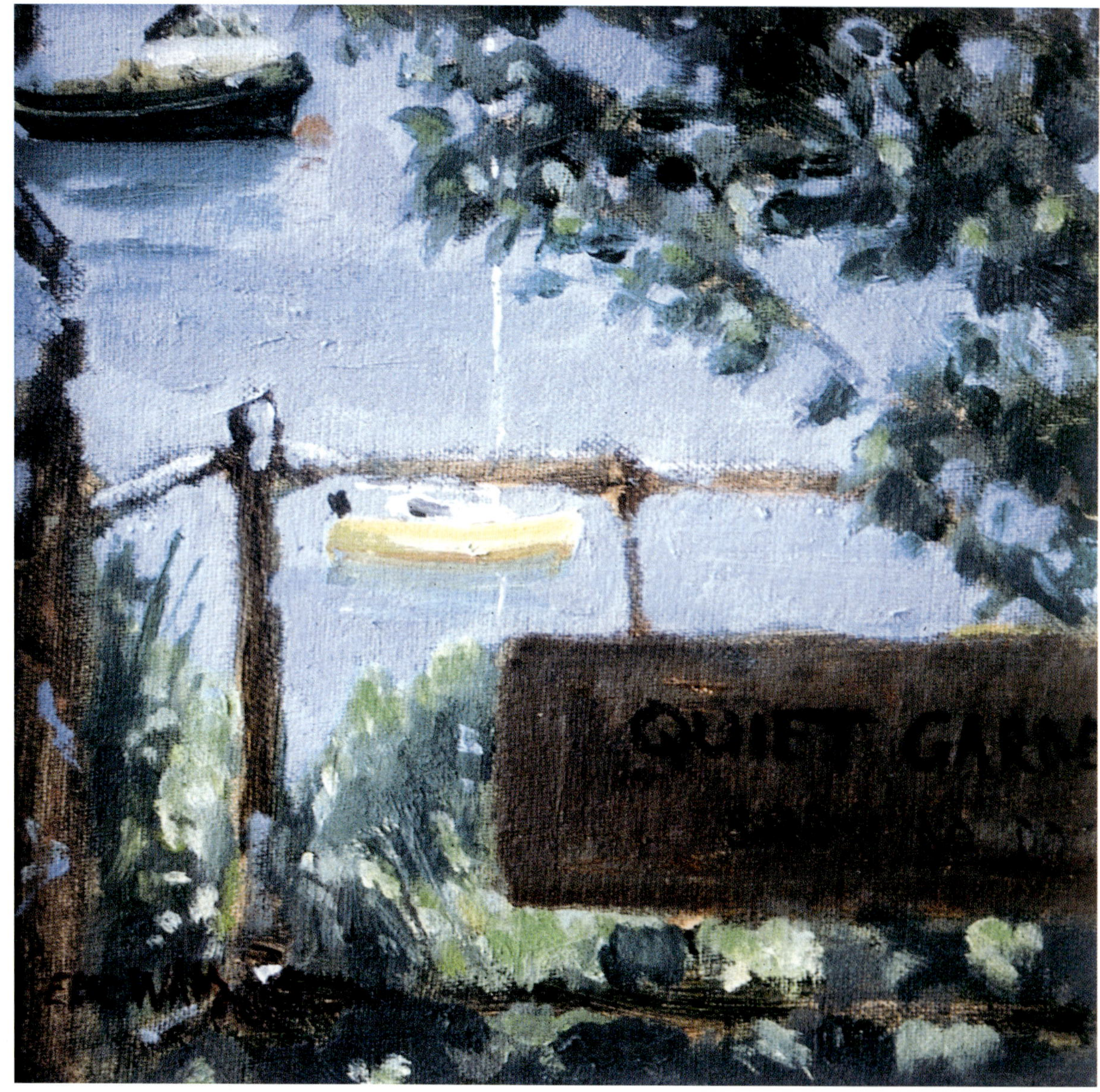

The Old Grammar School Garden, Fowey
Oil on panel, 19 x 19cm

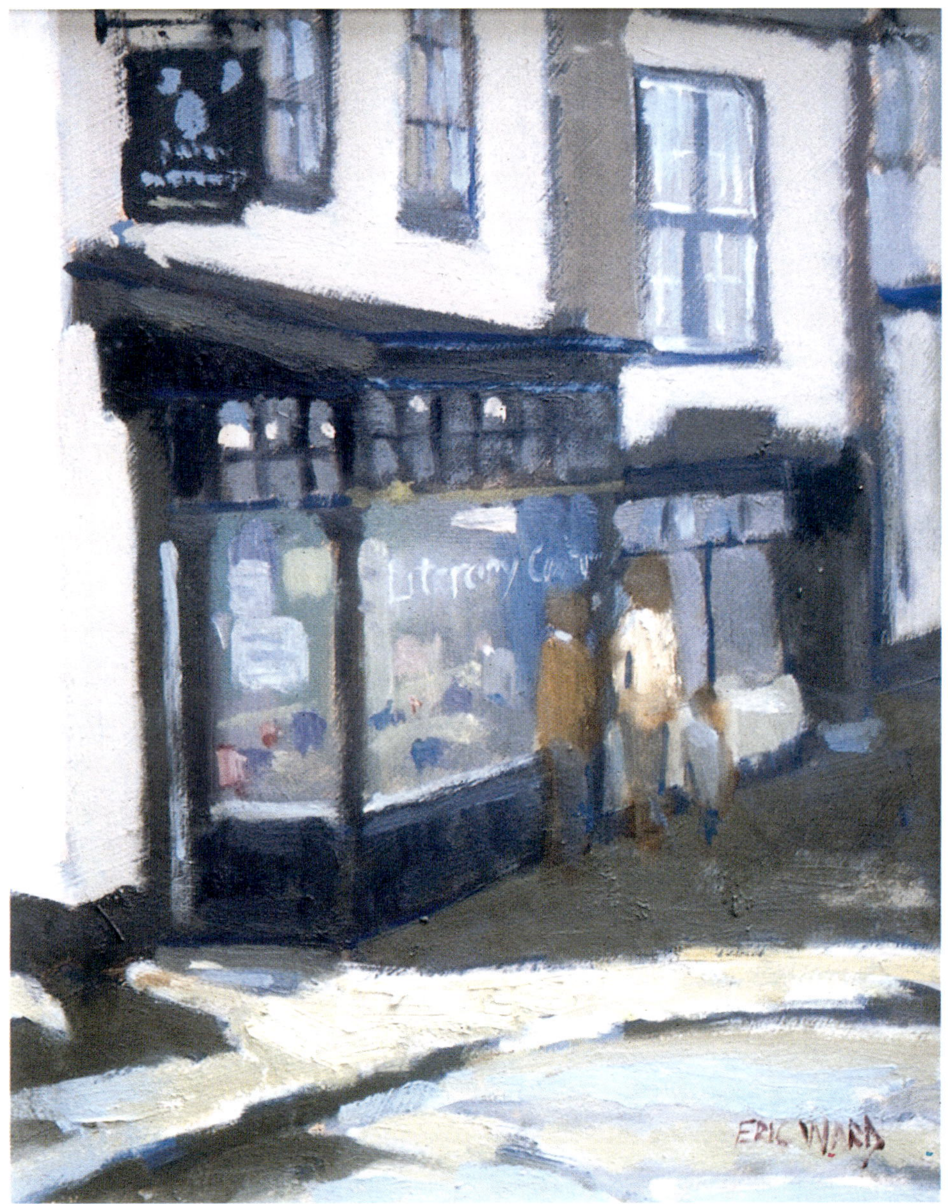

Daphne Du Maurier Centre, Fowey
Oil on panel, 25.4 x 20.3cm

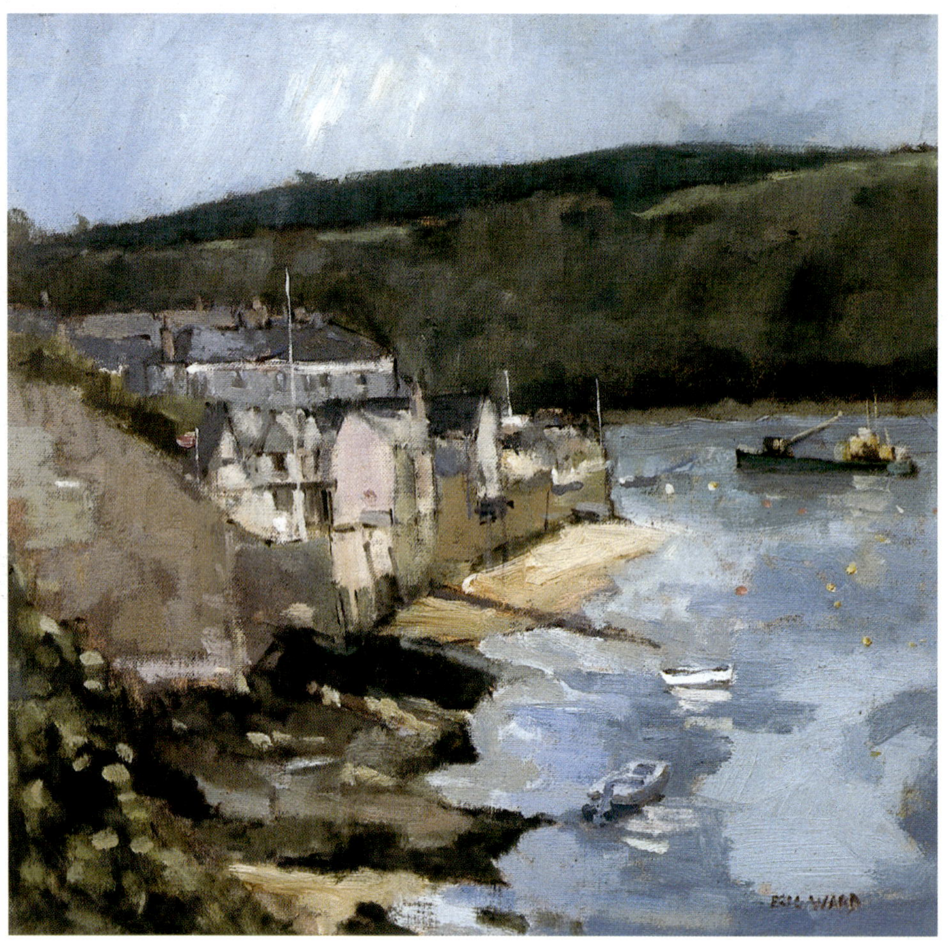

Along the River to Fowey
Oil on panel, 35.5 x 35.5cm

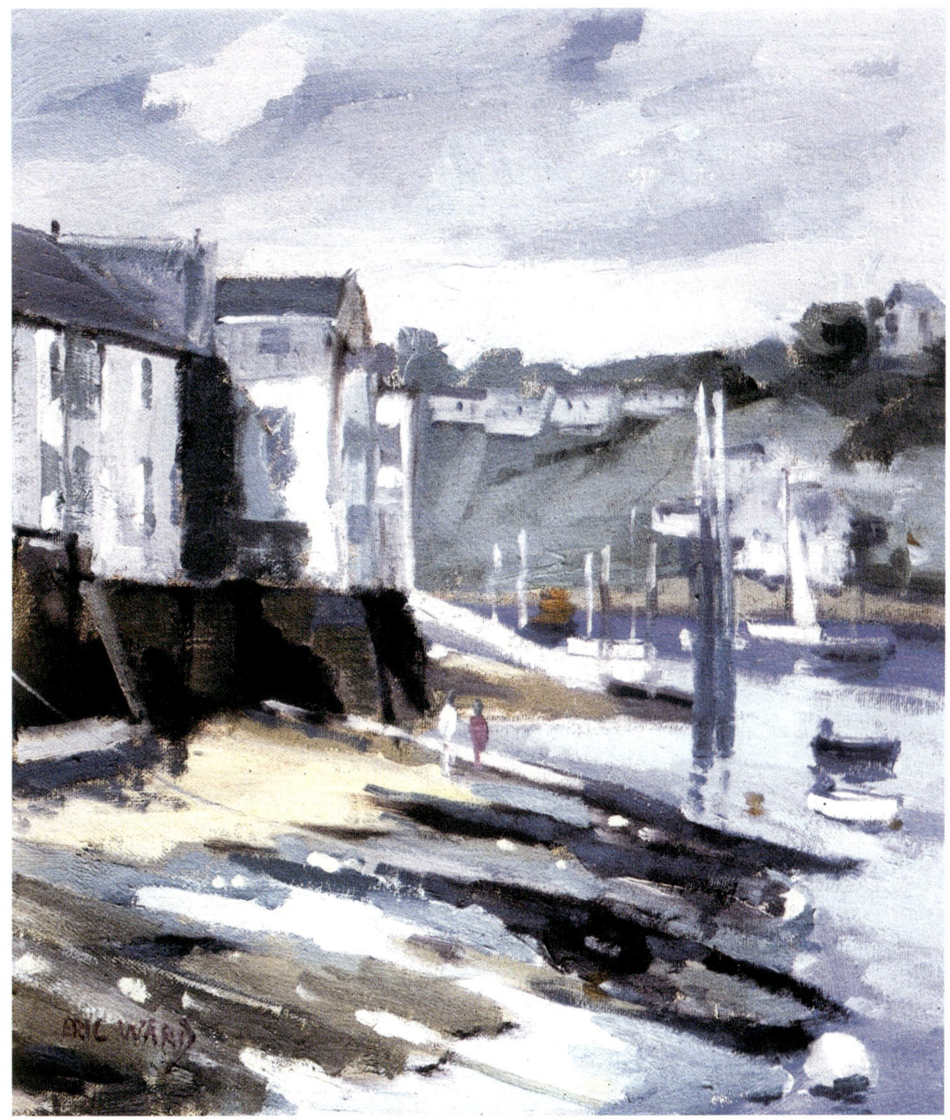

Along the River to Ferry Side
Oil on panel, 32.4 x 27.3cm

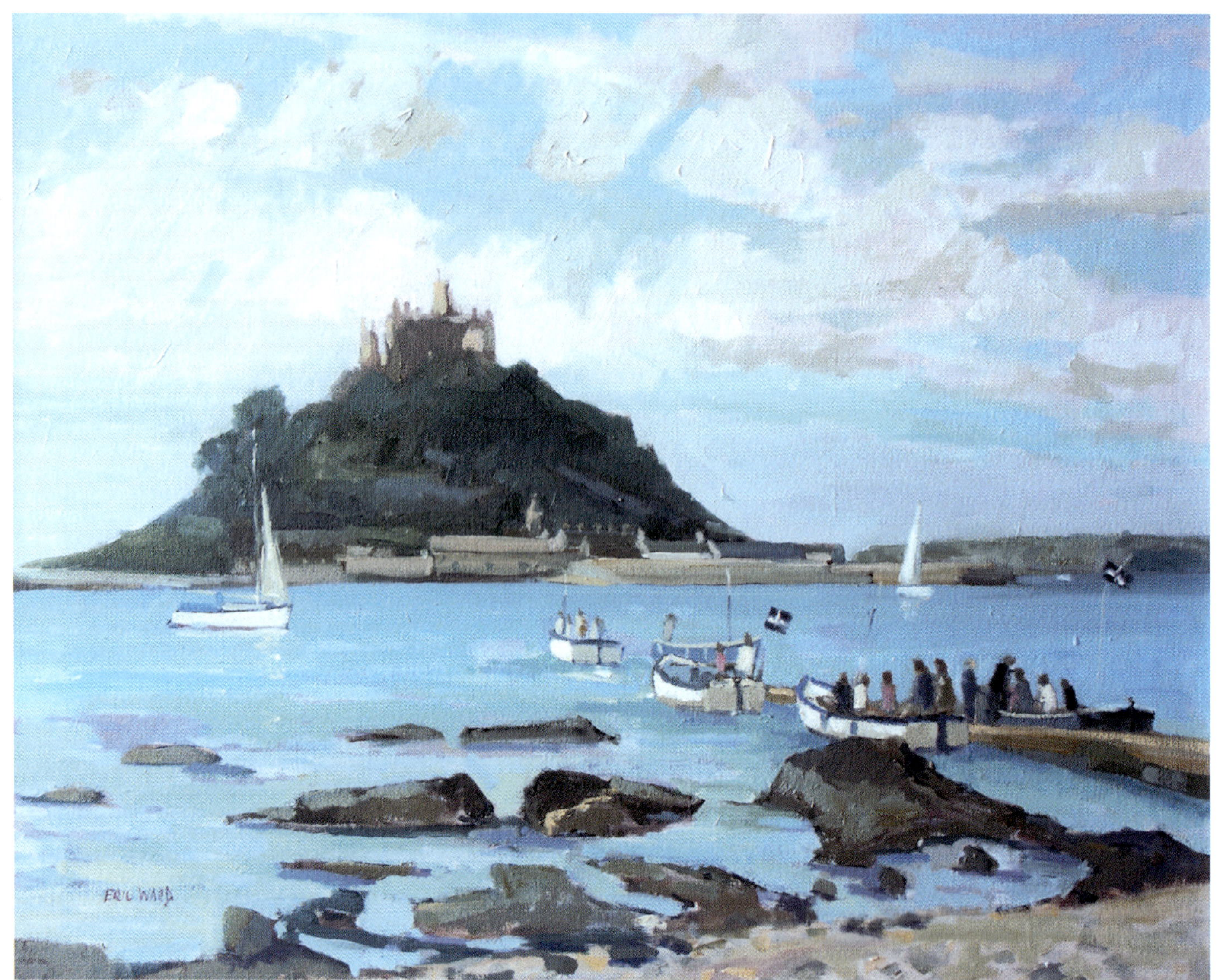

Sunny Day at St Michael's Mount
Oil on canvas, 50.8 x 60.8cm

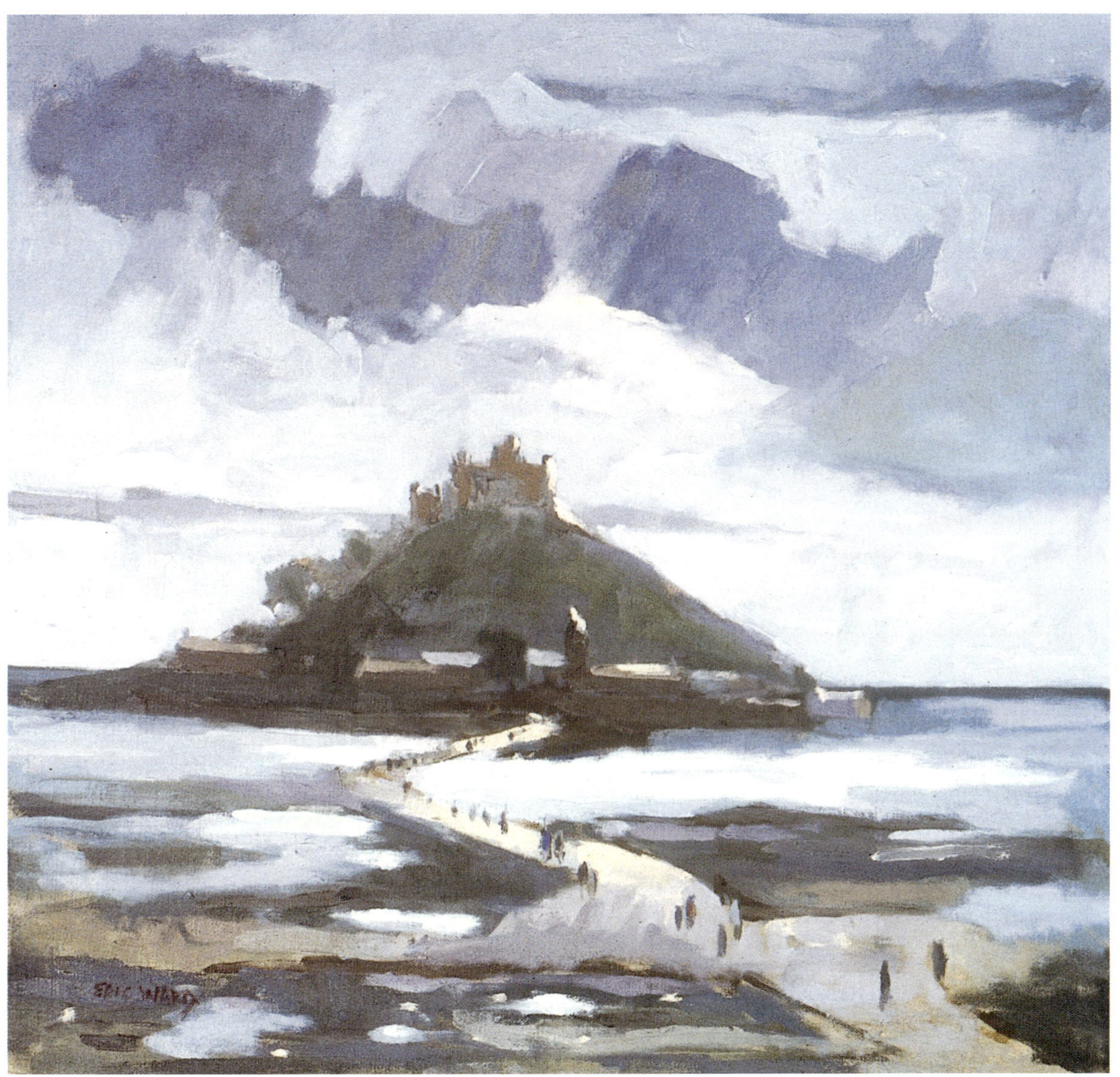

Stormy Day at the Mount
Oil on panel, 45.8 x 45.8cm

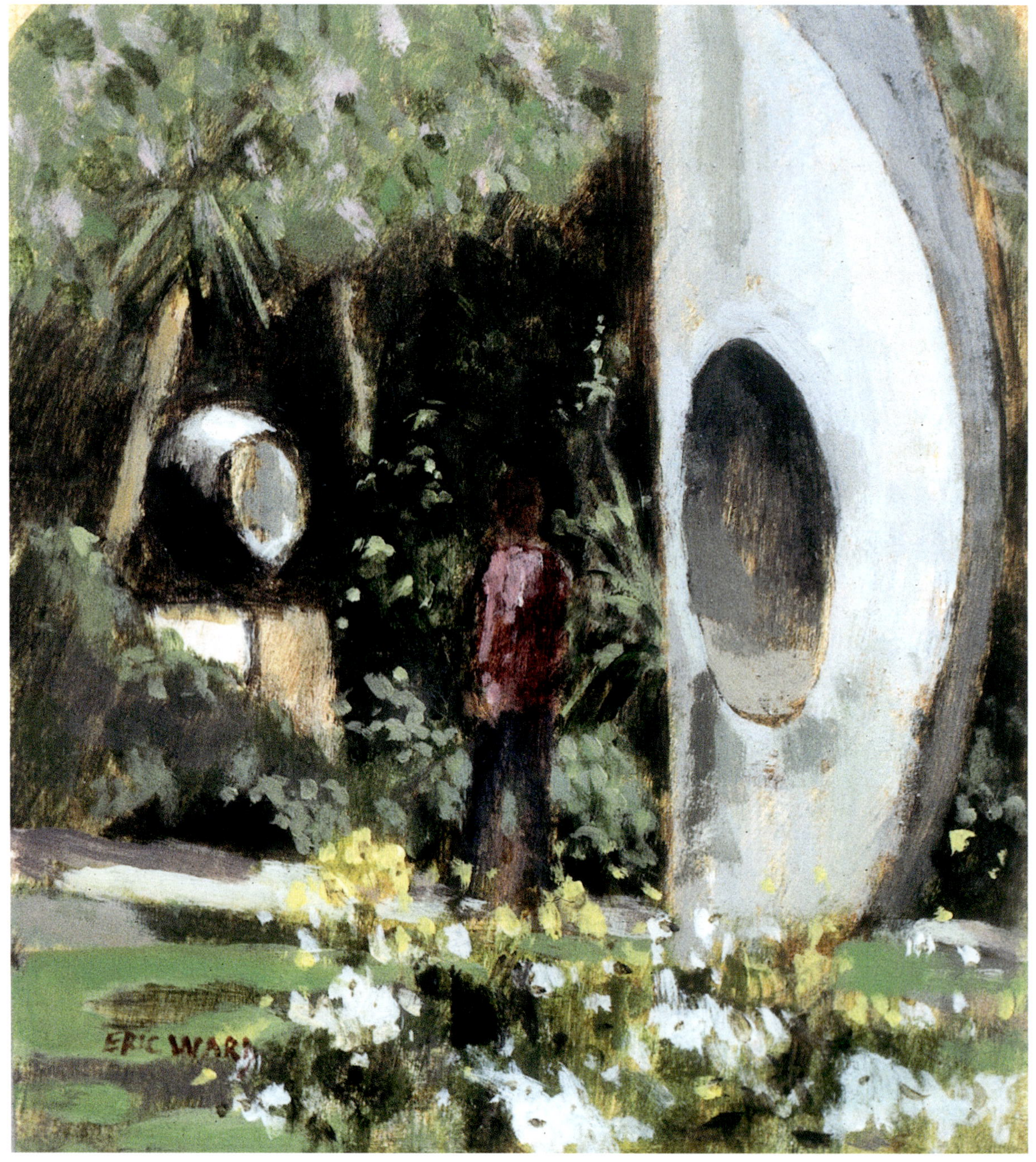

Barbara Hepworth Garden, St Ives
Acrylic on panel, 25.4 x 20.3cm

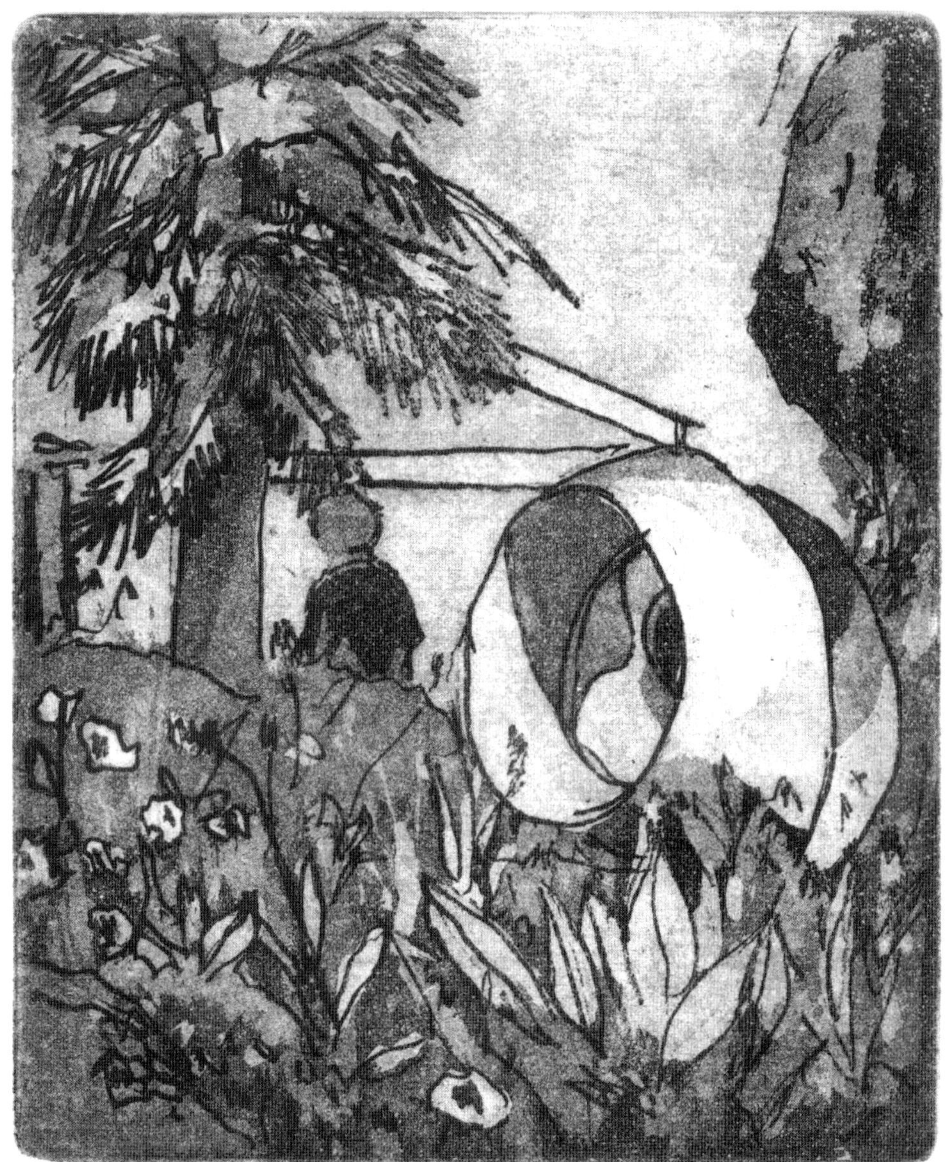

Barbara Hepworth Garden, St Ives
Etching, copper plate

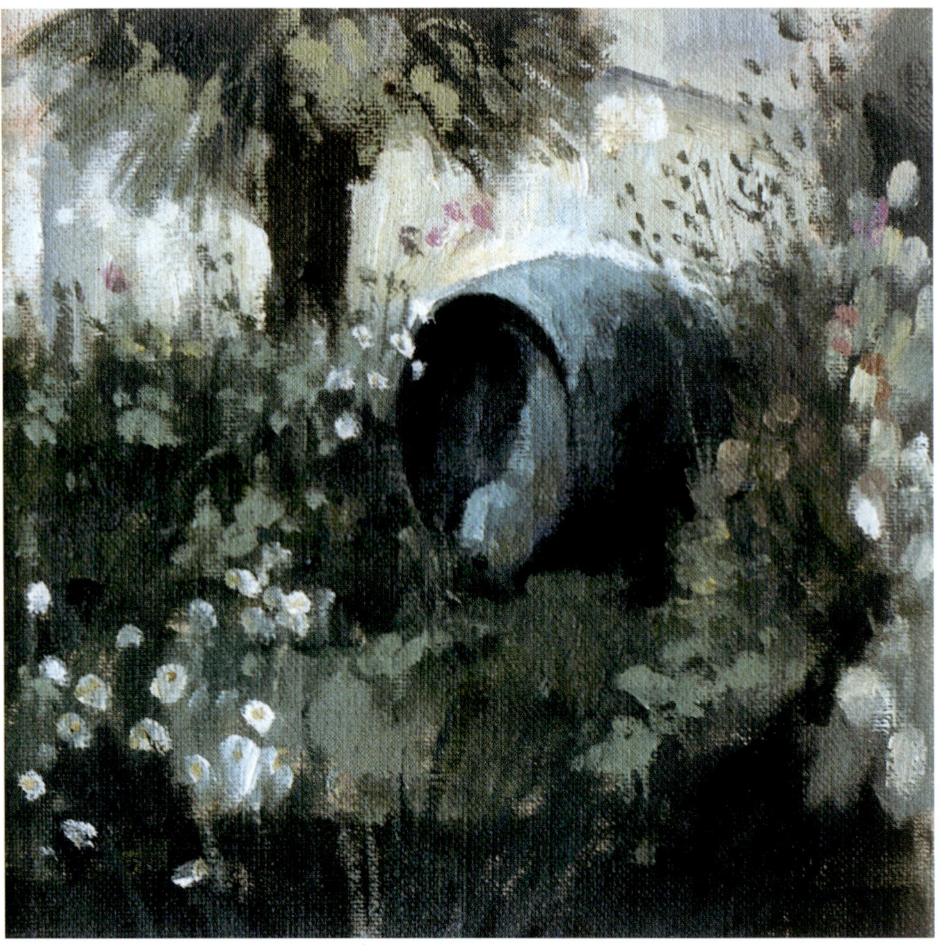

Autumn in the Barbara Hepworth Garden, St Ives
Oil on panel, 20.3 x 20.3cm

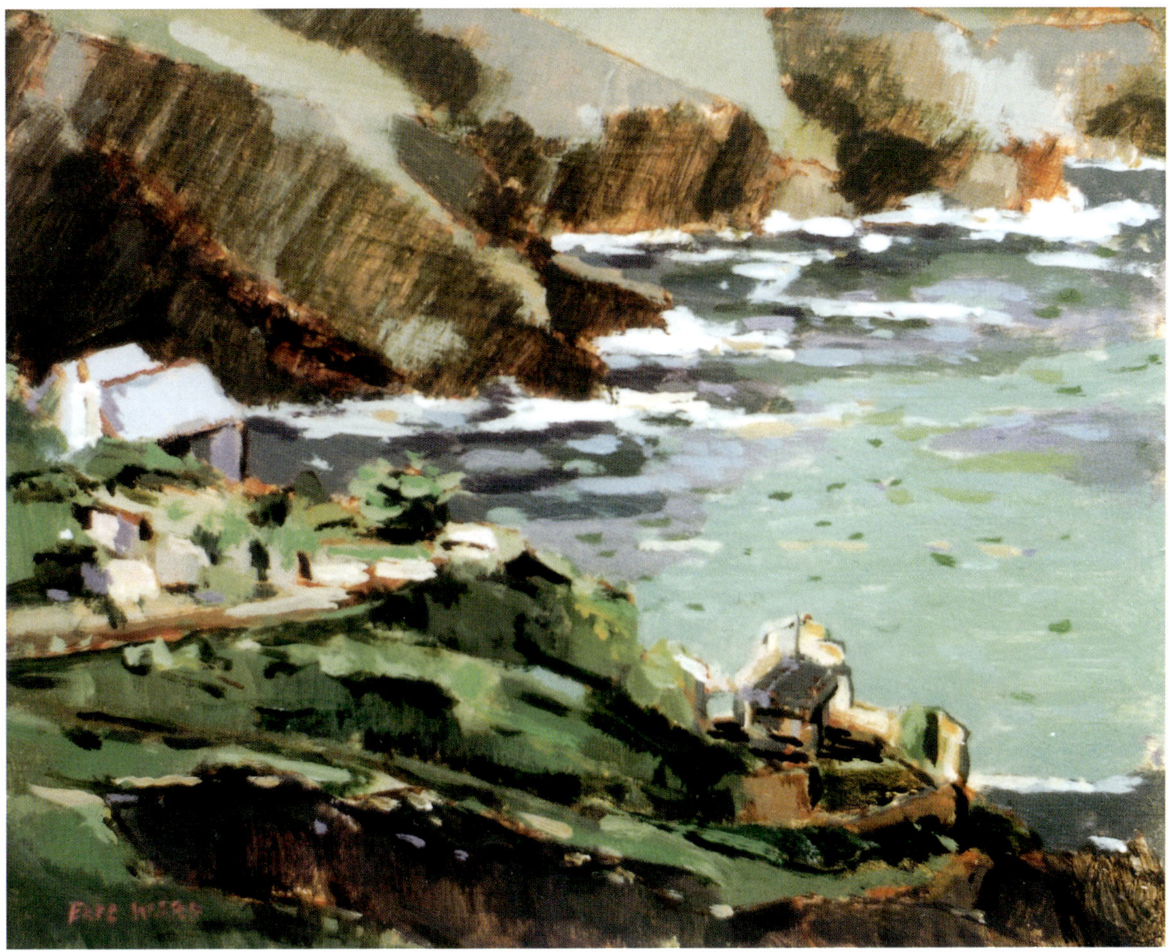

The Cove at Gurnard's Head
Acrylic on panel, 25.4 x 30.5cm

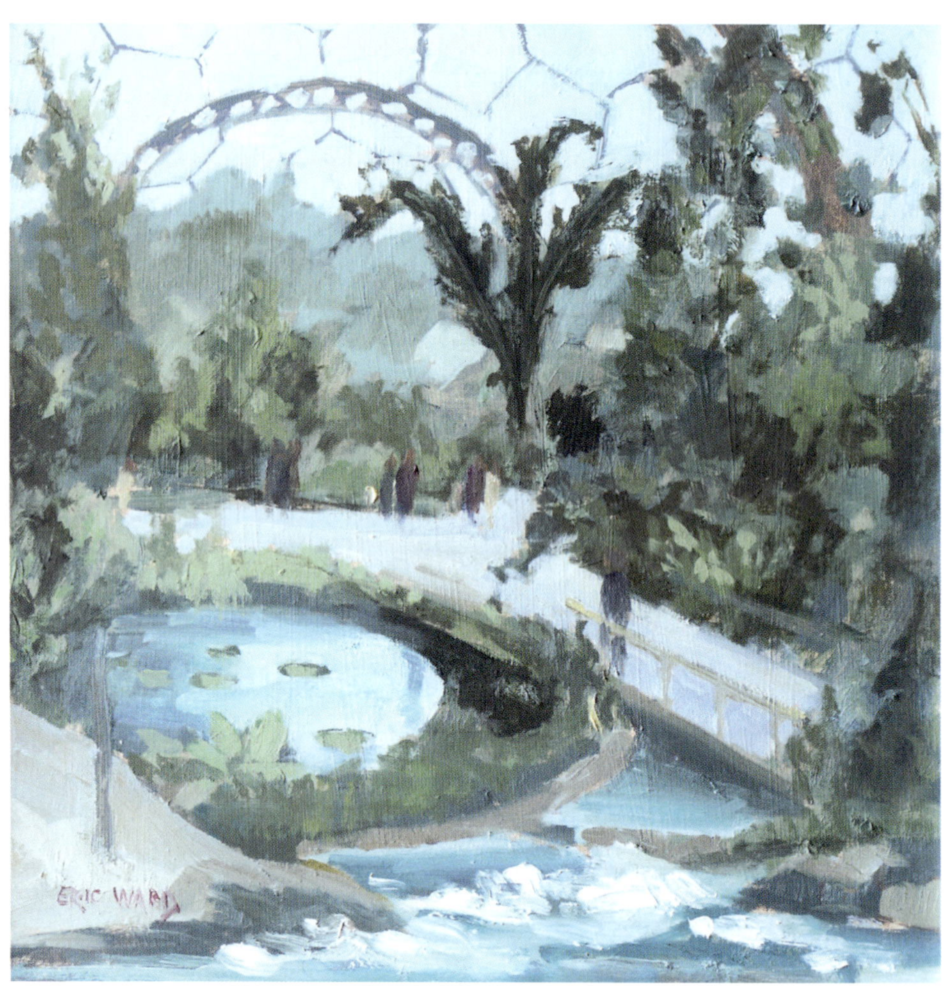

Eden
Oil on panel, 27.9 x 27.9cm

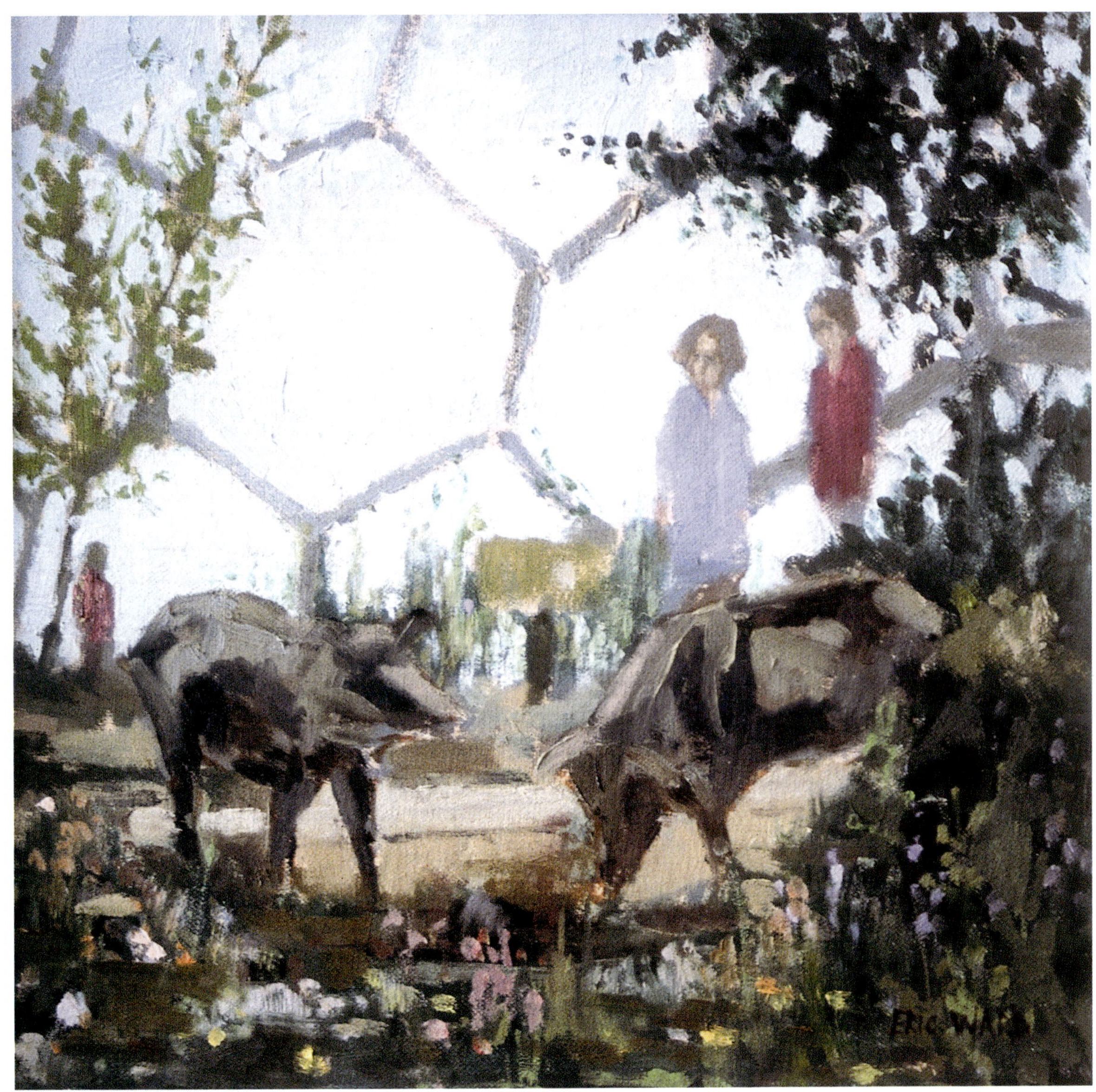

Orchard Pigs at the Eden Project
Oil on panel, 27.9 x 27.9cm

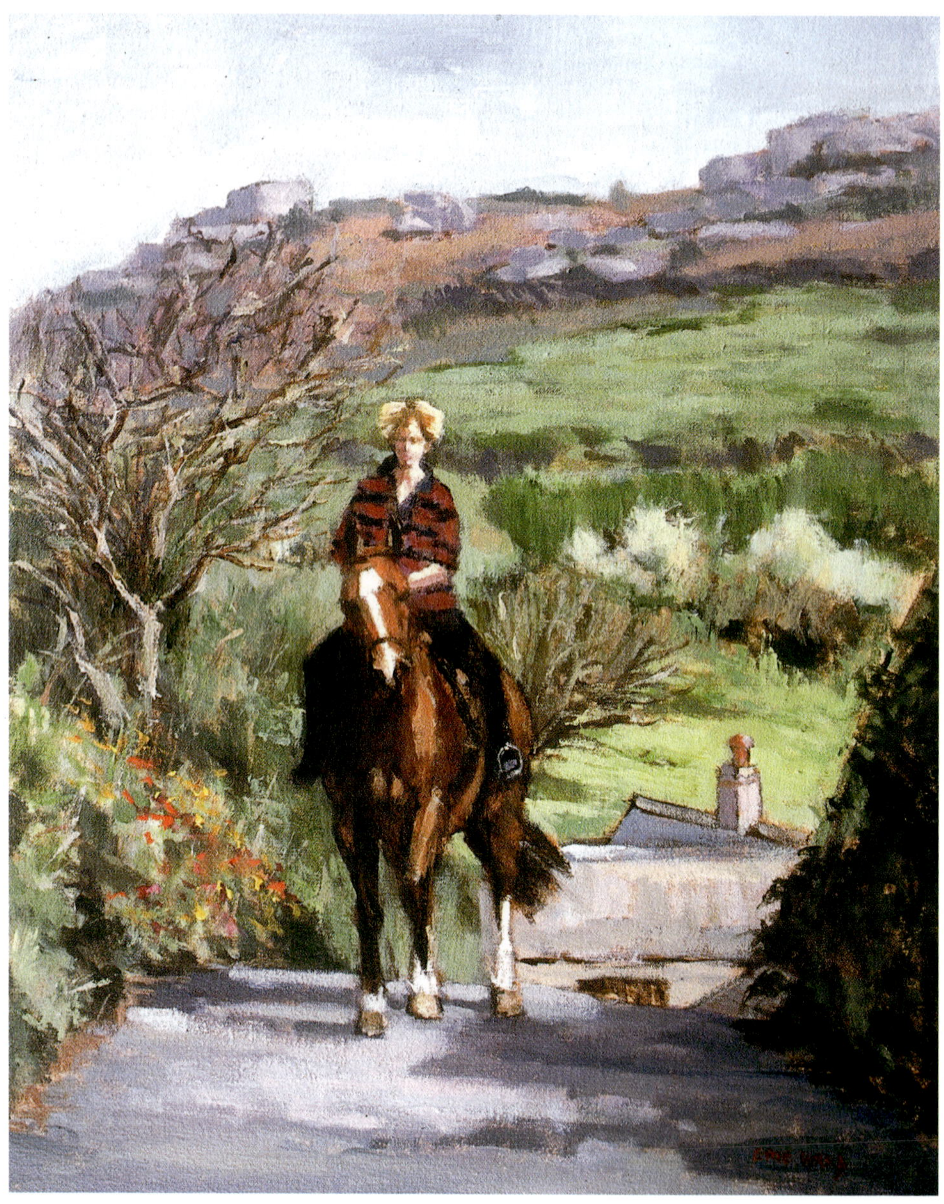

Morning Ride
Acrylic on canvas, 50.8 x 40.6cm

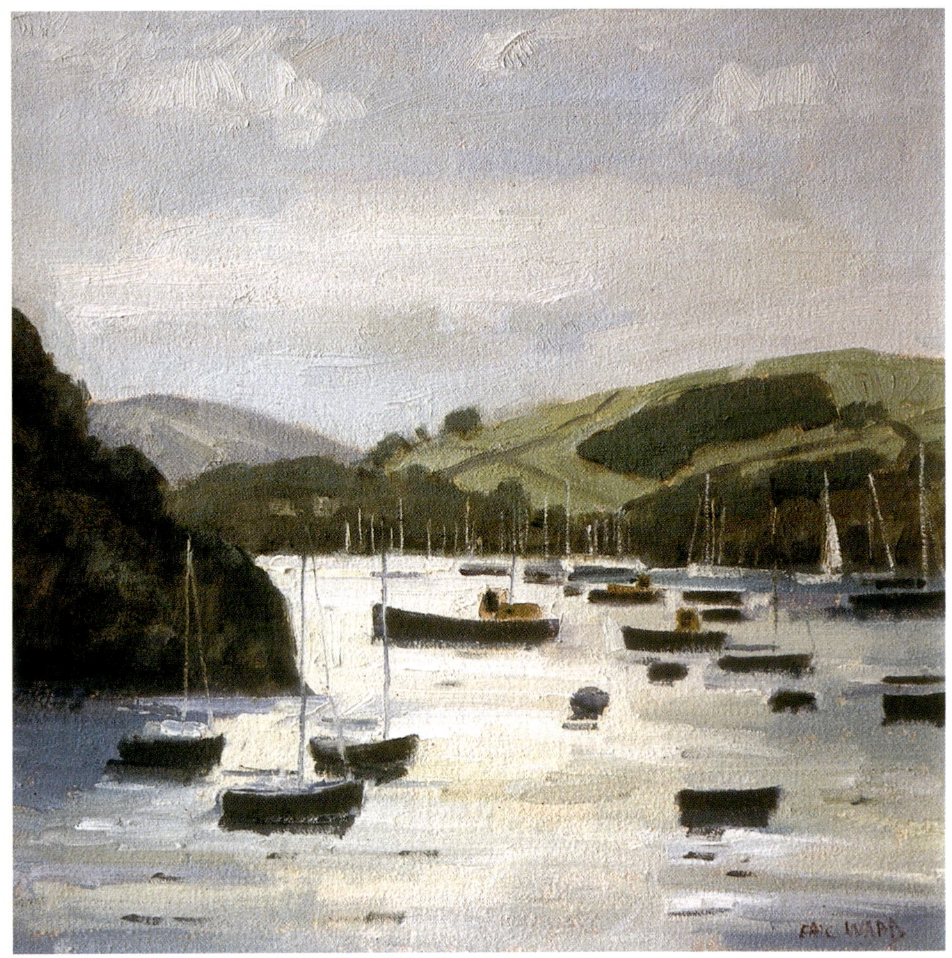

Morning Tide, Salcombe
Oil on canvas, 35.5 x 35.5cm

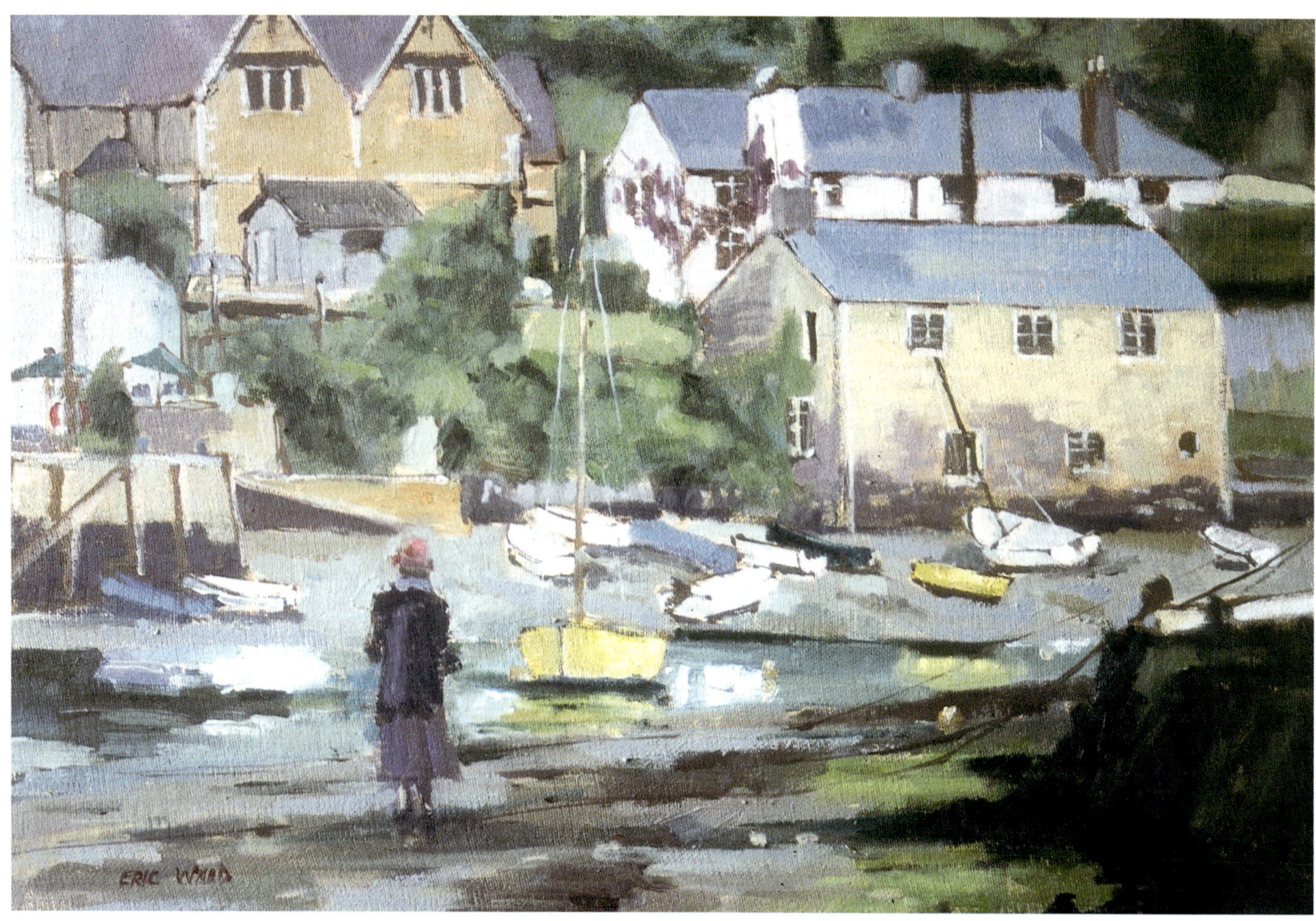

Noss Mayo
Oil on panel, 25.4 x 35.5cm

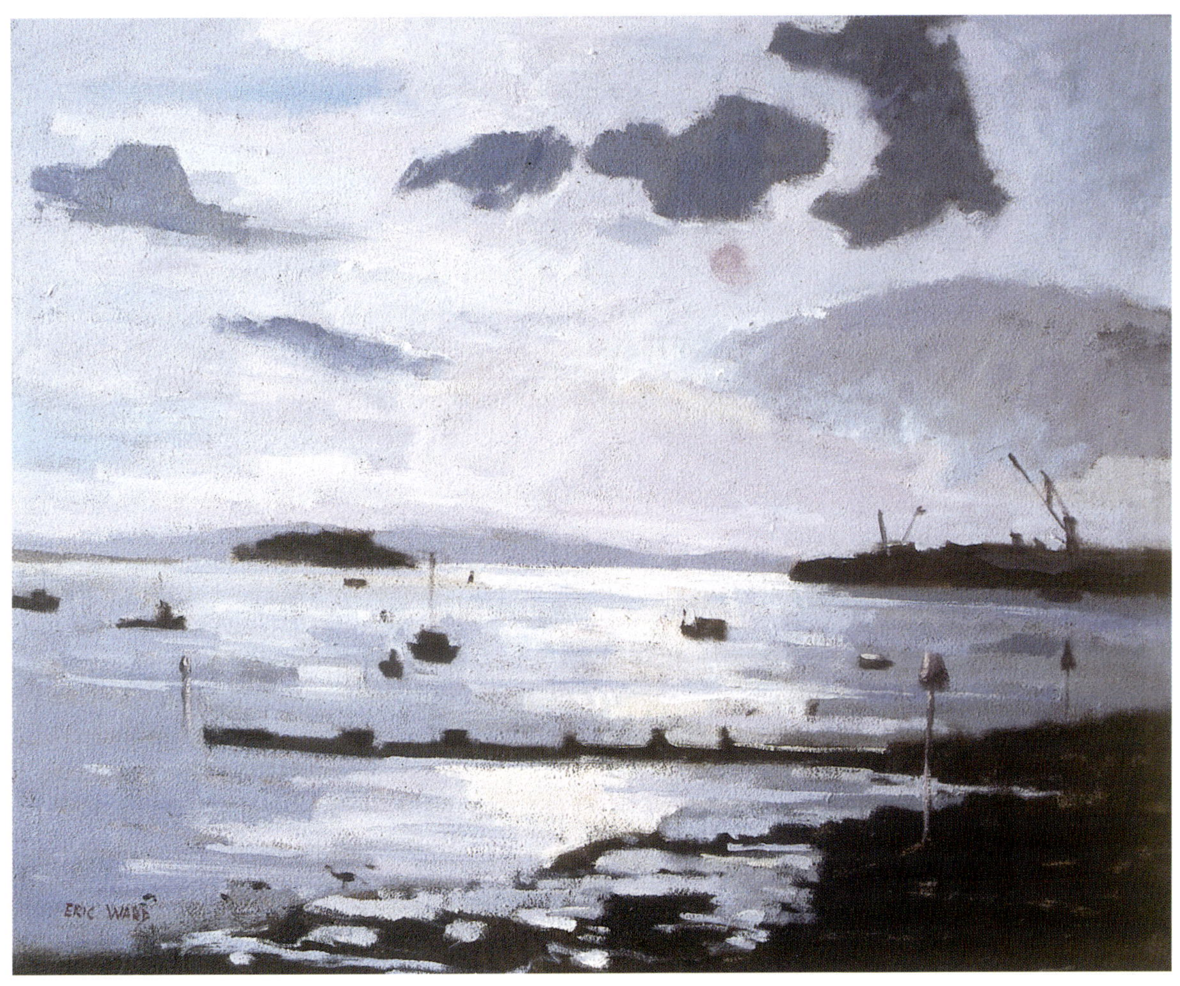

Poole Harbour with the Purbeck Hills, Evening
Oil on canvas, 50.8 x 60.8cm

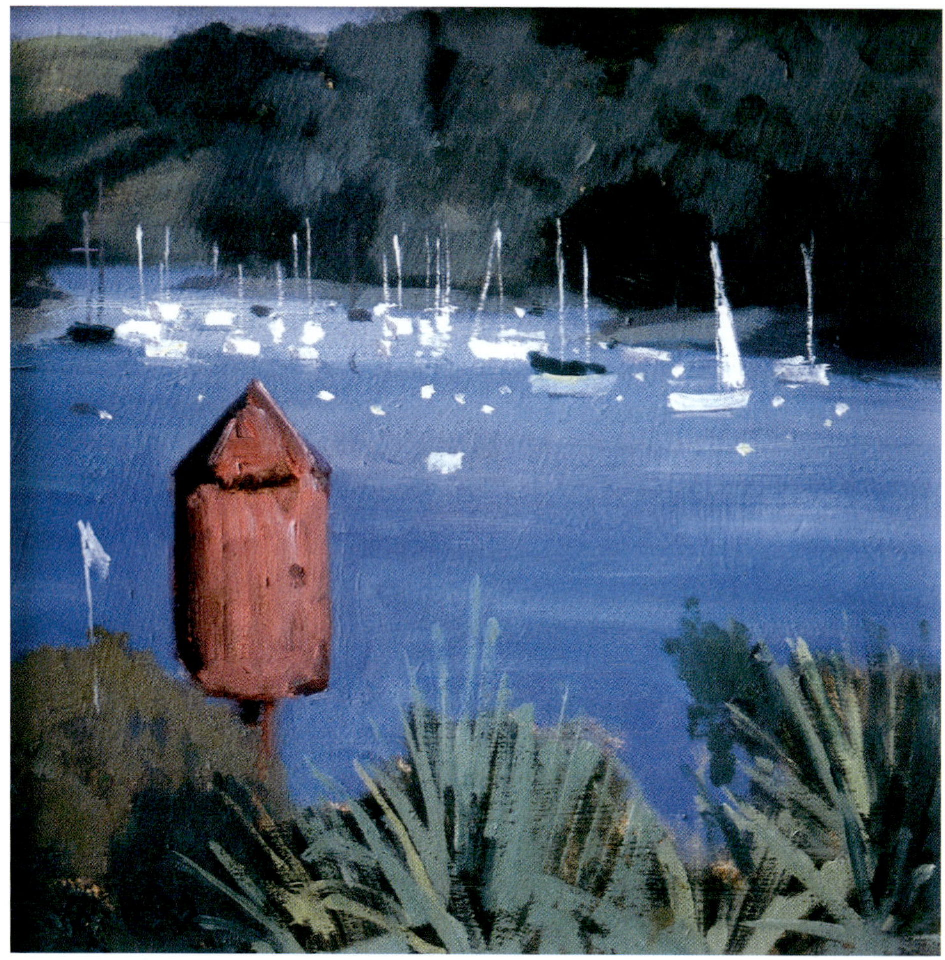

Boats at Moorings on the River Fowey
Oil on panel, 20.3 x 20.3cm

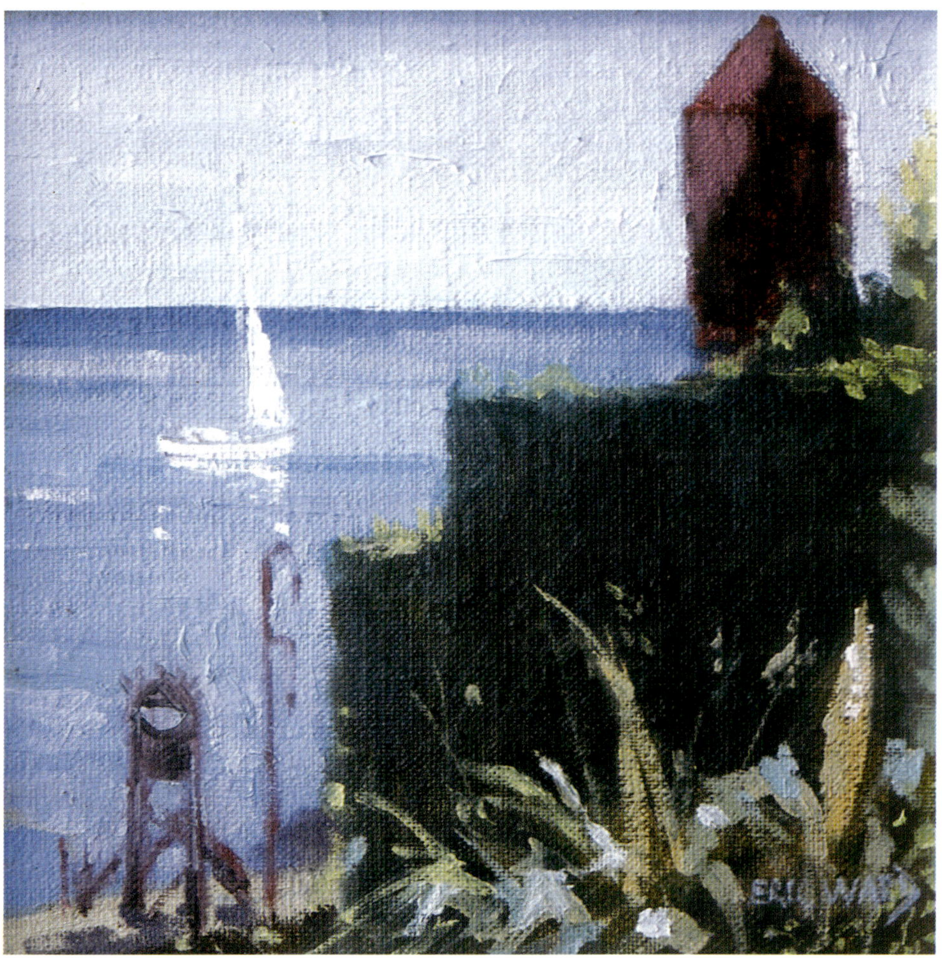

Port Hand Marker, Fowey
Oil on panel, 20.3 x 20.3cm

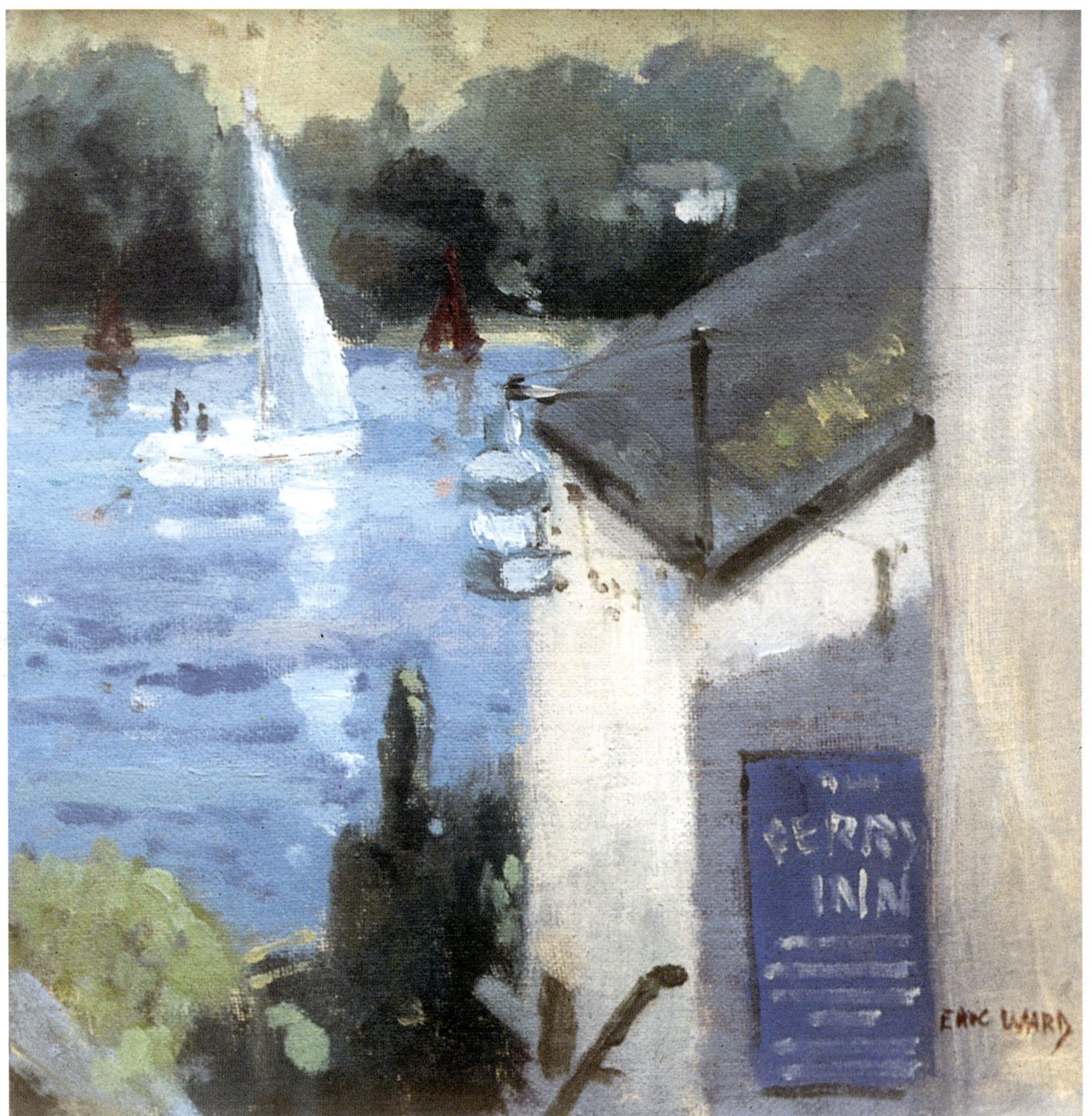

Ferry Inn, Salcombe
Oil on panel, 20.3 x 20.3cm